AF352185

ALEKSANDER LEDNICKI:
A POLE AMONG RUSSIANS,
A RUSSIAN AMONG POLES

Polish-Russian Reconciliation in
the Revolution of 1905

by
Andrew Kier Wise

East European Monographs, Boulder
Distributed by Columbia University Press, New York

2003

EAST EUROPEAN MONOGRAPHS, NO. DCXX

Aleksander Lednicki, c. 1905
Photograph courtesy of the
Polish Institute of Arts & Sciences of America, Inc. (New York)

Aleksander Lednicki, c. 1917
Photograph courtesy of the
Polish Institute of Arts & Sciences of America, Inc. (New York)

To My Parents,
Lester and Sue Wise

CONTENTS

ACKNOWLEDGMENTS

I would like to thank the individuals and institutions who have helped me as I researched and wrote this book, a revision of my doctoral dissertation.

For constant support and encouragement while a graduate student in the Corcoran Department of History at the University of Virginia, I owe a great debt to Woodford McClellan. Any depth of argumentation and clarity of writing is in large part due to his guidance as my dissertation advisor. I would like to thank two other professors at the University of Virginia, Walter Sablinsky and Eno Kraehe, for their support. For my early interest in Russian liberalism and the cultural milieu of revolutionary Russia, I am indebted to Charles Timberlake and Gennady Barabtarlo, my undergraduate advisors at the University of Missouri-Columbia.

For his advice during my stay in Moscow I thank Valentin Shelokhaev, whose suggestions concerning archival research in Moscow proved invaluable. From the earliest stages of my dissertation to the final stages of the book I received guidance and borrowed materials from Tracey Trenam, whose dissertation on Polish liberalism paved the way for my work.

Everyone at the Polish Institute of Arts and Sciences in America in New York was extremely helpful, allowing me complete access to the Lednicki archives housed at that institution. In particular Thaddeus V. Gromada and Jane Gromada Kedron deserve my thanks, as well as Feliks Gross, who shared his personal reminiscences and insights concerning Aleksander Lednicki. In addition, I thank Joseph W. Wieczerzak (Editor-in-Chief of *The Polish Review*) for publishing several of my articles. He also kindly granted permission for me to reprint portions of one article ("Polish Messianism and Polish-Russian Relations: The Influence of Adam Mickiewicz on Aleksander Lednicki") and one article in its entirety ("The Search for Slavic Unity: Aleksander Lednicki and the Russian Revolution of 1905"). I also thank Jean-Marie Volet, editor of *Mots Pluriels*, for permission to use material from an article entitled "A Pole Among Russians."

I thank the Pilsudski Institute in New York for use of its archives. Janusz Cisek was especially helpful. Research conducted in the Library of Congress was funded by a short-term grant from the Kennan Institute for Advanced Russian Studies of the Woodrow Wilson Center. Research was also conducted at a Summer Research Laboratory at the Russian and East European Center at the University of Illinois. The staff at the university's Slavic and East European Library were enormously helpful. I thank both institutions for their financial support.

Travel and research grants from Daemen College, as well as release time from teaching, helped me complete the book. I especially thank the Faculty Research Committee and Faculty Travel Committee for their support. In addition, the staff of Marian Library, especially Dorothy Lutgen, was wonderfully helpful in acquiring books through interlibrary loan.

Innumerable friends and family have offered support along the way. Most notable are Charles Evans, Meg Trott, Colum Leckey, Susannah Smith, and my brother John Wise. I thank Carroll and Olga Colley for their hospitality during my stay in Moscow. I am especially grateful to my in-laws, Lamberto and Diana Nobleza, for being gracious hosts during several research trips to New York.

I thank Stephen Fischer-Galati, Editor of East European Monographs, for accepting this book for publication.

Most important, I thank my wife Gloria, whose constant support and encouragement made the completion of this book possible.

INTRODUCTION

On the morning of 11 August 1934, Aleksander Robertovich Lednicki, a sixty-six year old lawyer, financier and ex-statesman, jumped out of a second-story window of his Warsaw home. His body was found at 5:45, lying on the asphalt of Pius XI Street. He was killed instantly by the fall, his head crushed. He had been distraught over allegations that he had betrayed Polish interests in negotiating a resolution to a Polish-French financial dispute.[1] Ever since he settled in Poland in 1918, after living most of his adult life in Russia, Lednicki had endured a long series of attacks on his patriotism. The Żyrardow Affair.[2] was the last straw: Lednicki no longer had the willpower to respond to the constant barrage of attacks on his honor, his Polishness, and his vision of Poland's future.[3] A devout Catholic who had contemplated the priesthood in his youth, Lednicki at last ended his torment by committing a mortal sin.

Lednicki was laid to rest in Warsaw on 16 August. More than a thousand friends and supporters attended the funeral conducted by Metropolitan Edward von Ropp, Lednicki's long-time friend and political ally. Many of those present were old friends: members of the former Polish colonies in Moscow and St. Petersburg, and Russian comrades in the liberation movement residing in exile in Warsaw. Professional colleagues from the Warsaw bar attended, and representatives of foreign governments, led by the French ambassador and the British consul general, also paid their respects to the former statesman who was once regarded as a candidate for top government posts in the new republic.[4] In their eulogies, mourners not only grieved over the death of a dear friend and colleague, but also paid tribute to a true champion of freedom for all peoples.[5]

Lednicki spent his entire life combatting chauvinism and extremism. His brand of pragmatic politics called for compromise and mediation rather than conflict and violence; the Second Republic never accepted the validity of these tenets. Lednicki and his fellow progressives who strove to create a liberal democracy in independent Poland were relegated to a minor role in an era of intolerance and rabid nationalism in a nation torn apart by ethnic strife, class conflict and partisan politics.

Aleksander Lednicki was a cosmopolitan liberal guided by his devotion to the principle of universal liberty. He was greatly influenced by the thinking of the Polish national poet, Adam Mickiewicz, whose "romantic universalism" called for the free cultural development of all peoples and "sanctified the pluralism of national cultures as an expression of unique and irreplaceable individualizations of human nature."[6] Most importanly, this doctrine stressed that universal progress could only be attained through the maturation of individual nations.[7] Lednicki wrote that

> in the thought of Mickiewicz, Polish patriotism may constitute only one part of a universal patriotism, love of one's homeland must serve as a prelude to a love of the great homeland of mankind.[8]

In his struggle to liberate Poland from tsarist Russia, Lednicki always insisted that Polish freedom could only be attained in combination with the liberation of all peoples of the empire. When the First World War made possible a radical redrawing of the map of Europe, Lednicki warned that Europe must address its nationality problems if the continent were ever to achieve a lasting peace.[9]

Lednicki's life experiences inculcated in him a keen awareness of the plight of non-Russians within the tsarist empire. A Polish Catholic nobleman, he grew up surrounded by Orthodox Belorussian peasants and Jewish townfolk. As a leader in the Russian liberation movement, he fought not only for Polish autonomy, but for the right of all national minorities to cultural and political self-determination. In the First Duma, he not only represented the people of Minsk, but was also entrusted by the Georgians with the task of defending their cause until provincial elections were held. Later, in the face of growing chauvinism in his homeland, Lednicki advocated a Poland not only for Poles, but for all peoples living within the borders of the new state.

Lednicki's passion for liberty was deeply rooted in the discrimination he suffered under the brutal policy of russification practiced by the tsarist regime. He resented the Russian government, its oppressive bureaucracy and arbitrary brand of justice. In part because of his legal training, Lednicki had a keen appreciation for the rule of law and the need for order in society. He preached against lawlessness and anarchy, whether on the part of the autocracy or the revolutionary movement. Despite defending dozens of political criminals and sheltering refugees from tsarist authorities, he never promoted violence. In a time and place characterized by extremism, he was distinguished by his unwavering democratic convictions.

Despite his distaste for tsarism, Lednicki was passionately devoted to the Russian nation. Lednicki believed that if the two great Slavic nations—Poles and Russians—could escape the tsarist yoke, they could coexist peacefully in a federated democratic republic. He blamed the Russian bureaucracy, an artifical construct "forced" on the Russian nation, for severing the organic ties of kinship between Slavic peoples.

Lednicki spent his life in Russia trying to renew those ties of Slavic kinship. He subscribed to the V. O. Kliuchevskii school of thought, which taught that Peter the Great had disturbed Muscovy's organic pattern of growth by promoting the westward expansion of his empire. Lednicki regarded Peter's determination to make Russia a Baltic power as "a tragedy for Poland, because Russia in its pressure on the North West sees in us [Poles] an enemy, who...obstructs its path; from the time of Peter it [the Russian state] has conducted decidedly anti-Polish politics."[10] Lednicki regarded Poland's war against the young Soviet state as a noble cause, for a Polish victory would blunt Russian expansion to the Baltic. Russian interest would then shift to the south, signifying a "turn from the ideology of Nikolai Karamzin, which embodies the politics of the All-Russian Emperors, to the ideology of Kluchevskii, representing the national-organic tendencies of the Muscovite tsars."[11] Above all, he insisted that Poland should liberate the peoples of his native Kresy from the Soviet grip, at last allowing them to freely pursue their national interests. "In this way," he promised, "we will settle a moral account with Russia."[12]

This work deals with the first part of Lednicki's life, from his childhood in Minsk through the period of the first Duma. I will not examine his role in the Provisional Government in 1917, when he served as President of the Liquidation Commission, the body established to oversee the dissolution of all ties between Russia and Poland, nor will I discuss at any length his participation in Polish politics during World War I and the period leading up to the establishment of the Second Republic. Rather, this work focuses on Lednicki's actions in Russia and Poland during the turbulent first years of the twentieth century. From 1900 to 1907, he was a central figure in the Russian and Polish liberation movements: he participated in the Union of Liberation, organized lawyers' unions in Russia and Poland, and founded the first liberal parties in both countries. His political machinations during these years were grounded in a firm belief that a democratic Russia would replace the autocracy and reform the empire into a federation of autonomous units. While he longed for Polish independence, Lednicki regarded federalism as the only just solution to the nationalities problem that was feasible at the time.

Lednicki heralded the Russian Revolution as a continuation of the French Revolution. The Revolution of 1905, he later wrote during the interwar period, "introduced into life the idea of the right of nations, as collective individuals having the same right as an individual man and citizen."[13] A vocal advocate for a united front in the struggle against tsarism, Lednicki called on all nations in the empire to come together in a joint effort to topple the old regime. It is a great irony that those characteristics which served him so well in the liberation movement — passionate belief in the equality of all men, sincere respect and appreciation for other cultures, and devotion to attaining a just settlement to the nationalities problem through peaceful means — prevented him from playing a major political role in the new Polish state in 1918.

ENDNOTES

1.   *The New York Times*, 12 August 1934; and *Gazeta Polska*, 12 August 1934.

2.   The Franco-Polish dispute centered on several large cotton and linen mills in the Warsaw suburb of Żyrardow. Lednicki was accused of favoring French shareholders in resolving the conflict. He was posthumously cleared of any wrongdoing. See Wieslaw Wladyka, *Działalność polityczna polskich stronnictw konserwatywnych w latach 1926–1935* (Wrocław: Zakład Narodowy imienia Ossolińskich Wydawnictwo Polskiej Akademii Nauk, 1977), 213–18.

3.   Aleksander's son, however, did defend his father's honor. Wacław Lednicki seriously wounded one of his father's accusors, Colonel Ignacy Matuszewski, in a duel fought on 22 August 1934. A former Finance Minister and a member of Piłsudski's clique, Matuszewski was, at the time, editor of *Gazeta Polska*. This paper had published articles highly critical of Lednicki's role in the Żyrardow Affair. See *The New York Times*, 23 August 1934 and *Segodniia*, 25 August 1934.

4.   *Segodniia*, 23 August 1934. Władysław Studnicki noted in his memoirs that "at the time of Steczkowski's ministry, Lednicki was universally regarded as the natural successor of Steczkowski for the post of premier. Lednicki knew about this, but he remained in Moscow...to bring help to the throng of refugees." Piłsudski Institute, Archiwum Władysława Studnickiego, Teka IV, Teczka 4 (incomplete typed copy of Studnicki's book *Ludzie, idée i czyny*), p. 1. Wacław Lednicki recalls that in spite of the efforts of supporters to convince his father to return to Poland to campaign for the post, he chose to stay in Moscow and help repatriate hundreds of thousands of Poles dislocated by the war. Wacław Lednicki, Pamiętniki (London: B. Świderski, 1963–7), 2: 456–59.

5.   Polish Institute of the Arts and Sciences in America (PIASA), Aleksander Lednicki Collection (006), folder 71. This folder contains accounts of the funeral from the Polish press. Also see *Paneuropa* 10 (October 1934), no. 8: 156.

6.   Andrzej Walicki, "The Conceptions of Nation in the Polish Romantic Messianism," *Dialectics and Humanism: The Polish Philosophical Quarterly 2* (Winter 1975): 104.

7.   Ibid.

8.   Aleksander Lednicki, "L'homme de la rue en Pologne et l'organisation de la Paix," *Revue Mondiale* (15 January 1932): 136–37. This article contains the text of a speech Lednicki delivered at a meeting of the pacifist league, "Amities Internationales."

9.   In a speech delivered during World War I, Lednicki argued that while the war could not possibly resolve all of Europe's conflicts, the nationalities problem had to be solved. He called for a new world order in which "an independent

Polish state would be one of the guarantees of stability and durability." See PIASA, Aleksander Lednicki Collection (006), folder 12.

10. Aleksander Lednicki, *Nasza polityka wschodnia* (Warsaw: Polskie Towarzystwo Wydawnicze "Zjednoczenie," 1922), 6.

11. Ibid., 9.

12. Ibid., 22.

13. Ibid., 37.

Chapter One

CHILDHOOD AND EDUCATION, 1866–1889

Aleksander Robertovich Lednicki was born 2 (14) July 1866.[1] on the Lednicki family estate near Minsk in the Northwestern Region (*Sevorozapadnyi Krai*) of the Russian Empire.[2] Referred to by Poles as the *Kresy* (Borderlands), the area was populated by many different ethnic and religious groups: Polish and Lithuanian Catholics; Russian, Ukrainian and Belorussian Orthodox; and Jews. According to the 1897 census, Poles made up only 4.9 percent of the population in these provinces, which had been part of the old Polish-Lithuanian Commonwealth.[3] Vastly outnumbered, *Kresy* Poles were confronted with an entirely different situation than residents of the Kingdom, which was more ethnically Polish. The *Kresy* Poles, however, had made peace with their minority status; Poles from the borderlands were known for their acceptance of other cultures. As the scholar Feliks Gross has noted:

In my own personal experience, Poles from the Eastern *Kresy*, from the frontierlands, even in my time, were more liberal and openminded toward religious and ethnic differences than those of the same social class and education in the Western provinces...In the old frontierland, they have learned to share destiny with others; good neighborhood is a way of life.[4]

Other scholars have made similar observations,[5] and it seems clear that Lednicki's upbringing and early education in the borderlands greatly influenced his personality and political outlook throughout his life.[6] Always a Polish patriot and champion of the Polish cause, Lednicki was above all tolerant and sensitive to the needs of all national minorities in the Russian Empire.[7]

Born into a family of petty Polish nobility, Aleksander was the only son of Robert and Rozalia Zawadzka Lednicki. Robert was the second son of Franciszek and Jozefa Adamowiczowna Lednicki. He and his older brother, Klemens, both suffered from poor health. Klemens graduated from Moscow University with a medical degree in the 1850s and practiced as a physician in a small town near Minsk before an early death from tuberculosis. Robert also suffered from this disease and was obliged to leave the gymnasium before graduation; he later served briefly as an office-worker in Minsk.[8]

Aleksander's mother, Rozalia, was the daughter of Wincenty and Tekla Zawadzki. After Wincenty's death, Rozalia's mother married Franciszek Karczewski, a judge. Little is known of Rozalia's life before 1863, when she took part in the Polish uprising, giving food, clothing and shelter to partisans. Despite his poor health Robert Lednicki also participated in the rebellion. For their patriotic efforts both were punished: Robert was arrested but escaped long imprisonment, while Rozalia was imprisoned for a year.[9] The two were married in 1865 and promptly travelled to Berlin, where Robert underwent treatment for tuberculosis and epilepsy. On their return to Minsk, Robert's condition gradually deteriorated; he died in 1870 at the age of 33.[10]

While it is impossible to determine fully the psychological impact of his father's death on the three-year-old Aleksander, the tragedy obviously affected the young boy's life. Suddenly burdened with the prospect of raising Aleksander and his younger sister Amelia by herself, the widow Rozalia moved to Lachowiec, the Lednicki family estate. Here Aleksander would come under the influence of his grandparents, who instilled in him the traditions and worldview of the *Kresy szlachta*, or gentry.

Perhaps most important of those traditions was a devout belief in Roman Catholicism. Aleksander's grandfather, Franciszek, was a zealous Catholic whose house was filled with religious icons and paintings; his grandmother, Jozefa, was quite mystical. She frequently "contacted" the spirits of her dead sons through mediums; these visitations seemed to soothe the grieving Jozefa and doubtless had a certain impact on the children. As Wacław recalls in his memoirs, his father had a life-long interest in seances and intercourse with spirits, especially after his wife's death in 1923.[11]

In addition to his religiosity, Franciszek had strong ties to the land. His devotion to his estate had a powerful impact on Aleksander, who at an early age "became familiar with the soil and the rural economy, and took part in work in the fields and meadows...becoming attached to the Belorussian landscape."[12] Aleksander learned by example from his grandfather and became imbued with the "spirit of democratism and tolerance, and a feeling of personal dignity."[13] By his own admission the possessor of "an innate merriment, even recklessness,"[14] Aleksander was exhorted by his grandfather not to "put off to tomorrow what you can do today," and instructed that if "you respect money it will respect you."[15] While these admonitions seem to have had little impact on Aleksander in his youth, as an adult he applied them assiduously.[16]

After Franciszek's death in 1880, the mood at Lachowiec changed considerably. Aleksander's widowed grandmother retired to another family property, leaving him and his mother to care for Lachowiec. More vibrant and better educated than her mother-in-law, Rozalia enlivened the old estate and cultivated a new atmosphere of refinement. More visitors, and of a different sort, came to the Lednicki home. Chief among them were the local intelligentsia, physicians, army officers and government officials. Aleksander's mother was also a devout Catholic, and priests continued to be frequent visitors. Rozalia organized amateur theatrical presentations and dance recitals at Lachowiec, with profits contributed to libraries that distributed books throughout the region.[17]

As Mieczysław Smolen notes, these "literary evenings" had a great impact on Aleksander.[18] His mother was also an avid reader and instilled in her son a love of Polish literature. As Aleksander later noted in his memoirs,[19] he undertook no systematic study of literature, but was exposed to the works of many Polish writers: Zygmunt Krasiński, Juliusz Słowacki, Mikolaj Rej, Jan Kochanowski, Kajetan Węgierski, Eliża Orzeszkowa, and especially Adam Mickiewicz.[20] Equally important, the greater presence of the Zawadzki clan, which had committed so much in the struggle for Polish freedom in 1863, redoubled the patriotic air of Lachowiec.

What emerges from a survey of Lednicki's early family life is a picture of a boy influenced by contradictory forces. While he was exposed to the literary and artistic world of his mother and her intellectual friends, Aleksander's grandparents strove to school him in the ways of the traditional *szlachta*, above all a love of Church and the Polish land. This goal was met: once he attained some affluence, Aleksander purchased estates and spent much time and effort supervising their revitalization. And throughout his life he remained a devout Catholic with close ties to the Church hierarchy in Poland. Catholic bishops and archbishops were frequent guests at the Lednicki home in Moscow.[21] It is worth noting that during his youth, while his comrades at the gymnasium came under the influence of the writings of the Russian radicals Dmitrii Pisarev, Nikolai Dobroliubov and Nikolai Chernyshevskii, Aleksander contemplated the priesthood.[22]

Grandfather Franciszek's aversion tc upheaval and change, typified by his denunciation of the uprising of 1863 as the unfortunate result of "the fury of hotheads,"[23] did not immediately affect Aleksander. While Aleksander's later schooling in the moderate politics of Warsaw Positivism had its roots in the teachings of his grandfather,[24] equally influential was the Zawadzki family tradition of romantic insurrectionalism. The visceral romanticism of the mature Lednicki, as well as the elements of radicalism evident in his political philosophy, can be traced to his mother's influence.[25]

Influential as they may be in the formation of one's character, family and geography are not the sole determinants in a person's life. In the case of Aleksander Lednicki, his years at the Minsk gymnasium (1878–1885) were equally important. He attended gymnasium during a period of intense russification in the *Kresy* and was punished several times for speaking Polish in school.[26] He was not a rebel, however, and graduated without succumbing to the radicalism which infected so many of his comrades.[27] When a conspiracy arose in the Minsk gymnasium in 1882 among a group of Polish students, he did not take part.[28]

Yet Aleksander and his friends did debate the issues of the day, especially the nationalities question.[29] Despite the attempts of the tsarist regime to emasculate young students politically, Aleksander and his classmates were aware of the intellectual trends of the day.[30] Above all, Aleksander was influenced by the school of thought known as "Warsaw Positivism," rooted in the tradition of "organic work," the Polish equivalent of the Russian "small deeds" doctrine. Positivist thinkers called on Poles to repudiate revolution in favor of economic and cultural development. In the words of the Enlightenment reformer Stanisław Staszic, "science, commerce, and crafts are the weapons you [Poles] need, otherwise you will perish."[31] Aleksander Świętochowski (1849–1938), the most influential positivist thinker, observed that the post-1863 generation wished "to extend work and learning in society, to discover new resources, to utilize existing ones, and to concern ourselves with our own problems and not those of others."[32]

Less enthralled with the romanticism of its fathers, the new generation sought a more secure foundation for Poland's future through the study of science and materialism. The uprisings of 1830–1831 and 1863 not only did not win independence but actually led to intensified russification. Tsarist policies were particularly harsh in the *Kresy* region, where de-polonization was actively pursued. The government also administratively integrated the Kingdom into the empire. Russian administrators replaced Polish ones, and the educational system underwent intensive reform: mandatory study of Russian language, history and geography was instituted in elementary and secondary schools in 1869, and in 1885 Russian became the official language of instruction in all subjects except Polish and religion.[33]

While grounded in the Polish tradition of organic work, Warsaw Positivism also borrowed from western intellectual trends. Henry Thomas Buckle was the new generation's first hero; his landmark *History of Civilization in England*[34] helped create a new worldview. For Buckle, the progress of European civilization represented the triumph of scientific knowledge over the forces of nature. He attempted to transform history into an empirical science that could be used to search for the conditions and laws determining the development of human society.

Equally influential was August Comte's positivist philosophy, which emphasized the observation of phenomena and the examination of their relationship to their causes and consequences. Comte's disciples believed that, by following his method of investigation, they could discover the laws governing the universe. Young Poles were first exposed to Comte's philosophy in 1868 through a synopsis of the new school of thought that appeared in the Polish press. Already embracing the notion of organic work, they readily adopted the empiricism of Buckle and Comte and applied it to the scientific investigation of Poland's social ills.[35] Comte's ideology of progress confirmed Poles' belief in the natural development and unity of society. In this way, Western thought provided an intellectual justification for the indigenous Polish tradition of organic work.[36]

In his youth Aleksander Lednicki was also captivated by positivism, especially the teachings of Aleksander Świętochowski and Włodzimierz Spasowicz (1829–1906). Referred to by one scholar as the "hetman of Warsaw positivists,"[37] Świętochowski had an enormous influence on Lednicki. The two would develop a close relationship that culminated in 1904 with the establishment of the Progressive-Democratic Union, the first liberal party in Poland. Świętochowski developed the notion that, in the absence of a state, every Pole was morally obligated to serve society. In lieu of a state, he argued, the Polish nation could survive through cultural and economic nationalism and social integration. Lednicki adhered to most of this doctrine but rejected the notion that social integration of the Polish nation required the eradication of ethnic differences. While an advocate of Jewish rights in his early years,[38] Świętochowski would later write that he "defended Jews when they wished to be Poles, and for these same reasons I do not defend them today, when they wish to be Jews, enemies of the Poles."[39] Throughout his life a defender of the rights of national minorities, Lednicki could not accept this view and the two men severed relations in the interwar period.

While Lednicki adopted many of Świętochowski's ideas, his spiritual kinsman was undoubtedly Włodzimierz Spasowicz. A renowned lawyer and co-founder with Erazm Piltz of the Polish-language journal *Kraj*, Spasowicz was (like Lednicki) a Polish "argonaut" who spent his adult life in Russia.[40] Their lives were remarkably similar: both from Minsk, they were successful lawyers in Russia and each worked in his place of residence—Spasowicz in St. Petersburg and Lednicki in Moscow—to further the cause of Polish-Russian conciliation. Devoted to a peaceful resolution of the Polish question, the two men were united by memories of Minsk where they spent their school years, united by the *Kresy* and a deep attachment to it. "They both saw and felt that it was precisely there that the finest political traditions of the Polish Commonwealth were preserved the best and the most faithfully, and these traditions inspired both...in their fight for Poland."[41]

The Minsk years were important for another reason: Aleksander's education at the local gymnasium had to a certain extent russified him. Although his home environment acted as a certain counterbalance, his absorption of Russian culture would affect him throughout his life. Like Spasowicz, Aleksander Lednicki had become "equally a Pole and a Russian,"[42] forever a "man standing on the border of two cultures—Polish and Russian."[43]

Yet at the same time, Aleksander's school days in Minsk must surely have made him acutely aware that he was different, that he was not Russian. As one biographer states, this experience "deepened in Aleksander a feeling of separateness in relation to Russian society."[44] This sensation of "otherness," along with his exposure to the plight of other non-Russian students, had a lasting effect. As an adult, Lednicki would be a staunch defender of equal rights for all national minorities in the empire.

Of particular importance was Lednicki's exposure to the plight of Jews. During his gymnasium years, 60 percent of the population of the city of Minsk was Jewish.[45] As Lednicki noted in a letter to the Ministry of Justice denouncing its handling of the Beilis Affair in 1911, he spent his youth

> among a large Jewish population, and at the time rumors circulated about the use of Christian blood by Jews in matzoh, but these rumors and these legends, from the earliest days of my life I regarded more than skeptically.[46]

Lednicki denounced the whole Beilis fiasco as "one of the most shameful pages in the history of [Ivan] Shcheglovitov's Ministry of Justice."[47] Throughout his life, Lednicki consistently promoted equal rights for Jews, earning their trust and confidence.[48]

In August 1885 Lednicki and two colleagues travelled to Moscow to begin their studies at the university. The young men evidently had debated whether to attend that institution, the university in St. Petersburg, or Kiev. According to his memoirs, Aleksander and his friends wanted to study medicine;[49] this eliminated St. Petersburg University, which did not have a medical school, from consideration.[50] It seems that Moscow was their final choice because one of the men had relatives in that city.[51]

The study of medicine was popular at the time, given the new ideal of service to the people.[52] Beyond the drive to engage in socially constructive work, Lednicki's decision was influenced by the fact that two of his uncles were physicians—his father's brother Klemens and his mother's brother Aleksander. However, all hopes were dashed when the young men reached Moscow and discovered that no more student spaces were available in the Faculty of Medicine. As a result, Aleksander enrolled in the Faculty of Natural Sciences.[53]

He arrived at a time of great change and upheaval in Russian higher education. Just as the gymnasiums placed a heavy emphasis on the classics, avoiding controversial, thought-provoking subjects, the 1884 University Statute introduced a similar curriculum into the universities. In the Juridical Faculty, to which Lednicki transferred after one semester, the teaching of foreign constitutional law was abolished and sensitive fields such as state law downgraded to the status of "secondary subjects." Students were not tested in these areas, which consequently provoked less intense study on their part. The focus was on less abstract fields of study, such as Roman and church law, rather than legal theory or comparative legal systems.[54]

Moreover, the new statute shifted power from faculty councils to the minister of education and his appointed curator. In addition to worsening the faculty-student ratio and producing higher fees, this more intrusive state presence made student life at the university highly volatile. The student body took it upon itself to defend the integrity of the institution; this resulted in frequent protests and clashes with university officials and police.[55] Lednicki witnessed many of these encounters and became active in student life, including the student judicial system.[56]

Such experiences undoubtedly accounted in large part for Lednicki's decision to transfer to the Juridical Faculty. In his memoirs, he noted that during the sixth year of gymnasium he began to contemplate a legal career. His interest in the law was piqued by his mother's stepfather, Franciszek Karczewski, a judge.[57] Later in life, Lednicki kept a collection of law books given him by his step-grand-father in his Moscow library.[58]

Many of his student colleagues shared Lednicki's choice of profession: the most significant change in enrollment patterns between 1880 and 1912 was the replacement of the Medical Faculty by the Juridical Faculty as the most popular. Several factors seem to have been involved in this development. Contemporaries regarded the study of law as a relatively easy way to obtain a lucrative degree, less difficult than the rigorous fields of medicine and the natural sciences. Especially under the new guidelines, which decreased the freedom of professors to change lectures from year to year, law students learned that they could skip classes and still pass year-end exams.[59]

But many young men had loftier reasons for pursuing a legal career. Lednicki's decision, for example, was motivated by his interest in social and political activism.[60] He was not unique in this regard; many young men of his generation, painfully aware of the oppression and arbitrariness of tsarism, resolved to struggle for the protection of human rights against tyranny.[61] As Vasilii Maklakov recalled:

> My brief experience in life had shown me that the chief evil of Russian life was the supreme role of arbitrariness in it...The defense of a person against lawlessness,—in other words the defense of the law itself—this was the substance of the legal profession's "societal" service. It was the goal I set as my own."[62]

Maklakov, Lednicki and many of their contemporaries would devote their lives to the task of bringing the rule of law to Russia.

While student unrest frequently erupted into disturbances, it was the subsequent state-sponsored repression that often politicized them.[63] One such disruption took place on 22 November 1887: at a public concert for the benefit of poor students a third year law student named G. Siniavski slapped the face of Inspector A. A. Bryzgalov, a hated university official.[64] Siniavski's action was planned by fellow students demanding the abrogation of the 1884 statute,[65] and they quickly showed support for their colleague by organizing protests against his arrest.[66]

Government reaction was swift and harsh; police and Cossack units suppressed the demonstrations. In the end, officials closed the university, hoping to end disturbances by beginning the Christmas vacation early. The whole affair left a lasting impression on the student body,[67] and Siniavski's bold act and the subsequent closing of the university precipitated Lednicki's transfer to the Demidowski Lyceum in Yaroslavl. There, in the relative calm of the provincial school, he finished his degree in 1889.[68] While Lednicki's role in the events of November 1887 is unclear, he later indicated that he was sentenced to an "administrative exile" from Moscow for his participation in the student disturbances.[69] Regardless of his role in the "Bryzgalov Affair," this event contributed to Lednicki's resentment of the tsarist government and its policies.

While protests were one form of expressing student discontent, the politicization of the student body did not always manifest itself so dramatically. Despite official concern, student activism did not lead inevitably to radicalism. For Maklakov, politicization meant liberal activism. The same can be said of Lednicki, who was not in the socialist camp.[70] For Lednicki, Maklakov and others of this generation, the dominant philosophical influences were non-socialist in nature: they adhered to the rationalism and scientism of Comte, Spencer and Mill.[71] A. A. Kizevetter recalled that he and his colleagues at Moscow University "didn't dream of becoming revolutionary heroes; *legal* social work attracted us; but on this legal footing we all prepared ourselves for a struggle for our ideals, a patient, persistent and unwavering struggle."[72] With a belief in the philosophy of "small deeds" and a commitment to incremental change, many men of the 1880s embarked on careers in which they could change the status quo in a non-violent manner.[73]

Lednicki's decision to enter the Juridical Faculty at Moscow University proved pivotal. It exposed him to such constitutionalists as Maksim Kovalevskii, and participation in meetings of the Moscow Juridical Society introduced him to other liberals. Viktor Alexandrovich Gol'tsev, vice president of the society and future editor of *Russkaia mysl'*, would later become Lednicki's close political collaborator in attempts to forge closer relations between Russian and Polish liberals. Of special importance was Lednicki's relationship with the president of the society, Sergei Muromtsev, who greatly influenced the formation of Lednicki's political outlook.[74] Muromtsev was in fact one of Lednicki's role models, for he symbolized the type of "lawyer-activist" that the young Pole was destined to become. Lednicki later wrote that

> Muromtsev blazed the trail for the Russian legal profession toward the Western European model of lawyers—political activists guiding the life of the country, tireless fighters for more perfect forms of government and social existences, and added a Russian name to the Pantheon of glorious European activists:...Muromtsev—builder of constitutional forms in Russia.[75]

The Juridical Society's meetings almost always had a political character. Under the guise of a scientific gathering, society members discussed topics otherwise off limits. "The Juridical Society," A. A. Kizevetter noted, "undoubtedly played not a small role in the popularization of constitutional ideas in Russian society."[76] Lednicki was certainly one youth who became imbued with the spirit of constitutionalism.

Lednicki's experiences at the Juridical Society indirectly affected him in another way. At a lecture given by the Moscow University professor A. I. Chuprov in 1886, Lednicki met a fellow Pole who would change his life.[77] Bronis Peczlewicz led a study group consisting of Polish students from three institutions of higher learning located in Moscow: the University, the Technical School and the Agricultural Institute.[78] About one hundred students belonged to the Polish *zemliachestvo*,[79] which at the time had its own library of 2,000 books and 4,000 rubles in savings.[80] Ostensibly a self-help organization, the Polish group, like all *zemliachestva*, provided an arena for the discussion of different political and social views.[81]

The Polish circle was essentially divided into two political camps: nationalists and socialists. Lednicki joined the nationalist group: the russified Pole from Belorussia was coming to terms with his heritage. Formally educated at Russian institutions, Lednicki had undertaken little serious study of Polish culture and history. Encouraged by his new roommate Peczlewicz, and intimidated by those in the group with a better command of Polish, Lednicki embarked on an intense self-education in all things Polish. As his son later noted, it was quite ironic that only in Moscow, the center of old Russia, would Aleksander Lednicki experience the "definitive crystalization of his *polskosc.*"[82]

It was also in Russia that Lednicki became politicized. Like many members of the petty Polish nobility, he had gone there in search of professional training. Many, like Lednicki, also sought employment there. These well-educated Poles had a sense of historical awareness of Poland's fate. Possessing a certain pride in their social standing, they also bitterly resented the fact that, despite their noble lineage and higher education, they were not first-class citizens.[83] For Aleksander Lednicki, the years at Moscow University proved important for another reason. He established life-long relationships with prominent liberal constitutionalists, with whom he later helped establish the Constitutional Democratic Party (Kadets), Russia's first liberal party. It was during this time that he became friends with fellow university students Princes Petr and Pavel Dolgorukov (1866–1927). Scions of a wealthy Russian family that traced its lineage back to ancient Rus', the princes would later become Lednicki's close political collaborators. Both brothers were sensitive to the Polish issue, but Petr was particularly instrumental in bringing Russian and Polish liberals together in the period 1903–1905.

The more radical of the two brothers, Petr spent most of his time at the family estate in the Sudzha district of the Kursk province, while Pavel lived in the family palace in Moscow. In late 1902, Petr was banned from public activity for five years because of his participation in oppositional politics. Ironically, the punishment allowed him to devote all of his time to clandestine activities; no longer able to work in the zemstvos, he played an integral role in the emerging liberation movement. He served as chief treasurer for the Union of Liberation and functioned as its liaison with other opposition groups.[84] His proselytizing activities eventually led to discussions with Lednicki on the Polish problem; on 25 November 1904, Petr hosted the first meeting between zemstvoists and Polish liberals at the Dolgorukov palace in Moscow.

Lednicki also worked closely with Pavel Dolgorukov on the Polish issue. During World War I, when Lednicki was becoming more assertive in his demands, Pavel attended Russo-Polish conferences hosted by his old friend.[85] Pavel remained on good terms with his Polish colleagues long after the Poles had gained their independence from Russia; in the interwar period he frequently travelled to Warsaw to visit friends. On one occasion in the early 1920s, Dolgorukov recalled, he "was greeted in Warsaw, as a friend of the Poles, since our party [Kadets] was the first to proclaim the autonomy of Poland, and from the turn of the century I had met with many Polish activists at Russo-Polish conferences in Warsaw and at my home in Moscow."[86]

Lednicki joined several discussion groups at the university, where he read the works of Spencer, Mill and Buckle.[87] It was also there that he became fully aware of his Polish heritage. And it was also "exactly there, at those meetings of student associations, both Russian and Polish, that the great social activist, which [he] remained until his death, was born."[88]

ENDNOTES

1.   1 All dates in this text will be given in Old Style, with New Style dates given in parentheses when pertinent.

2.   Jan Zaprudnik, "Political Struggle for Byelorussia in the Tsarist State Dumas, 1906–1917" (Ph.D. diss., New York University, 1969), 17–23. The provinces which were included under this rubric varied. In this study I shall use this term in reference to five specific provinces: Mogilev, Vitebsk, Minsk, Vilno and Grodno.

3.   Ibid., 24. Belorussians were by far the largest ethnic group in the Kresy, totaling 63.5% of the population. They were followed by Jews (14.2%) and Russians (5.9%). For a graphic depiction of the territorial claims of the various nationalities, see Norman Davies, *God's Playground: A History of Poland* (New York: Columbia University Press, 1982), vol. 2, *1795 to the Present, 67*.

4.   Feliks Gross, "Kresy: The Frontier of Eastern Europe," *Polish Review* 23 (1978), no. 2: 12.

5.   Andrzej Micewski, *Roman Dmowski* (Warsaw: Verum, 1971), 14–17.

6.   This thesis is shared by others. See Mieczysław Smolen, "Działalność polityczna Aleksandra Lednickiego w Rosji: 1905–1918" (Ph.D. diss., Jagiellonski Uniwersytet, 1979), 32.

7.   Professor Feliks Gross, who personally knew Lednicki and worked with him at the First Pan-European Congress held in Vienna in October 1926, notes that he was very sensitive to the Jewish question and the plight of other national minorities. In Gross' words, Lednicki "did not have a prejudiced bone in his body." Interview by author, New York City, 21 October 1993.

8.   W. Lednicki, *Pamiętniki*, 1: 245.

9.   Ibid., 245–49. Two of Rozalia's brothers also were involved in the rebellion and were punished with exile to Siberia. See Polish Institute of Arts and Sciences in America (PIASA). Waclaw Lednicki Collection (007). Folder 240, "Russo-Polish Relations. Revised edition," p. 5.

10.   W. Lednicki, *Pamiętniki*, 1: 245.

11.   Ibid., 1: 246–49; 2: 258, 579.

12.   Ibid., 1: 250.

13.   Ibid., 258.

14.   Ibid., 264.

15.   Ibid., 258.

16.   This notion is seconded by Smolen. See his "Działalność polityczna," 28–29.

17.   Polish Institute of Arts and Sciences in America (PIASA), Aleksander Lednicki Collection (006), folder 73, p. 24. This folder contains a photocopy of an incomplete biography of Lednicki written by Włodzimierz Dzwonkowski. Henceforth this manuscript will be referred to as "Dzwonkowski." This biographical sketch has also been published in Włodzimierz Dzwonkowski, *Rosja a Polska* (Warsaw: Oficyna Wydawnicza Interim, 1991): 11–208. Also see Smolen, "Działalność polityczna," 30.

18.   Smolen, "Działalność polityczna," 30–31.

19.   A photocopy of Aleksander Lednicki's autobiography is contained in the Aleksander Lednicki Collection (006), folders 65–66, housed in the archives at the Polish Institute of Arts and Sciences in America (New York City). These memoirs were written while he was imprisoned in 1908. Wacław's *Pamiętniki* contain extensive sections of his father's notes, which will be the version referred to in this work as "W. Lednicki, *Pamiętniki* (A. Lednicki, *Memoirs*)."

20.   W. Lednicki, *Pamiętniki*, 1 (A. Lednicki, *Memoirs*): 261. Aleksander Lednicki knew several parts of Mickiewicz's epic *Pan Tadeusz* by heart. While this in itself was not unusual for a Pole at that time (or the present), the impact of Mickiewicz on Lednicki was deeper than that of an appreciation for a great national poet. In many of his speeches and writings throughout his life, Lednicki refers to Mickiewicz, whose belief in the necessity of man's joint struggle for freedom and the pan-European ideal he shared. See A. Lednicki, *Mowy polityczne. Przed zwołaniem dumy* (Kraków: Świat Słowianski, 1906), 100; *Z lat*

wojny: Artykuły, listy, przemówienia (1915–1918) (Warsaw: Nakładem Księgarni F. Hoesicka, 1921), 125–27; and *Paneuropa* 2 (1926), no. 11/12: 16.

21. W. Lednicki, *Pamiętniki*, 1: 169.

22. Ibid., 264.

23. Ibid., 250.

24. Smolen, "Działalność polityczna," 29.

25. In his memoirs, Wacław Lednicki points out that the two greatest Polish liberals living in Russia—Aleksander Lednicki and his spiritual mentor Włodzi-mierz Spasowicz—both came from romantic backgrounds and found themselves in positivist circles. They were positivists who remained romantics at heart throughout their lives. See *Pamiętniki*, 1: 332–33. This spiritual dualism was expressed by Lednicki in a speech delivered to the Kraków Economic Society on 22 February 1922, in which he claims to "have a deep sentiment for the idea of Polish romanticism, which gladdened the cheerless years of our bondage. But when the material truth is concerned, the study of the basis of economics, this is difficult; one ought to tear oneself away from poetry, take a pencil and abacus in hand and with a lancet of analysis establish the truth." See A. Lednicki, *Nasza polityka wschodnia*, 60–61.

26. W. Lednicki, *Pamiętniki*, 1: 261.

27. Aleksander Lednicki later recalled that "there were [at this time] Russian revolutionary circles in Minsk, to which I and several of my colleagues belonged. I did not actively participate in such circles, but I was under their strong influence. If I had not possessed an innate merriment, and even recklessness, which often drew me away to dances and ladies, then with certainty I would have also entered such an organization." See W. Lednicki, *Pamiętniki*, 1 (A. Lednicki, *Memoirs*): 264. Lednicki's school days were wild ones, capped by a year of partying during his eighth class at the gymnasium, a period during which he lived apart from his mother in private quarters shared with another Polish student. This year of merriment was described by Lednicki as days of "wantonness and debauchery: cards, drinking and finally, women." Ibid., 265–66.

28. PIASA, Aleksander Lednicki Collection (006), folder 73 (Dzwonkowski), p. 21; also Smolen, "Działalność polityczna," 33.

29. W. Lednicki, *Pamiętniki*, 1: 264–65.

30. The tsarist educational system emphasized classical studies and mathematics; the goal was to keep students too busy to think about politics. Obviously, this did not always work. See Allen Sinel, *The Classroom and the Chancellery: State Educational Reform in Russia under Count Dmitry Tolstoi* (Cambridge: Harvard University Press, 1973), 151.

31. Stanislaus A. Blejwas, *Realism in Polish Politics: Warsaw Positivism and National Survival in Nineteenth Century Poland* (New Haven: Yale Concilium on International and Area Studies, 1984), 7.

32. Ibid., 4. The quotation is from the article "My i wy," *Przęgąd Tygodniowy* 44 (1871): 357.

33. Blejwas, *Realism in Polish Politics*, 57–58.

34. This book first appeared in Polish translation in Lwow in 1862. For more on Buckle's impact on Polish thought, see Andrzej Feliks Grabski, "Warszawscy entuzjasci H. T. Buckle'a. Z dziejów warszawskiego pozytywizmu," *Kwartalnik historyczny* 76 (1969): 853–64.

35. Blejwas, *Realism in Polish Politics*, 68–72.

36. Norman Naimark, "Warsaw Positivism and the Origins of Polish Marxism," *Canadian-American Slavic Studies* 10 (1976): 333.

37. Blejwas, *Realism in Polish Politics*, 85.

38. Świętochowski maintained a strongly assimilationist attitude, asserting that Jewish talent was a resource the Polish nation could ill afford to squander. For a more detailed discussion of the positivists' attitude toward Jews, see Stanislaus Blejwas, "The Jews in the Theory and Practice of Polish Positivism," in *Proceedings of the Conference on Poles and Jews: Myth and Reality in the Historical Context*, ed. Harold B. Segal (New York: Institute on East Central Europe, Columbia University, 1986), 111–139; Henryk Grynberg, "The Jewish Theme in Polish Positivism," *Polish Review* 25 (1980), no. 3/4: 49–57; and Magdalena Opalski, "The Concept of Jewish Assimilation in Polish Literature of the Positivist Period," *Polish Review* 32 (1987), no. 4: 371–83.

39. Cited in Blejwas, *Realism in Polish Politics*, 247, f.n. 56. Roman Dmowski, whose intellectual development was also strongly influenced by Świętochowski, fully embraced this concept. Dmowski's ideology of integral nationalism, which placed emphasis on the interests of the nation above group (class or ethnic) interests, was opposed to those Jews who retained their unique identity. See Peter A. Witkowski, "Roman Dmowski and the Thirteenth Point" (Ph.D. diss., Indiana University, 1981), 20–21; and Alvin Marcus Fountain II, *Roman Dmowski: Party, Tactics, Ideology 1895–1907* (Boulder: East European Monographs, 1980), 109–11.

40. Spasowicz's biographer, Janina Kulczyck-Saloni, uses this term in *Włodzi-mierz Spasowicz. Zarys monograficzny* (Wrocław: Ossolineum, 1975), 9. On Spasowicz, also see Maciej Jankowski, *Być liberalem w czasie trudnym: Rzecz o Włodzimierzu Spasowiczu* (Łódź: Ibidem, 1996).

41. W. Lednicki, *Pamiętniki*, 1: 335. Lednicki regarded himself as a student and follower of Spasowicz. Lednicki followed Spasowicz in making Russian society the target of all efforts for change. Both men refrained from petitioning the tsarist government, hoping instead to convince Russian society that a just solution to the Polish problem was in its best interest. Younger and much more skilled politically, Lednicki carried this program to its logical conclusion through his activities in the Kadet party, the first Duma and the Provisional Government. Lednicki's role as Spasowicz's "spiritual heir" was even recognized by Lednicki's political foe, Erazm Piltz, who on his death bequeathed a portrait of Spasowicz—painted by Repin—to Lednicki. Piltz had collaborated with Spasowicz on the newspaper *Kraj*, and had been Lednicki's political ally at

the turn of the century. See Ibid., 325–38.

42. Kulczycka-Saloni, "Włodzimierz Spasowicz," 6.

43. Piłsudski Institute, Archiwum Władysława Studnickiego. Teka IV, Teczka 4, p. 1.

44. Smolen, "Działalność polityczna," 32.

45. Michael Hryhory Voskobiynyk, "The Nationalities Question in Russia in 1905–1907: A Study in the Origin of Nationalism, with Special Reference to the Ukrainians" (Ph.D. diss., University of Pennsylvania, 1972), 55.

46. PIASA, Aleksander Lednicki Collection (006), folder 2.

47. Zygmunt Wasilewski, *Proces Lednickiego. Fragment z dziejów odbudowy Polski 1915–1924* (Warsaw: Skład główny w Księgarni Perzynski, Niklewicz i Sp., 1924), 385. Lednicki was asked to take part in the defense of Beilis by the Moscow rabbi Jakub Mazeh. Lednicki declined, suggesting that Russian lawyers were needed to make the defense more effective. See Aleksander Lednicki, "Pamiętniki". Ed. Zbigniew Kozinski. *Biuletyn biblioteki Jagiellonskiej* 41 (1991): 154–55.

48. Ironically, while Lednicki's reputation as a champion of Jewish rights was a political liability in his homeland, it gained him much support abroad. In a confidential memo to Lord Cecil, dated 22 December 1917, Jewish activist Lucien Wolf pressed the British government to support Lednicki's bid for political supremacy in Poland. He argued that "a friendly combination of Poland, Lithuania, and Ukrainia is quite possible on the Lednicki basis of the independence of each of those countries and of national autonomy for the minorities within their frontiers, while such a powerful combination is excluded by all the essentials of M. Dmowski's policy...[this] should be made the starting point of discreet negotiations for an entente with M. Lednicki." See PIASA, Aleksander Lednicki Collection (006), folder 17. Photocopy of British Foreign Office document, FO 371/3019, contained in the Public Records Office. The British liberal press also demanded a reevaluation of the government's Polish policy. The *Manchester Guardian* of 7 December 1917 called on the Foreign Office to support Lednicki, arguing that Dmowski stood "for Jingoism and reaction." The *Guardian* labelled Dmowski the "father of modern Polish anti-Semitism."

49. W. Lednicki, *Pamiętniki*, 1: 267.

50. Samuel D. Kassow, *Students, Professors, and the State in Tsarist Russia* (Berkeley: University of California Press, 1989), 24.

51. W. Lednicki, *Pamiętniki*, 1: 267.

52. Lednicki and his comrades may also have been influenced by literary figures, in particular Bazarov, the protagonist of Ivan Turgenev's *Fathers and Sons*, who was preparing for a medical career. The appeal of the nihilist Bazarov to youths of that time is evident in Aleksander's statement that "if not for fear [of punishment] at the gymnasium, with certainty everyone would have worn long hair and blue glasses." Waclaw Lednicki concludes that this is a reference to Bazarov. See his *Pamiętniki*, 1 (A. Lednicki, *Memoirs*): 264.

53. Ibid., 267–69.

54. Kassow, *Students, Professors, and the State*, 31.

55. Ibid., 43–57.

56. W. Lednicki, *Pamiętniki*, 1: 268–69. One of Lednicki's acquaintances at the University, Aleksandr Amfiteatrov, later recalled Lednicki as a bright and serious student who took part in political meetings, but who also enjoyed an active social life. See *Segodniia*, 3 September 1934.

57. Ibid., (A. Lednicki, *Memoirs*): 271.

58. W. Lednicki, *Pamiętniki*, 1: 247.

59. Kassow, *Students, Professors, and the State*, 58–59, 76.

60. Smolen, "Działalność polityczna," 39. Lednicki had apparently witnessed the brutal suppression by police and Cossacks of a student demonstration in his first year at Moscow University. Undoubtedly this further politicized Lednicki and played a role in his later pursuit of a legal career. See PIASA, Wacław Lednicki Collection (007), folder 240, "Russo-Polish Relations," 11–12.

61. Many prominent men in the liberation movement were lawyers, including Lednicki, Leon Petrażicki, Sergei Muromtsev, Vasilii Maklakov, Maksim Winaver, Fedor Rodichev and N. V. Teslenko. See Jonathan E. Sanders, "The Union of Unions: Political, Economic, Civil, and Human Rights Organizations in the 1905 Russian Revolution" (Ph.D. diss., Columbia University, 1985), 524.

62. Vasilii Maklakov, *Iz vospominanii* (New York: Izdatel'stvo imeni Chekhova, 1954), 220. Translated in Sanders, "Union of Unions," 525.

63. George Fischer, *Russian Liberalism: From Gentry to Intelligentsia* (Cambridge: Harvard University Press, 1958), 56.

64. One eyewitness, however, maintains that it was not so much Inspector Bryzgalov's behavior which motivated Siniavski as the oppressive conditions in general which stemmed from the University Statute of 1884. The tsar and much of the Muscovite elite were in attendance, so this concert presented Siniavski with a good opportunity to draw attention to his cause. See G. Rostovtsev, "Studencheskie volneniia v Moskovskom universitete v 1887 r.," in *Moskovskii universitet v vospominaniiakh sovremennikov* (Moscow: Izdatel'stvo Moskovskogo Universiteta, 1956), 326–35. For information about other incidents involving Bryzgalov, see Kassow, *Students, Professors, and the State*, 74.

65. Robert Jean Burch, "Social Unrest in Imperial Russia: The Student Movement at Moscow University, 1887–1905" (Ph.D. diss., University of Washington, 1972), 22–24.

66. Rostovtsev, "Studencheskie volneniia," 330. Siniavski was later sentenced to three years hard labor. See Burch, "Social Unrest in Imperial Russia," 23.

67. Vasilii Maklakov, for example, recalls the episode as a turning point in his life: "For the first time in my life I had seen a person who was sacrificing his whole life for something. Involuntarily there passed through my mind my mother's stories about saints who live in this world and what we read about 'martyrs' who did not want to renounce their faith. I felt that I was seeing such a 'martyr'

with my own eyes. It was one of those impressions which in youth do not pass without an impact...This dim emotion possessed not only me apparently. Everyone wanted to do something..." See *Iz vospominanii*, 61–62. Translation in George Fischer, *Russian Liberalism*, 55.

68. W. Lednicki, *Pamiętniki*, 1: 277–78. Interestingly, Lednicki's future wife, Maria Odlanicka, also witnessed the event. She was present to perform in her first public concert.

69. *Gosudarstvennaia Duma pervago prizyva. Portrety, kratkiia biografii i kharakteristiki deputatov.* (Moscow: Knigoizdatel'stvo "Vozrozhdenie," 1906), 40.

70. PIASA, Aleksander Lednicki Collection (006), folder 73 (Dzwonkowski), p. 32; and W. Lednicki, *Pamiętniki*, 1: 271.

71. Fischer, *Russian Liberalism*, 69–70. Paul Miliukov noted that he him-self "succeeded in remaining independent of the influence of both main currents ruling over the minds of the Russian intelligentsia of the last quarter of the nine-teenth century, populism and Marxism. This I owe before all else to circumstances beyond my control: that I belong to the generation that is younger than the gener-ation of the 'seventies which was enthusiastic about populism, but older than the generation of the 'eighties and 'nineties, which pledged allegiance to Marx."

72. A. A. Kizevetter, *Na rubezhe dvukh stoletii. (Vospominaniia 1881–1914)* (Prague: Orbis, 1929), 170.

73. Sanders, "Union of Unions," 525.

74. Muromtsev's photo stood on Lednicki's desk next to that of Spasowicz. In 1911 Lednicki headed Muromtsev's funeral committee. W. Lednicki, *Pamiętniki*, 1: 336, 400–04. Smolen maintains that the "spiritual fatherhood of Muromtsev and Kovalevski" influenced Lednicki's political career, determining his liberal activism. See "Działalność polityczna," 40.

75. A. R. Lednitskii [Lednicki], *Iz proshlago* (Moscow: V. I. Voronov, 1917), 46. This booklet contains the text of Lednicki's speech delivered on the occasion of the fiftieth anniversary celebration of the Moscow bar on 23 September 1916.

76. Kizevetter, *Vospominaniia*, 25–26.

77. W. Lednicki, *Pamiętniki*, 1: 271.

78. Zygmunt Łukawski, *Ludność polska w Rosji 1863–1914* (Wrocław: Wydawnictwo Polskiej Akademii Nauk, 1978), 127. Unlike the zemliachestva made up of Russian students, the groups consisting of non-Russians were city-wide and not restricted to students at the university. See Kassow, *Students, Professors, and the State*, 77.

79. Formally banned by authorities, *zemliachestva* were self-help and self-education groups consisting of students from the same home district or the same nationality.

80. Łukawski, *Ludność polska w Rosji*, 127; also W. Lednicki, *Pamiętniki*, 1: 272.

81. Kassow, *Students, Professors, and the State*, 79.

82. W. Lednicki, *Pamiętniki*, 1: 275. *Polskość* is defined by one scholar as something more than Polishness or Polish character. "It can signify everything that the dictionary says, but it also signifies, as it were, something more, something elusive. *Polskość* signifies the very essence of being a Pole." See Jerzy Jedlicki, "Holy Ideals and Prosaic Life, or the Devil's Alternatives," in *Polish Paradoxes*, ed. Stanislaw Gomulka and Antony Polonsky (London & New York: Routledge, 1990), 41. For a rebuttal to those who accused Lednicki of not being "Polish," see the transcript of his attorney's speech at the trial of Zygmunt Wasilewski, whom Lednicki charged with slander in 1924, in Eugeniusz Smiarowski, *Mowy obroncze* (1920–1925) (Warsaw: M. Borkowski-Marzałkowski, 1926), 142–270, especially 168–74.

83. Tracey Trenam, "Without a Free Poland, a Free Russia Cannot Be! Polish Liberals in the Russian Empire, 1904–1907" (Ph.D. diss., Columbia University, 1994), 55–56.

84. Galai, *Liberation Movement*, 154–55.

85. Other Russian participants at these meetings included Prince Dmitri Shakhovskoi, Maklakov, Fedor Kokoshkin, Pavel Miliukov, Fedor Rodichev, Vladimir Nabokov, and Evgenii Trubecki. See Leon Kozlowski, *Rewolucja rosyjska i niepodległość Polski: Geneza aktu 30 marca* (Warsaw: Zjednoczenie, 1922), 26. Kozlowski wrote that "in the Lednicki salon, Moscow met Warsaw."

86. Prince Pavel Dmitri Dolgorukov, *Velikaia razrukha* (Madrid: Imp. Rafael Taravilla Paul, 1964), 245. On this particular occasion, Lednicki organized a large reception for Dolgorukov, who stayed on as a house guest. Lednicki also remained in contact with Petr Dolgorukov; see their correspondence in GARF (Prazhkii arkhiv), F. 5086, op. 1, d. 1.

87. According to Lednicki, Buckle's *History of English Civilization* was among his favorite books; in fact, he cites it as one reason for his switch to the Juridical Faculty. See W. Lednicki, *Pamiętniki*, 1: 276.

88. Ibid.

Chapter Two

LAWYER AND POLISH ACTIVIST, 1889–1903

Having fled the highly charged atmosphere of Moscow University, Lednicki flourished in the peaceful surroundings of Yaroslavl. Concentrating more on his studies than on politics, he graduated with a law degree in the spring of 1889. His thesis, entitled "Joint Stock Companies," revealed an early interest in the business world. Trained in the law of finance and possessing a knack for making money, Lednicki would amass a huge fortune. After overcoming a penchant for wild spending, by the turn of the century his material resources were "truly unlimited."[1]

In the fall of 1889 Lednicki married Maria Odlanicka-Poczobutt Kriwonosow, whom he had met while a student in Moscow. The Polish colony in Moscow at that time numbered about 7,500, and it maintained close relations with Polish students at the university and other schools in the city.[2] Amateur theatrical productions, balls, concerts and fundraisers for destitute students were held at the homes of prominent Poles, at which students and their compatriots comingled. It was at one such event that Aleksander first met Maria, probably in 1887. Smitten, he became a regular at functions of the Moscow Polish colony; he continued to participate in its activities even after his transfer to Yaroslavl in order to pursue his courtship.

Like many other Polish Muscovites, Maria was the offspring of mixed parentage; her mother was Polish and her father Russian.[3] Considered Orthodox under Russian law, she was in fact a devout Catholic.[4] Aleksander's desire to accentuate her Polishness induced the young couple to marry in secrecy. They travelled to Narva for their wedding; Maria's birth records were in Moscow, and the lax authorities at Narva allowed her to register as "Maria Odlanicka, Catholic Pole."[5] This was an illegal act, one that would cause the couple much grief. In fact, Lednicki's marriage to a "Russian" would haunt him his whole life: to his political opponents in interwar Poland, in particular, it offered further proof of his total russification.[6]

In the short term, however, Aleksander's marriage proved beneficial. Perhaps because of her bourgeois background, Maria possessed a strong work ethic and was frugal with her own limited financial resources. Meanwhile, Aleksander still retained his youthful ways; during the first years of his marriage he continued to gamble and carouse with his companions, neglecting his work and his family's finances. Lednicki enjoyed having a good time, and he had a taste for the finer things in life. A non-smoker, he always kept the best Havanna cigars on hand for guests.[7] He frequently rented a private room at the Sandunovskii baths in Moscow, where he escaped to relax and recuperate.[8] He forever retained his passion for the high life: in his later years he particularly enjoyed playing roulette and baccarat in Monte Carlo and Biarritz.[9]

Over time, Maria instilled in her husband a greater sense of responsibility; the birth of their first child, Waclaw, in 1891 no doubt helped in his maturation. A talented musician, Maria abandoned any dreams of a career to devote all her time to her family. Waclaw later remembered the Lednicki home as an idyllic household in which his mother provided a peaceful environment. Lednicki suffered from occasional migraine headaches, and Maria strived to prevent them by insisting on absolute quiet for her husband when he was working.[10] Lednicki worked late, often until 2 a.m., then slept for seven or eight hours. When he awoke, Maria read him the papers in bed, especially the news on Russian and foreign politics.[11]

An equally important factor in Lednicki's metamorphosis was his employer, the civil lawyer Nikolai S. Trostianskii. Aided by his wife's connections in the Russian legal community, Aleksander began work as an apprentice in Trostianskii's office shortly after his marriage. He served as an assistant lawyer for several years, becoming the office chief in 1893. The following year he ended his apprenticeship, and on Trostianskii's death in 1896 he assumed control of the firm. During these years, Aleksander experienced a change of character. Lednicki's son, Waclaw, speculates that Trostianskii may have served as an authority figure for Aleksander, who lost his own father at the age of three and his grandfather not long thereafter. There may be some validity to this theory, for it is clear that by the time of his mentor's death Aleksander had abandoned his profligate ways and had become "a fanatic for work."[12]

Indeed, those early admonitions by grandfather Franciszek regarding the value of work had finally taken effect, for Aleksander was now a workaholic. As Adam Szafkowski—one of Lednicki's legal assistants from 1905 to 1918—recalled, "He was a titan of energy and work."[13] For the "new" Aleksander, a strong devotion to work constituted a major part of his personality, and he apparently had little regard for those who chose to ignore productive activity, which he came to consider one's moral obligation.[14] This conviction was undoubtedly also grounded in his long-held belief in the tenets of Warsaw Positivism, which called on Poles literally to work their way to political independence. Armed with considerable native intelligence and talents and the motto, "One cannot live without work," he would do very well in the business world.[15]

While not yet widely known among the general public, Lednicki had already earned quite a reputation in legal circles by the time he inherited Trostianskii's practice. In 1896, Vasilii Maklakov, just graduated from Moscow University's Juridical Faculty, set about searching for a patron in whose office he could enroll as an assistant. Already possessing the attributes that would bring him great fame as a criminal lawyer, Maklakov was highly regarded by his teachers. The famous jurist F. N. Plevako had known Maklakov as a student, and immediately offered him a position. Fearful of becoming lost in the crowd at the bustling offices of Plevako, Maklakov looked elsewhere. He turned to a local Justice of the Peace, who advised him:

Don't go to a celebrity: they will not teach you. Don't go to
an unknown man: you won't find work there. Go to some-
one, who is still not a celebrity, but soon will be. I have in
mind such a man. It is Lednitskii...He will go far.[16]

Maklakov followed this advice, and became Lednicki's first official assistant.

While Maklakov soon moved on to establish his own practice, he and Lednicki enjoyed an enduring friendship. Often a guest at Lednicki's home in Moscow or at his estate near Smolensk, Maklakov later noted how "at evenings at his [Lednicki's] home, where the flower of Muscovite magistrates, lawyers and intelligentsia gathered, I was able to observe how his popularity grew."[17] Indeed, Lednicki's name appeared frequently in the press and he quickly attained public recognition for his involvement in major cases. He had a wide circle of clients, mainly among rich landowners, industrialists, and merchants.[18]

By the time of the first Russian revolution, Lednicki was one of the wealthiest and most widely-recognized lawyers in all of Russia. In 1902 he was elected to the Lawyers' Council of Moscow, an honor bestowed on only a dozen or so of the most accomplished lawyers in that city. Members of the council had enormous influence among their fellow attorneys and the public at large. Lednicki received permission to argue cases before the Senate, the highest court in the empire. From 1900 to 1905, he also taught a legal seminar at Moscow University.[19] With his increasingly busy schedule, he usually deferred most of his caseload to his assistants in order to concentrate chiefly on the most lucrative civil lawsuits; he also occasionally handled some criminal and political cases.[20]

Lednicki parlayed his status and reputation into a public career, which always took three paths: work for the welfare of Poles living in Russia, especially among the Polish colony in Moscow; cooperation with political and cultural organizations in Poland; and political action among Russian society regarding the Polish question.[21]

In constant flux, the Polish colony in Moscow was traditionally difficult to organize. Many Poles would go to Moscow for their higher education, then return to Poland after graduation. Others, however, did remain permanently, pursuing lucrative professional careers. Yet residency in Russia had a high cost; russification, and often total assimilation, caused many Poles to lose their national identity.[22] This further complicated efforts to consolidate the Polish colony. Social differentiation also posed a problem in developing a sense of community among Poles in Moscow, for members of the professional intelligentsia had little in common with their working-class compatriots.[23]

One common denominator was their Catholicism, and it was around the Church that the colony began to coalesce. On 16 December 1885, the Roman Catholic Relief Society held its first meeting in Moscow. Originally founded to help the children of destitute Poles and to facilitate the acclimation of new members of the colony, the society gradually widened the scope of its activities. It did so at the urging of Lednicki, who from 1890 was the secretary of the society and represented the interests of the younger generation of Poles living in Moscow. In 1896 he assumed the presidency, marking a new period of increased activity for the society and the Polish community in Moscow.[24]

Under Lednicki's leadership, the society established a reading room, a library and an orphanage, and it provided free medical and legal aid to destitute Poles. Increased membership and consequently more funds made such activities possible. The society's original membership of 73 soon grew to about 200. It remained at that level for several years, but by 1904 its roster had swelled to include some 579 full and adjunct members.[25] In 1886, membership dues, one-time gifts and amateur theatrical productions raised about 3,000 rubles. By 1903, the annual income had risen to 23,562 rubles.[26]

Lednicki's fund-raising efforts also reached beyond the Moscow colony. In celebration of the 100th anniversary of the birth of Adam Mickiewicz in 1898, Lednicki organized a drive to collect funds for a fellowship in the poet's name for Polish students to be established at Moscow University. The effort raised six thousand rubles, largely donations from merchants and industrialists living in Polish communities around the empire. Many engineers, doctors and lawyers also contributed, as did a number of *Kresy* landowners.[27] These same groups would support Lednicki throughout his political career; many contributors were members of the Roman Catholic Relief Society or the Polish Committee for the Relief of War Victims, an organization Lednicki established during World War I.[28]

As a result of his activities among the Polish colony in Moscow and other Russian cities, Lednicki became one of the most prominent Poles in Russia. His home became a center of Polish cultural activities. Lednicki and his wife hosted costume balls and other fund-raising functions for the colony. Maria also headed the organization "Lutnia" (Lute), an association of amateur musicians and choral groups which the Roman Catholic Relief Society established in 1902.[29] The Lednicki home also functioned as a sort of political salon, where Poles—and Russians—gathered to discuss current issues.[30] It was in these informal gatherings that Lednicki pursued a rapprochement between Poles and Russians. Poles in Moscow, indeed throughout the empire, would come to know him as a tireless advocate of the Polish cause.

Lednicki's reputation for aiding Poles in distress soon spread well beyond Moscow. For example, in 1902 the Polish writer Eliza Orzeszkowa[31] called on him to help her raise funds for the care of the aged Maria Konopnicka[32] In her letters, Orzeszkowa points to his work as a tireless Polish activist as her reason for contacting him.[33] Further, Lednicki often helped Poles accused of political crimes escape the wrath of Russian authorities.[34]

Lednicki's activism carried him well beyond the confines of the Polish colony, and by the mid-1890s he had become active in Russian liberal circles. His goal was to popularize the Polish cause; by making Russian society aware of Poland's plight, he hoped to gain support for Polish autonomy. In 1894, he succeeded in drawing the Roman Catholic Relief Society into contact with Russian charitable groups, but Russian authorities prevented any real cooperation between Poles and Russians.[35] While such efforts served to highlight the particular problems of Poles in Russia, they also publicized the Polish question in general. In no small measure due to Lednicki's influence in Moscow society, Russians were becoming more aware of the Polish issue.

While many of his Russian friends were professional colleagues such as Maklakov, Lednicki also became acquainted with Moscow's creative community at the Moscow Literary-Artistic Club. It was probably here that he met the Symbolist poets Valerii Briusov and Dmitrii Merezhkovskii.[36] Lednicki's friendship with Briusov developed into a relationship with a political twist. During the First World War, Lednicki arranged for Briusov to tour Poland as a war correspondent for *Russkiia vedomosti* (Russian News)[37] In this way, Briusov served

Lednicki's political agenda, propagandizing the Polish cause among the readers of *Russkiia vedomosti*.[38] Briusov stayed in Poland, mainly Warsaw, from late August 1914 until mid-May 1915, with one brief visit to Moscow in January. During this time, he wrote some seventy-five articles as a war correspondent.[39] Briusov also penned several poems while in Poland. They evoke images of Slavic unity in the face of the German onslaught. He dedicated one poem, entitled "V Varshave," to his friend and benefactor, Aleksander Lednicki.[40]

In his crusade for Polish autonomy, Lednicki found a staunch supporter in Viktor Aleksandrovich Gol'tsev (1850–1906), editor of *Russkaia mysl'* and by the turn of the century a veteran of anti-government activism.[41] After receiving his law degree from Moscow University in 1872, Gol'tsev pursued a career in academia. His future as a scholar was cut short, however, after the police, acting on false accusations regarding his political activities, deemed him a subversive character. Ironically, as a result he focused all his energies in political activism. He published liberal journals critical of the tsarist regime, and actively participated in the zemstvo movement. He attended the first zemstvo congress held in Moscow in 1879.[42] Later, he served as vice-president of the Moscow Juridical Society.

Lednicki became acquainted with Gol'tsev at meetings of this society. Moreover, the two men belonged to the same liberal social circles in Moscow in the 1890s.[43] They were on familiar terms by 1900, when *Russkaia mysl'* dispatched Lednicki to report on the five-hundred-year anniversary of the founding of the Jagiellonian University in Kraków. In his first article in the Russian press, Lednicki not only commented on the celebration, but also criticized the oppressive conditions in Poland and Russia.[44]

Under the guidance of Gol'tsev and his co-editor, Vukol Lavrov, *Russkaia mysl'* published many articles on Poland. Gol'tsev was enthusiastic about Polish-Russian brotherhood, while Lavrov was one of the most prolific translators of Polish literature. He translated all the novels of Henryk Sienkiewicz and Eliża Orzeszkowa and many of the works of Maria Konopnicka, Bolesław Prus, Stefan Żeromski and other leading Polish writers. He maintained a particularly close relationship with Orzeszkowa.[45] Lednicki himself helped popularize Polish literature in Russia, by contributing literary reviews to

Russkaia mysl'. In a 1903 article on the works of Maria Konopnicka, he praised her for promoting the "great principle of the democratic movement," which he believed "the whole civilized world obeys with greater and greater force."[46]

Lednicki and Gol'tsev cemented their friendship with a mutual passion for a just solution to the nationalities problem. In a 1901 speech in Moscow, Gol'tsev quoted N. S. Soloviev in arguing that, while "the nationality question for many nations is a question of their existence...the nationality question in Russia is a question not of existence, but of a *deserving existence*."[47] Lednicki later hailed his friend as an advocate for the freedom of all Slavic nations, calling him "one of the most zealous organizers of the Polish-Russian congresses [of 1904 and 1905]. He was weak, but he took part—he was one of the few who did not oppose a separate constituent assembly in Warsaw...."[48] At Gol'tsev's funeral in Moscow on 22 November 1906, Lednicki delivered an emotional eulogy, declaring it his "sacred duty... to swear before all, that this Russian name will not be forgotten."[49]

Gol'tsev evidently had great respect for his friend, for in 1903 the aging editor decided to turn over control of *Russkaia mysl'* to Lednicki. Such a move required the approval of tsarist authorities; subsequently, the *Okhrana* (tsarist secret police) undertook an investigation to determine the "moral qualities, political reliability, acquaintances, occupations, means of living, positions in society, kindred ties, personalities and ages" of Lednicki and his proposed coeditor, Dmitrii Stepanov Gorshkov.[50] Lednicki's bid for control of the influential thick journal was rejected. Police reports cite his "dealings with liberals of extremist tendencies" as the primary reason for denying him this privilege.[51] Lednicki later recalled with bitterness that it was Minister of Interior von Plehve who barred his acquisition of *Russkaia mysl'*. To him, as to many in the liberation movement, the hated minister became a living symbol of arbitrary bureaucratic oppression.[52]

Because of his influence within the Moscow Polish colony, his reputation throughout Poland, and his close relations with the leaders of the emergent Russian liberation movement, by the turn of the century Aleksander Lednicki was the "Polish ambassador accredited by Russian society."[53] Lednicki was uniquely qualified for this role, for he was a man of two worlds. As Paul Miliukov wrote at the time of his close friend's death, although "a great Polish patriot, 'Alexander Robertovich' was regarded by his Moscow friends as a genuine Russian intellectual."[54] Lednicki was also an admirer of the Russian people and firmly believed in the decency of the Russian nation.[55] The tsarist autocracy's relentless oppression of all peoples of the empire—including the Russians—motivated his social and political activism.

Like Adam Mickiewicz, Lednicki believed that the struggle for liberty was universal, and that Polish freedom could only come hand in hand with that of other nations.[56] For Lednicki, this was no abstract concept: he seems to have been innocent of any trace of chauvinism. In his law offices, for example, he employed not only Poles but also Russians, Jews, Ukrainians and Lithuanians. During his last years in Moscow, his chief legal assistant was Pietr Andriejewicz Pietrowski, a russified Ukrainian married to a russified Pole, who also participated in Lednicki's actions on behalf of the Polish cause.[57] For Lednicki, multiculturalism was a natural way of life.

It was because of his apparent russification and his multicultural outlook that Lednicki's Polishness, his *polskość*, came to be questioned by political opponents. Zygmunt Wasilewski, publicist and political ally of the chauvinistic leader of the National Democrats, Roman Dmowski, maintained that Lednicki was "a man not able to define his nationality."[58] Wasilewski charged in the interwar period that Lednicki's return to Poland was purely an act of expediency, and that he felt no kinship with other Poles. He regarded Lednicki as a sort of human chameleon: "when there was not a Polish state but there was a Russian state, Lednicki passed himself off as a Russian. While today [1924], when there is no Russian state but a Polish state, he passes himself off as a Pole."[59]

Other Polish critics commented on Lednicki's inherent Russianness, which he still retained as an elderly man living in Poland. One acquaintance recorded his revulsion upon meeting Lednicki in 1925, noting that "his accent appeared to be not of Wilno, like that of Pilsudski...but Muscovite; his clothing was something from Moscow or Petersburg, and his mentality also seemed completely foreign to me."[60] Yet it was this outward Russianness and his mastery of the Russian language that enabled Lednicki to ingratiate himself with his colleagues in Moscow.[61] It was only on his permanent return to Poland after the Bolshevik Revolution that these characteristics became liabilities.

Wacław Lednicki devoted much of his later life defending his father's integrity, constantly endeavoring to prove Aleksander's *poskość*. Wacław recalls that a distinctly Polish atmosphere pervaded the Lednicki home in Moscow, site of many functions of the Polish colony. Frequented by Poles of all sorts, especially clergymen, it served as "a [Polish] island in the surrounding Russian sea."[62] Nagorski argued that "despite his permanent residence in Moscow he [Lednicki] always lived a Polish life."[63] In fact, Lednicki abhorred those who abandoned their *polskość*; for example, he criticized those Poles who attended the elite schools for sons of the upper nobility in St. Petersburg, where future tsarist officials were groomed. To Lednicki, the presence of Poles in these schools was "a compromise, a silent resignation from national ambitions."[64]

"National ambitions," the desire to promote the Polish cause, was Aleksander Lednicki's *raison d'être*. Initially this desire was manifested in his cultural activism. Poles in the late 19th century felt the increasing pressure of russification and responded by acting to preserve their national cultural traditions. This was especially the case for those who lived in Russia, struggling to preserve their *polskość* in a hostile environment. Influenced by the philosophy of Warsaw Positivism, which called for the strengthening of a nation's cultural and material wealth as a necessary precursor to political independence, Poles embraced the notion that "the most vital, most important foundation of every nation is its culture, its language."[65]

As a youth in the *Kresy*, Lednicki was raised in an environment of Polish patriotism. As a university student in Moscow, he intensified his Polishness through self-education, immersing himself in the study of Polish history, culture and language. Even at this time, his Russian colleagues "became accustomed to respect him, to respect his *Polskość* — this young Polish gentleman compelled [them] to bow low before the Polish standard."[66] Indeed, Lednicki fit the image of Roman Dmowski's "modern Pole," striving to fulfill his duties as defender of all things Polish.[67]

With the coalescence of the Russian liberationists into an organized movement at the turn of the century, Lednicki decided the time was ripe to defend not only Polish culture, but actively to solicit support for political demands, including autonomy for the Kingdom. Aided by his intimate contacts with leading constitutionalists, the ambitious young Pole with a passion for politics went about orchestrating a rapprochement between Russian and Polish liberals.[68]

ENDNOTES

1.　W. Lednicki, *Pamiętniki*, 1: 139–40. By 1914, Lednicki was a multimillionaire, largely because of his lucrative law practice. He owned several estates totalling about 15,000 acres. He bought the estate Borek in 1896. Located near Smolensk, it included 1,600 acres and was valued in 1916 at 400,000 rubles. The more palatial Bortkuszki-Platerowo, purchased in 1913, was situated near Wilno. Lednicki also owned homes in Minsk, Warsaw and Moscow. In 1898 he purchased his home at No. 8 Krivonikol'skii Lane in Moscow for 80,000 rubles. After considerable renovation it consisted of 25 rooms. See *Pamiętniki*, 1: 357, 478–79.

2.　Walentyna Najdus, *Polacy w rewolucji 1917 roku* (Warsaw: PWN, 1967), 39.

3.　Aleksander Lednicki recalled in his memoirs that the Polish colony in Moscow during his student years contained many such households; according to him about one-half of the Polish elite in Moscow were part Russian, if not also Orthodox. Russification was in many cases complete, and he reported meeting many Poles who could no longer speak Polish. See W. Lednicki, *Pamiętniki*, 1: 272–74, 281–82.

4.　Maria's "Orthodoxy" upset Lednicki's mother and sister, who vehemently opposed the marriage. Ibid., 341–42.

5.　Ibid., 299.

6.　The young couple's secret was revealed quite early in the marriage. Lednicki's first major legal case (while the exact date is unclear, it must have occurred sometime in the mid-1890s), a complicated one dealing with a dispute over a large estate, pitted him against a fellow Polish lawyer by the name of Kozłowski. Having found out that Lednicki had illegally falsified his marriage records, Kozłowski threatened to report the incident to the authorities. Lednicki responded by confessing his act directly to the Vice Governor of Moscow, Boratynski, and A. V. Stepanov, the local procurator. Their support of Lednicki, resulting in the dismissal of any charges against him, reveals the good relations Lednicki had already established with the elite of Russian society and the Russian legal community. See Ibid., 303–07.

7. Ibid., 437.

8. Ibid., 62.

9. Ibid., 345.

10. Ibid., 339.Lednicki's hectic schedule undoubtedly exacerbated his condition, and he frequently sought cures by the sea. He responded well to such treatments. He was particularly fond of Kissingen; in July 1914, despite the recent assassination of Archduke Ferdinand in Sarejevo, Lednicki vacationed there with his family because he needed the rest. Lednicki returned to Russia only after Austria issued its ultimatum to Serbia on 23 July. Lednicki regarded the departure that same day of General A. A. Brusilov, his frequent bridge partner at the resort, as a bad omen. See W. Lednicki, *Pamiętniki*, 2: 336. In his search for a healthier lifestyle, Lednicki evened toyed with vegetarianism for a while, until his private physician convinced him to forego such a drastic conversion. Ibid., 1: 518.

11. Ibid., 350.

12. Ibid., 301–02, 346.

13. Ibid., 352.

14. For example, Lednicki hated spending time at the Poczobutt estate, Cialosz, at which prevailed a "truly Oblomov" atmosphere. Ibid., 131–32.

15. Dzwonkowski cited figures given by Adam Szafkowski, who maintained that Lednicki earned 240,000 rubles per year after paying expenses and salaries for the 32 lawyers he employed. His chief assistant earned 24,000 rubles per year —a hefty sum at a time when the vast majority of lawyers made between 2,000 and 10,000 rubles annually. Only .5% of all lawyers in Russia earned between 20,000 and 50,000 rubles per year. To place Lednicki's income (excluding any revenue from his estates or investments) in greater perspective: the average physician earned 1,200 rubles annually, while full professors earned about 3,000 rubles. See PIASA, Aleksander Lednicki Collection (006), folder 73 (Dzwonkows-ki), p. 47. Cited in Smolen, "Działalność polityczna," 44; W. Lednicki, *Pamiętniki*, 1: 361–62. Also see Sanders, "Union of Unions," 528; and Kassow, *Students, Professors, and the State*, 34 and 61.

16. Maklakov, *Iz vospominanii*, 234.

17. V. A. Maklakov, "F. I. Rodichev i A. R. Lednitskii," *Novyi zhurnal* 16 (1947): 245. For anecdotes relating to Maklakov's visits, see Wacław's childhood recollections in V. Lednitskii, "Vokrug V. A. Maklakova (Lichnye vospominaniia)," *Novyi zhurnal* 56 (1959): 225-28.

18. Smolen, "Działalność polityczna," 44.

19. Ibid., 45; also see PIASA, Aleksander Lednicki Collection (006), folder 73 (Dzwonkowski), p. 57.

20. W. Lednicki, *Pamiętniki*, 1: 351, 365–66; see also Alexander Kerensky, *Russia and History's Turning Point* (New York: Duell, Sloan and Pearce, 1965), 76. Lednicki argued for those who were accused of crimes and could afford to hire an established lawyer, but he also handled a number of *pro bono* cases.

21. Zygmunt Nagórski, "Aleksander Lednicki (1866–1934)," *Zeszyty historyczny* 1 (1962): 29. This article is also included in Nagórski's *Ludzie mego czasu. Sylwetki* (Paris: Księgarnia Polska w Paryżu, 1964).

22. In his memoirs, Aleksander Lednicki recounted his encounters as a student with many Poles in Moscow who could no longer speak Polish. He recalled one in particular, a lawyer named Edmund Falkowski, who broke into tears when Lednicki began speaking to him in Polish. It was the first time he had heard Polish in 20 years. See W. Lednicki, *Pamiętniki*, 1 (A. Lednicki, *Memoirs*): 273–74.

23. Smolen,"Działalność polityczna," 46.

24. Ibid., 48; PIASA, Aleksander Lednicki Collection (006), folder 73 (Dzwonkowski), p. 78. The population of the Polish colony was also growing. In 1907 it numbered 14,000, and by 1914 about 20,000 Poles lived in Moscow. See Najdus, *Polacy w rewolucji*, 39.

25. Łukawski, *Ludność polska w Rosji*, 141.

26. Ibid.

27. M. Namyslowska, ed., "Historia stypendium im. Adam Mickiewicza przy uniwersytecie moskiewskim," in *Puszkin: 1837–1937*, 2 vol., ed. A. Bruckner, B. Lepki, J. Tyc, et al. (Kraków: Nakładem Polskiego Towarzystwo dla Badań Europy Wschodniej i Bliskiego Wschodu Skład Główny, 1939), 2: 73–82. A total of 270 people donated from 30 kopecks to 100 rubles.

28. Ibid., 79.

29. PIASA, Aleksander Lednicki Collection (006), folder 73 (Dzwonkowski), p. 83.

30. Łukawski, *Ludność polska w Rosji*, 146.

31. Eliża Orzeszkowa (1841–1910), Polish populist novelist and publicist, spent most of her life in her hometown of Grodno, in the former Grand Duchy of Lithuania. Her writings are full of characters whom she met in the provinces: peasants, petty gentry and Jewish villagers. Her writings promoted equal rights for women and Jews. Polish patriot and democrat, she participated in the uprising of 1863; however, she also later established schools and publishing houses in Wilno, in the spirit of Positivist "organic work." Published collections of her correspondence with the leading minds of Poland and Europe reveal a wealth of information. Of particular importance was her relationship with Vukol Lavrov and Viktor Gol'tsev, editors of *Russkaia mysl'*. See Czesław Miłosz, *The History of Polish Literature*, 2d ed. (Berkeley, Los Angeles, London: University of California Press, 1983), 303–08.

32. Maria Konopnicka (1842–1910), was a popular poet and short story writer whose works dealt chiefly with the plight of the oppressed: peasants, workers and Jews. She became friends with Orzeszkowa while both attended a Catholic boarding school in Warsaw. During her many troubled times, Konopnicka was supported by her old friend; it was in an attempt to help that Orzeszkowa wrote to Lednicki. Ibid., 318–20.

33. Eliża Orzeszkowa, *Listy zebrane*, ed. Edmund Jankowski (Warsaw:

Wydawnictwo PAN, 1981), vol. 9: 347–49, 421–22. Lednicki had great respect for Orzeszkowa and her writings, and he often quoted her works with regard to the democratic spirit in Polish literature and the struggle against antisemitism. For example, see A. Lednicki, *Mowy polityczne*, 26–27.

34. As late as the 1950s, a Pole named Henry Korab-Janiewicz donated $1,000 to the Polish Institute of Arts and Sciences in America "in commemoration of the great Polish patriot and noble man, Aleksander Lednicki." Lednicki had saved Korab-Janiewicz, then a boy of 16 and a member of a Polish conspiratorial group, from Siberian exile in 1915. See W. Lednicki, ed., *Adam Mickiewicz in World Literature* (Berkeley and Los Angeles: University of California Press, 1956), viii–ix. Unsubstantiated, and vehemently denied by Wacław Lednicki, is one scholar's contention that Lednicki helped Feliks Dzierżyński flee Russia in 1899. In *Man of Terror: Dzherzhynski* (London: Peter Owen Limited, 1956), 58–59, Bernard Bromage maintains that after escaping from Siberia, Dzierżyński "somehow...found a fellow-countryman, an attorney named Lednicki, who gave him money and food. A few days later he was on the train for Wilno." See also W. Lednicki, *Pamiętniki*, 2: 452.

35. Smolen, "Działalność polityczna," 49–50; also Smolen, "Aleksander Lednicki (1866–1934). Pierwsze kroki na niwie społecznej i politycznej," *Prace historyczne* 92 (1990): 58–59.

36. W. Lednicki, *Rosyjsko-polska 'entente cordiale,' jej początki i fundamenty 1903–1905* (Paris: Instytut Literacki, 1966), 14. One memoirist recalled that after the Bolshevik Revolution "Merezhkovskii met many of his acquaintances from Petrograd and Moscow in Warsaw. Among them were close friends such as A. P. [sic] Lednicki, the Polish patriot and distinguished public leader..." See Karol Wędziagolski, *Boris Savinkov: Portrait of a Terrorist*, ed. Tadeusz Świętochowski, tr. Margaret Patoski (Clifton, NJ: The Kingston Press, 1988), 158–59.

37. Lednicki arranged for his friend's safe conduct to Wilno and accommodations there, and most likely other Polish cities as well. See Rukopisnyi Otdel, Gosudarstvennaia Biblioteka im. V. I. Lenina (RO GBL). Valerii Iakovlevich Briusov Collection. F. 386, k. 92, ed. kh. 2a, l. 3. In a letter written to the president of Wilno, Michal Weslanski, dated 12 August 1914, Lednicki asked that he take care of "our friend, the well-known writer Valerii Briusov."

38. N. Ashukin, ed. *Valerii Briusov v avtobiograficheskikh zapisiakh, pis'makh, vospominaniiakh sovremennikov i otzyvakh kritiki* (Moscow: Federatsiia, 1929), 325.

39. Joan Delaney Grossman, "Autumn 1914: A Russian Poet in Poland," in *Language, Literature, Linguistics: In Honor of Francis J. Whitfield on his Seventieth Birthday, March 25 1986*, ed. Michael S. Flier and Simon Karlinsky (Berkeley: Berkeley Slavic Specialties, 1987), 72–88.

40. This poem, dated 24 August 1914, first appeared in *Russkiia vedomosti*, and is in Briusov's collected works. See V. Ia. Briusov, *Sochineniia*, 2 vols.

(Moscow: Khudozhestvennaia literatura, 1987), 1: 325.

41.   On *Russkaia mysl'* in general, and Gol'tsev's role in particular, see E. V. Startskova, *"Russkaia mysl',"* in *Literaturnyi protsess i russkaia zhurnalistika kontsa XIX—nachala XX veka. 1890–1904: Burzhuazno-liberal'nye i modernistskie izdaniia* (Moscow: Nauka, 1982), 44–90.

42.   Shmuel Galai, *The Liberation Movement in Russia 1900–1905* (Cambridge: Cambridge University Press, 1973), 17.

43.   Judith Zimmerman, "Between Revolution and Reaction: The Russian Consti-tutional Democratic Party: October, 1905 to June, 1907" (Ph.D. diss., Columbia University, 1967), 18–19.

44.   See *Russkaia mysl'* 21 (October 1900): 9–10, 225–30. See also W. Lednicki, "Cracow Celebration—A Retrospective Presentation of Aleksander Lednicki's Report," *Polish Review* 9 (1964), no. 2: 5–18.

45.   Zbigniew Baranski, *Literatura polska w rosji na przełomie XIX i XX wieku* (Wrocław: Prace Wrocławskiego towarzystwa naukowego, 1962), 58–59.

46.   A. R. Lednitskii, "Mariia Konopnitskaia," *Russkaia mysl'* 24 (April 1903): 14. Also see A. G. Piotrovskaia, *Tvorcheskii put' Marii Konopnitskoi* (Moscow: Izdatel'stvo Akademii Nauk SSSR, 1962), 265–68.

47.   V. Gol'tsev, "Natsional'nyi vopros v XIX veke. (Iz politicheskago nasledstva proshlago stoletiia)," *Russkaia mysl'* 22 (March 1901): 152. Emphasis in original. A signed copy of this speech is in Gol'tsev's collection in the Lenin Library. See RO GBL, f. 77, k. 20, ed. kh. 4, ll. 1–36.

48.   A. Lednicki, *Z lat wojny*, 174.

49.   Ch. Vetrinskii, "Viktor Aleksandrovich Gol'tsev. Biograficheskii ocherk," in *Pamiati Viktora Aleksandrovicha Gol'tseva. Stat'i, vospominaniia, pis'ma*, ed. A. A. Kizevetter (Moscow: N. N. Klochkova, 1910), 91.

50.   GARF, f. 63, op. 24, d. 403, l. 3. Report dated 31 December 1903. Gorshkov was a thirty-one year old Russian lawyer living in rented quarters on the Arbat. He was known to associate with men under police surveillance.

51.   GARF, f. 63, op. 24, d. 403, l. 28. Report dated 13 May 1904. This surely referred to his participation in liberal circles gathered around the journal *Osvobozhdenie*.

52.   See Lednicki's autobiographical statement in *Russkiia vedomosti: 1863–1913. Sbornik statei* (Moscow: Tipografiia "Russkikh Vedomostei," 1913), 102. On the liberals' hatred for von Plehve, see Anna Geifman, *Thou Shalt Kill: Revolutionary Terrorism in Russia, 1894–1917* (Princeton: Princeton University Press, 1993), 338. According to Lednicki, von Plehve's assassination in July 1904 was the "harbinger of a revolutionary storm." See A. Lednicki, *Z lat wojny*, 71.

53.   W. Lednicki, *Pamiętniki*, 2: 217–18.

54.   Paul Milyukov, "Alexander Lednicki," *Slavonic and East European Review* 13 (1934/1935): 677.; also Pawel Milukow, "Aleksander Lednicki jako rzecznik polsko-rosyjskiego porozumienia," *Przegląd współczesny* 18 (1939): 25.

55.   Even during his life in interwar Poland, Lednicki retained his appreci-

ation of Russian culture and his friendly attitude toward the Russian people. See PIASA, Aleksander Lednicki Collection (006), folder 71, "Aleksander Robertovich Lednits[k]i—listki vospominanii."

56. This sentiment is expressed in his only speech translated into English, contained in Krystyna M. Olszer, ed., *For Your Freedom and Ours: Polish Progres-sive Spirit from the 14th Century to the Present*, 2d ed. (New York: Frederick Ungar Publishing Co., 1981), 142–44. This same volume includes excerpts from Mickiewicz's works on this theme.

57. W. Lednicki, *Pamiętniki*, 1: 176–78.

58. W. Lednicki, "Aleksander Lednicki (oszczerstwa i prawda)," *Zeszyty historyczny* 1 (1962): 69.

59. Wasilewski, *Proces Lednickiego*, 88.

60. W. A. Żbyszewski, "Dwaj Ledniccy," *Kultura* 22 (1968), no. 8/9: 156.

61. Trenam, "Without a free Poland," 57. Apparently, Russian politicians favored the polished Russian of Lednicki to the broken Russian of Roman Dmowski and other National Democrats from the Kingdom.

62. W. Lednicki, *Pamiętniki*, 1: 24.

63. Nagórski, "Aleksander Lednicki," 29.

64. W. Lednicki, *Pamiętniki*, 1: 72.

65. Lesław Sadowski, *Polska inteligencja prowincjonalna i jej ideowe dylematy na przełomie XIX i XX wieku* (Warsaw: Państwowe Wydawnictwo Naukowe, 1988), 177.

66. W. Lednicki, *Pamiętniki*, 1: 277. These are the words of V. A. Amfitieatrov—a colleague of Aleksander's at Moscow University—written at the time of Lednicki's death in 1934 and published in the Russian emigre newspaper *Segodniia* in Riga.

67. The credo of the modern Pole, according to Dmowski: "I am conscious of a collective national life of which I am a part—because, simultaneously with my own affairs and interests, I am aware of the national problems, the interests of Poland as a whole...I am a Pole: so with all my spiritual life I participate in its existence, its emotions, thoughts, needs, strivings and aspirations...I am a Pole: so I have Polish duties—the better man I am the higher they are and the more I subscribe to them." See Roman Dmowski, "A Modern Pole," in *The Meaning and Uses of Polish History*, ed. Adam Bromke (Boulder: East European Monographs, 1987): 127–28.

68. Żbyszewski maintained that politics, not the law, was Lednicki's true passion. See "Dwaj Ledniccy," 157. This contention was supported by W. Lednicki, who stated that the proceeds from his father's law practice went not to personal aggrandizement, but to finance his socio-political work on behalf of Poland. See *Pamiętniki*, 1: 351.

Chapter Three

LEDNICKI THE LIBERATIONIST, TO NOVEMBER 1904

There were several factors behind the political mobilization of Russian society in the years before 1905. Judith Zimmerman has cited bankrupt government policies and bureaucratic oppression, combined with the emergence of a politically mature professional middle class, as the two main causes for the emergence of the liberation movement,[1] while Klaus Frolich has maintained that the economic crisis of the early years of the new century was the "final motivating factor" for political activism.[2] The intelligentsia had long possessed a certain "social self-consciousness and cultural missionary conviction" that had developed as they were exposed to the backwardness of Russian society and the oppressive nature of the tsarist regime, which thwarted their social activism at every turn.[3] Lawyers were especially outspoken in their disaffection with autocracy, demanding a constitution and a government that would obey the rule of law. Their activism was part of the larger "liberation movement," which sought to free Russian society from the yoke of tsarist oppression. Democratically-minded lawyers and other free professionals joined with zemstvo radicals to form the liberal wing of the opposition in the years before the 1905 revolution.

In 1901, Ivan Petrunkevich and Petr Struve agreed to publish a new organ of the liberation movement. With Struve as editor, the first issue of *Osvobozhdenie* appeared in Stuttgart on 18 June (1 July) 1902.[4] As part of a campaign to support this venture, "Friends of Liberation" (*Druz'ia Osvobozhdeniia*) circles were established throughout Russia. They served as centers for those who aimed to

replace tsarism with a constitutionalist regime. Members of these circles shared these demands and tactics: 1) a constitution for Russia; 2)
a constituent assembly elected by universal suffrage; and 3) the use of
peaceful means to pressure the government for reforms. In addition,
many, including Lednicki, believed they should coordinate their
efforts with those of the radical socialists — hence the doctrine of "no
enemies to the left."[5]

Radical elements among the liberal opposition also wanted to
establish closer ties to like-minded groups in Finland, Poland and
other regions of the empire. Struve led the search for allies: in the
first issue of *Osvobozhdenie*, he called on all nationalities of the
empire to join the liberation movement. In early 1903, he invited
Leon Wasilewski, a member of the PPS (*Polska Partiia Socjalistyczna*,
or Polish Socialist Party), to write a series of articles for
Osvobozhdenie on the current situation in Poland. Wasilewski was
highly critical of the Russian liberation movement, however, and
would not provide a link to the oppositionists in Poland.[6] Struve also
made efforts to establish ties with the Finns, arranging a series of discussions in Helsinki in July 1903 between Petr Dolgorukov and
Finnish leaders.[7]

The success of *Osvobozhdenie*, and the popularity of the circles
of "friends," resulted in the transformation of the radical-democratic
wing of the liberation movement into the Union of Liberation.[8] The
Union was born at the Schaffhausen Conference, held 20–22 July
(2–4 August) 1903 in the Swiss town of that name on Lake Constance.
Twenty-one representatives were present, including both zemstvo
radicals and members of the professional intelligentsia. Among the
participants were such future political allies of Lednicki as Prince Petr
Dolgorukov, Ivan Petrunkevich, Fedor Rodichev, and Prince Dmitri
Shakhovskoi. Because the liberation movement included people of
disparate views, the conference decided not to establish a political
party but rather to form a union of persons who could at least agree
on the crucial constitutional issue. The liberationist Ariadna Tyrkova-
Williams defined the Union as "a kind of war coalition of diverse
groups, monarchists and republicans, liberals and socialists, temporarily united to carry on a guerilla fight against the common enemy
—autocracy."[9] Until the formation of the Kadet party in October

1905, when the electoral campaign for the First Duma neccesitated a more tightly controlled organization, the Union would serve as the "conspiratorial co-ordinating centre of the Liberation Movement."[10]

Subsequent to the formation of the Union of Liberation, moderate zemstvo constitutionalists led by Pavel Dolgorukov created the Union of Zemstvo-Constitutionalists. Its main function was the advocacy of constitutionalism within zemstvo assemblies and at all-zemstvo congresses.[11] The Union of Liberation leaders decided that this sister organization was needed for those zemstvoists who did not want to participate in any conspiratorial activities.[12]

The Union of Zemstvo-Constitutionalists first met on 8 November 1903. Members of this group, along with several invited representatives of the radical-democratic intelligentsia, resolved to convene a congress of the Union of Liberation in St. Petersburg as soon as possible. Attended by about fifty delegates, the congress met 2–5 January 1904.[13] It promulgated the first programmatic statement of the liberation movement. The congress recognized the right of all national minorities to self-determination; the Union thus became the first liberal organization in Russia to give such prominence to the divisive nationalities issue. The *osvobozhdentsy* resolved that

> in the sphere of national questions, the Union recognizes the right of self-determination of different nationalities entering into the composition of the Russian state. In relation to Finland, the Union supports the demand for the restoration of the constitutional status which existed in the country until its illegal abrogation during the current reign.[14]

The otherwise vague statement specifically mentioned the status of Finland because Petr Dolgorukov's discussions with Finnish opposition leaders during the summer of 1903 had elicited great enthusiasm among the Russians.

Finland thus occupied a preeminent place in the minds of those at the congress who were concerned with the nationalities question. Finland served as a model for the Russians, for it possessed those Western liberal institutions which they wanted in a reformed empire. But the Finns moved slowly in their dealings with the Russians, reluctant to commit themselves to a movement for empire-wide reform. Their interests were parochial, with all efforts focused on a return to the *status quo* before the curtailing of Finnish autonomy. This had begun in earnest in 1899, when N. I. Bobrikov was appointed governor-general. No Finnish leader actively participated in the Russian opposition movement, nor did any aspire to join the Union of Liberation or any other Russian organization.

The Poles differed from the Finns in this regard, for many opposition leaders were open to the possibility of cooperation with the Russians. Some, like Lednicki, explicitly linked the Polish drive for autonomy to the Russian liberation movement. As Lednicki constantly pointed out, the two nations had a history of fighting the autocracy together. "For your freedom and ours," the phrase coined by Adam Mickiewicz, once again became the slogan of Russians and Poles aiming to topple the tsarist regime. Slavic kinship, a factor stressed by Lednicki and many of his Russian allies, was another key element missing from the Russo-Finnish relationship.

It was difficult, however, for Russian *osvobozhdentsy* to find common ground with the best-organized political group in Poland, the National Democrats. The NDs and their leader, Roman Dmowski, refusing to recognize Russian concerns as consequential, were unable to divest themselves of their narrow nationalism.[15] The National Democrats also cared little about the fate of other national minorities within the empire, believing the Polish cause best served through abstention from contact with less-developed national movements. Besides, political aspirations among ethnic groups living in the lands of the former *Rzeczpospolita* would only weaken Polish claims to those regions.[16]

In their search for Polish allies, Russian opposition leaders inevitably came to regard Aleksander Lednicki as the man most willing and able to commit himself fully to both the Polish cause and the Russian liberation movement. Equally at home in Moscow, Minsk or Warsaw, he was in a unique position to open channels of communication for the Russians with liberals in the Polish Kingdom and the *Kresy*. As Terence Emmons has noted, Lednicki "seems to have combined the nationalist and 'all-Russian' orientations in near parity."[17]

The emergence of an organized political movement among supporters of *Osvobozhdenie* was a signal to Lednicki to begin proselytizing among friends, colleagues and potential political allies in Russia and Poland. His son later recalled that, around 1903, his father had frequent conferences with Russian friends, noting that "these meetings, often large, created in the household a certain atmosphere of vigilance."[18] The suspicions were well-founded, for the *Okhrana* had already begun to scrutinize Lednicki's activities. Surveillance reports confirmed *Okhrana* suspicions that Lednicki was "among the main leaders" of a clandestine anti-government camp which began to coalesce in 1903.[19] Not only did authorities find that he was on intimate terms with leading *osvobozhdentsy* and zemstvo activists, but he was also regarded as a leading political agitator among the Moscow bar.[20]

He was probably introduced to *Osvobozhdenie* supporters by either Prince Petr Dolgorukov or Prince Dmitrii Shakhovskoi, both of whom were very influential political activists in Moscow.[21] As noted above, Lednicki had known Dolgorukov and his twin brother Pavel since their student days at Moscow University.[22] Lednicki's close friend Viktor Gol'tsev probably introduced him to Shakhovskoi. The two quickly became friends; Lednicki's son recalls that Shakhovskoi was a frequent guest in their home.[23] Shakhovskoi would play a key role in Lednicki's campaign to forge an alliance between Russian and Polish liberals. He was well-equipped for this part, having spent his childhood in Warsaw, where he learned the Polish language. As Waclaw Lednicki noted, "this Warsaw period in his life undoubtedly influenced his attitude to the Polish question and to the nationality question in general."[24]

Interestingly, Lednicki would later deny membership in the Union.[25] This was no doubt part of an effort to re-write the history of his life in Moscow. In interwar Poland, his political career ground to a halt because of accusations that he was too "Russian."[26] These charges were based on the knowledge that Lednicki had been a member of Russian political organizations, such as the Kadet party and the Union of Liberation. Antoni Marylski, himself a participant at the "Russian" zemstvo congresses in 1905 as a delegate from the Kingdom, later maintained that it was inconceivable that

> a Pole under German occupation could belong to any sort of
> German group, or belong to an Austrian group under Austrian

occupation. Pan Lednicki, however, managed as a Pole to belong to a Russian group.[27]

Marylski denounced this feat as an act of "political hermaphroditism."[28] Disregarding any moral judgements on Lednicki's political acts, it seems clear that he was the man with "the best contacts both with Russian Constitutionalists...and with the Polish underground."[29] In the fall of 1903, the *osvobozhdenets* Lednicki travelled to Kraków to meet with leaders of the Polish opposition movement.

In Kraków, Lednicki organized a conference with leaders of the National Democratic Party. He met with Roman Dmowski, Jan Popławski, Tadeusz Grużewski, Zygmunt Makowiecki, and Zygmunt Balicki,[30] at whose house the meeting was held. They discussed cooperation with the Russian liberation movement and the development of organized Polish action in Russia.[31] Dmowski had just recently issued the "October Program," a doctrinal and tactical bible for the National Democrats. A *volte face* for Dmowski, it came about in part because of his more hopeful attitude about the possible success of the Russian liberation movement. Above all, however, Dmowski was driven to seek concessions from the Russians by his fear of German aggression. He considered the Russians politically and culturally weaker than the Germans and therefore less of a threat to Poland. It did not matter to Dmowski whether concessions came from the tsar or a new constitutional regime: his only concern was the fate of Poland. Dmowski pondered cooperating with the liberal opposition only when it seemed that it had a chance to succeed.[32]

In the end, Lednicki could not gain Dmowski's unqualified approval for agitation among the liberal elements in Russia. The conference with *Endecja*[33] leaders, however, was a minor political victory for him. Wacław Lednicki believed that his father's efforts at the Kraków conference contributed to Dmowski's decision to participate in further discussions with the Russian liberals, leading to his attendance at the Paris conference of opposition parties in October 1904.[34] As a result of discussions at Kraków, Zygmunt Balicki would later take part in the Russo-Polish Congress, hosted by Lednicki in April 1905. Balicki also participated in debates on the Polish question at the Zemstvo-Municipal Congress of November 1905.[35] Apparently,

Lednicki's argument at Kraków convinced the *Endecja* leadership of the vitality of the liberation movement.

But Dmowski would never fully respond to the overtures of Russian liberals. He later convinced National Democratic deputies to the First Duma not to sign the Vyborg Manifesto,[36] and as leader of the Polish Koło he refused to cooperate with the Kadets in the Second and Third Dumas.[37] As a result, he never earned the trust and admiration of Russian liberals. On the other hand, Lednicki was well-liked by his fellow *osvobozhdentsy* and was generally regarded as their true Polish friend and ally.

These political machinations presaged the Lednicki-Dmowski feud of later years. As Lednicki became more influential within the liberal camp in Russia, culminating in 1917 with his elevation to a cabinet post in the Provisional Government, Dmowski's jealousy was transformed into hatred.[38] As president of the Liquidation Commission established by the new government to oversee the elimination of all legal ties binding the Polish Kingdom to Russia, Lednicki would openly combat Dmowski not only in Russia and Poland, but also in Great Britain, France, Switzerland and the United States.[39] Dmowski was willing to use all means to discredit Lednicki in the eyes of his fellow Poles and the Allies, labelling him a "half-Jew", a Mason, and a pro-German pacifist.[40]

Dmowski's determination to destroy his rival did not abate after Lednicki's return to Poland. In addition to questioning his rival's patriotism, Dmowski belittled Lednicki's early political influence. He testified at the Wasilewski-Lednicki slander trial that "before the outbreak of the Japanese War and the revolutionary movement I had not heard of Pan Lednicki" and that they only became acquainted in 1904. Wasilewski's lawyer argued that "before 1905 nothing was heard of Lednicki in Poland. He was known only in Russia...The public life of Lednicki developed in Russian society and on the ground of Russian affairs."[41] Those connections with the elite of Russian society that served Lednicki so well in promoting the Polish cause during his life in Moscow would later prevent him from playing a major political role in the Polish republic. He would forever be branded a "Russian" Pole.

In his attempt to build an empire-wide liberation movement, Lednicki did indeed concentrate on gaining the support of radical constitutionalists in Moscow and Petersburg. This made good political sense, for Lednicki's circle of friends in the two capitals represented the elite of Russian liberalism—Gol'tsev, Muromtsev, Maklakov, Petr and Pavel Dolgorukov, Princes Evgenii and Sergei Trubetskii, Ivan Petrunkevich, Fedor Rodichev, Fedor Kokoshkin, Dmitrii Shakhovskoi and Vladimir Nabokov. These men would play a major role in any constitutionalist regime that replaced the autocracy. In addition to moving in the same social circles, they were connected politically. They cut their teeth as activists in the zemstvo movement, and took the lead in organizing the zemstvo congresses of 1904–05. In addition, they participated in the Union of Liberation, and later they formed the nucleus of the Kadet Party.[42]

Lednicki's efforts coincided with the outbreak of the Russo-Japanese War, which was precipitated by the attack on Port Arthur on 26–7 January 1904. As the war continued, defeats in the Far East spurred the opposition to step up criticism of the tsarist regime. The *osvobozhdentsy* clamored for peace and political reform, and many in the liberation movement hoped for a Russian defeat that would hasten the disintegration of the autocracy.

In the meantime, oppositionists began to mobilize: in the 26 April 1904 issue of *Osvobozhdenie*, a letter to the editor called for a conference of all opposition leaders, including those representing non-Russian parties.[43] Encouraged by the growing discontent throughout the empire, radical leftists tried to push the teetering government into the abyss. On 3 June Bobrikov was murdered, and on 15 July the widely detested von Plehve was assassinated. Many in Lednicki's circle despised the man most closely associated with reactionary opposition to reform in Russia. Prince Shakhovskoi was so outraged by von Plehve's behavior that shortly before his assassination, he argued that "Plehve ought to be killed...It is time for Plehve to be killed."[44] In the Struve household, news of the hated minister's murder caused "jubilation as if this were news about a victory over an enemy."[45] So important was the death of this symbol of oppression that Lednicki later likened the news to the "announcement of a revolutionary storm."[46]

These acts of terror at last drove Nicholas to grant concessions. On 11 August 1904 the tsar abolished corporal punishment and cancelled peasants' redemption payments.[47]   On 25 August, after the Russian defeat at Lyu-Yang, Nicholas named Prince P. D. Sviatopolk-Mirskii the new Minister of Interior. This was greeted with enthusiasm by the liberal camp, for the minister was viewed as a reformer. Sviatopolk-Mirskii spoke of change and expressed a "confidence in society." His feeble attempts at reform failed to satisfy the growing appetite of the opposition, however, and he only managed to increase demands for real change.[48]

What might have been considered acceptable concessions before the war were now regarded as pitiful attempts on the part of a weakened regime to halt the inexorable march of revolution. Not only had the war energized the opposition movement: it precipitated its gradual shift to the left. This drove many *osvobozhdentsy* to embrace the notion of an alliance with the revolutionary left.[49] As the reaction to Plehve's murder attests, the liberals were not entirely ill-disposed to the use of violence.

Lednicki was keenly aware of the growing radicalization of the Russian liberation movement. In his search for Polish partners, he moved from nationalists to conciliationists and eventually to socialists.[50] Finally, in December 1904, Lednicki would create his own radical-democratic party of progressive constitutionalists in Warsaw. The formation of the *Związek Postępowej-Demokratyczny* (ZPD or *Pedecja*), the Progressive-Democratic Union, filled a void in the Polish political spectrum. The Russian liberals would at last have a group with which they could work in creating a unified Russo-Polish liberation movement.

Just as the opposition movement in Russia proper became more radicalized throughout 1904, the borderlands became increasingly unsettled. In fact, anti-government protesters were particularly vocal in the Kingdom. On 1 March the Polish Socialist Party organized mass demonstrations in which marchers shouted the slogans "Down with the war," "Down with Tsarism," and "Long live an independent socialist Poland."[51] Clashes with police and Cossack units became frequent as the war dragged on, and the growing economic crisis and the looming threat of mobilization drove the Poles to the brink of revolution.[52]

Like their Russian counterparts, the invigorated Polish liberals began to organize. The first issue of the progressive monthly "*Kuznica*"

(The Smithy) appeared in March 1904, heralding the formation of a liberal organization by the same name in Warsaw committed to cooperation with the Russian *osvobozhdentsy*. The *Kuznicy* (those people gathered around the journal of the same name) advocated the restructuring of the Russian empire into a federation of autonomous regions. In June, the journal began to explicitly call for Polish autonomy.[53]

The politicization of society was evident in conferences and congresses, such as those held by the zemstvoists and zemstvo-constitutionalists in 1904 and 1905. These gatherings increasingly assumed an "all-Russian" character, including not only Russian delegates, but also national minorities from all over the empire. The first attempt to fortify the opposition movement by embracing those non-Russians engaged in national-liberation struggles was the "Conference of Oppositional and Revolutionary Organizations of the Russian Empire." Convened at the behest of Konni Zilliacus, leader of the Finnish Party of Active Resistance, the conference took place in September-October 1904 in Paris. The congress brought together representatives of two opposition groups from Russia—the Union of Liberation and the Socialist Revolutionaries (SRs)—and six parties from the borderlands: the National Democrats and the PPS from the Polish Kingdom; Zilliacus' Party of Active Resistance; the Latvian Social Democratic Workers' Party; the Georgian Socialist-Federalist Revolutionary Party; and the Armenian Revolutionary Federation. Pavel Milliukov, Petr Struve and Petr Dolgorukov represented the Union of Liberation. Other Russian delegates included the SRs Viktor Chernov and Evno Azev: the latter doubled as a government agent.[54] The ND leaders Roman Dmowski and Zygmunt Balicki attended, and Witold Joldko, Kazimierz Kelles-Krauz, Aleksander Malinowski and Jozef Pilsudski represented the PPS.[55]

The Poles had already taken steps to strengthen relations with the Russian opposition movement. Lednicki had tried, with only limited success, to convince the *Endecja* to join forces with Russian progressive forces in late 1903. In August 1904, the PPS organized a conference of progressive intelligentsia. Held in Zakopane, it represented an attempt by socialists to consolidate the Polish liberation movement under the auspices of the PPS. At this point the Russian oppositionists were interested in opening channels of communication with any Polish group. Consequently, the Pole Aleksander Więckowski went to Zakopane as an emissary of the Union of Liberation. His efforts undoubtedly paved the way for PPS participation at the Paris Conference.

Więckowski was a former member of the National League who lived and worked in St. Petersburg. In 1904 he was affiliated with the socialist movement, but in December he joined Lednicki's Progressive-Democratic Union. A strong supporter of Lednicki's initiatives for greater cooperation between Russian and Polish progressives, he became the main ZPD propagandist in Petersburg.[56] Perhaps Więckowski was dissuaded from further cooperation with the Socialists by discussions at Zakopane, where opinion was divided on the issue of cooperation with the Russians. Więckowski could report, however, that many participants called for cooperation with the Russian constitutionalists as the best method to achieve their political goal, Polish autonomy with a separate constituent assembly in Warsaw.[57] There was evidently enough interest in the notion of a Russo-Polish entente that several Socialists, including Piłsudski, travelled to Paris for discussions with the *osvobozhdentsy*.

Discussions at the Paris Conference focused on three issues that dominated debates throughout the revolutionary period: the nature of the future political regime of the empire; the nationalities question; and the means of struggle to effect change.[58] The meetings revealed that, aside from a shared hatred of the tsarist regime, there was little common ground on which to build a unified political movement. No reconciliation could take place between those who favored using any means necessary to bring down the tsarist regime and those who continued to promote—at least publicly—a peaceful transition to democracy. Despite a long debate and the presence of a large Polish contingent, the congress passed over the highly contentious issue of autonomy for the Kingdom in silence. Once again, the Finnish right to autonomy was heartily reaffirmed, while the fate of all other nationalities in the empire was described in general terms.[59]

Miliukov drafted the conference resolutions, which stated that

[n]one of the parties represented at the meeting, in uniting for concerted action, thinks for a moment of abandoning any point of its particular program, or of the tactical methods of

struggle, which are adapted to the necessities, the forces, and the situation of the social elements, classes, or nationalities whose interests it represents. But, at the same time, all declare that the principles expressed below are recognized by all of them:

1. The abolition of the autocracy; revocation of all the measures curtailing the constitutional rights of Finland.

2. The substitution for the autocracy of a democratic regime based on universal suffrage.

3. The right of every nationality to decide for itself; freedom of national development, guaranteed by the law; suppression of all violence on the part of the Russian government, as practiced against the different nationalities. In the name of these fundamental principles, the parties represented at the conference will unite their efforts in order to hasten the inevitable fall of absolutism, which is equally incompatible with the realization of all the ulterior purposes pursued by each of the parties.[60]

Miliukov believed at the time that this declaration marked "the climax of the political movement in Russia," and served to "isolate the government in its struggle with the Russian opposition."[61] Miliukov's participation in this conference was his first attempt to address the nationalities problem, which he had virtually ignored up to that time.[62]

Miliukov soon travelled to the United States, where he had recently begun a series of lectures. In December, he gave a talk at the Lowell Institute in Boston, in which he discussed the difficulties encountered at Paris in negotiating an agreement among the various parties representing different ideologies and nationalities.[63] When Miliukov returned to Russia the following spring, he sought new partners in his search for allies among the empire's national minorities. Miliukov's growing interest in this matter would soon draw him to Lednicki's side. Over the next decade, the two men would work closely on the Polish issue, in the process becoming close personal friends and political collaborators.

While Miliukov and other *osvobozhdentsy* were talking with Polish nationalists and socialists at the Paris Conference, however,

Lednicki was opening lines of communication with Polish moderates. He held talks with those Poles known as "*ugodowcy*" (conciliationists), who had long advocated a peaceful resolution to the Polish-Russian dispute. Many conciliationists, in fact, were not averse to dealing with the tsarist regime for concessions. Lednicki, of course, did not share that sentiment. Nevertheless, he met with them at the urging of the Russian zemstvoists, who like the members of the Union of Liberation were interested in closer relations with Polish groups.[64]

Undoubtedly, the limited success of the Kraków conference played a role in Lednicki's willingness to preach his doctrine to such an audience. In addition, he was already well-acquainted with many in the conservative camp. He was on intimate terms with Erazm Piltz and Włodzimierz Spasowicz, the editors of *Kraj*, which for years had been the leading liberal-conservative Polish-language newspaper in Russia.[65] After discussions with Piltz and Spasowicz, Lednicki arranged for a conference to be held at the latter's home in Warsaw.[66]

Among those in attendance were Count Adam Krasiński, a representative of the Warsaw aristocracy; Stefan Wydżga, a member of the middle gentry; Ludwik Straszewicz, correspondent for the daily *Kurier Polski*; and Spasowicz. As one scholar points out, these men shared Lednicki's "outlook and milieu."[67] Adam Krasiński (1870–1909), for example, had been one of the main organizers of the Maria Konopnicki jubilee in 1902. He moved in the same social circles as many important Polish writers, including Eliża Orzeszkowa and Henryk Sienkiewicz. Lednicki probably came to know Krasinski through his secretary, the minor poet Kazimierz Przerwa Tetmajer.[68] According to Straszewicz, everyone knew Lednicki, for he was "already at this time well-known from his bold speeches at political trials."[69]

At the Warsaw meeting, Lednicki spoke enthusiastically about the Russian zemstvoists. He claimed that they were prepared to fight for the liberation of all those in the empire who were living under bureaucratic oppression. He stressed the dominant liberal themes of human rights and the rule of law. Lednicki argued that it was the duty of those present to travel to Russia to inform their Russian counterparts of the state of affairs in the Kingdom.[70]

The conference represented a huge success for Lednicki, who was encouraged to communicate Polish grievances to the Russian oppositionists. He subsequently informed zemstvo activists of the Poles' willingness to hold talks with the Russians. As a result, he and Prince Shakhovskoi were entrusted with the task of organizing a future Russo-Polish conference. Initially set to convene in Moscow at the start of November 1904, the conference was postponed to coincide with the upcoming zemstvo congress.[71]

While Lednicki made preparations for the Russo-Polish conference, the Union of Liberation held its second congress 20–22 October in St. Petersburg. The Union's leadership called on members to pressure zemstvoists to embrace fully the demand for a constitution. The congress also urged liberal professionals to form unions; this effort would lead to the formation of the Union of Unions in 1905. Finally the executive council announced plans for a "banquet campaign" to coincide with the fortieth anniversary of the judicial reforms.[72]

Lawyers were among the first to answer the call to establish professional unions. The government opposed any such efforts, so lawyers and other professionals trying to form unions had to hold secret discussions. These illegal "congresses" became the usual way in which the opposition movement coordinated its political activity.[73] Lawyers held an *ad hoc* congress in Moscow as earlier as 15 February 1903. Dominated by members of the Union of Liberation, the assembly resolved that the "fight for political freedom" should be the guiding principle for lawyers.[74]

The lawyers' politicization increased during the following year, and in October 1904, Lednicki helped organize the First All-Russian Congress of Lawyers.[75] It consisted of two large meetings, one at Maklakov's home and the other at Lednicki's on 20 October. The goal was the creation of a lawyers' union whose members would share the common goal of a constitution for Russia. The leaders of the congress urged participants to support an open demand for a constitution, but many balked at the idea of supporting an "illegal" act.[76] Nevertheless, Lednicki and others subsequently petitioned Sviatopolk-Mirskii for constitutional reform.[77]

On 4 November, assistant lawyers of the Moscow court district met to discuss similar issues. They called on the upcoming zemstvo congress to demand a legislature based on the "four-tailed" vote: universal, equal, direct and secret suffrage. Senior Moscow lawyers met on 20 November and despite a generally more conservative outlook evidenced in their actions one month earlier at the lawyers' congress, they passed a resolution in favor of a constitutional form of government. Six days later, the Moscow Council of Lawyers elected an executive body that included Lednicki and his fellow *osvobozhdentsy* Sergei Muromtsev and N. V. Teslenko. They promptly demanded state reform as a necessary precondition for justice in Russia.[78] The lawyers' movement, like the liberation movement as a whole, was becoming increasingly radical. In January 1905, the tragedy of Bloody Sunday served as the necessary catalyst for the formation of a lawyers' union.[79]

The second congress of the Union of Liberation in October had also called for a "banquet campaign" to disseminate the gospel of constitutionalism among the populace. As Prince Shakhovskoi noted, the Union sought to unite "the bulk of the country's intelligentsia around the constitutional banner."[80] The banquet campaign consisted of thirty-eight banquets in twenty-six cities, during the period from 5 November 1904 to 8 January 1905.[81] Participants at these political rallies stressed several major themes, including the demand for the four-tail vote, amnesty to political prisoners, and an end to the war.[82] The crucial issue of the four-tail vote came to serve as the dividing line between democrats and liberals.[83]

Just as the *osvobozhdentsy* were increasing their propaganda efforts throughout Russia in the cause of constitutionalism, the Second Zemstvo Congress convened in St. Petersburg from 6–9 November. Like their counterparts in the Union of Liberation, the zemstvoists continued to balk on the nationalities matter. The thorny Polish question remained the main stumbling block for the promulgation of any far-reaching resolution of this vexing problem. There was no problem in recognizing Finland's special status, however, for it merely entailed a return to the situation before the campaign of russification launched in 1899.

The question of Polish autonomy was considerably more complex. Consequently, the zemstvoists passed over the Polish matter in silence. Point seven of the congress' resolutions stated that "the individual, civil and political rights of all citizens of the Russian Empire must be equal," and paragraph nine addressed the issue of decentralization, noting that "local self-government should be extended to all parts of Russia."[84] The Polish question did not yet have a special place in the liberal agenda. The Finnish problem remained the only nationality matter to be specifically addressed by the zemstvoists. Realizing that only direct Polish-Russian contacts would force Russian liberals to issue programmatic statements concerning Polish autonomy, Lednicki decided to force the issue by sponsoring deliberations on the matter. It was "at these meetings that Russians and Poles for the first time engaged in political discussions on the delicate theme of Russian-Polish affairs."[85]

ENDNOTES

1.   Zimmerman, "Between Revolution and Reaction," 1–2.

2.   Klaus Frolich, *The Emergence of Russian Constitutionalism 1900–1904* (The Hague: Martinus Nijhoff Publishers, 1981), 28. The author maintains that the heightened social conflicts which occured during this period of economic crisis upset any feelings of security held by liberal professionals and those active in the zemstvo movement, spurring them to further challenges of the relationship between state and society. Ibid., 45–6.

3.   Ibid., 35.

4.   *Osvobozhdenie* was well-financed; a trust fund of 100,000 rubles was established for its publication before the first issue appeared. See E. D. Chermenskii, *Burzhuaziia i tsarizm v pervoi russkoi revoliutsii*, 2d ed. (Moscow: Izdatel'stvo Mysl', 1970), 27.

5.   Galai, *Liberation Movement in Russia*, 117–18.

6.   Wojciech Bu_at, "Korespondencje Leona Wasilewskiego na lamach 'Oswobozdienija'," *Z pola walki* 19 (1976), no. 1: 167–70. For a full discussion of Wasilewski's ideology and activities in Russia, see Henry John Antkiewicz, "Leon Wasilewski: Polish Patriot and Socialist" (Ph.D. diss., The Ohio State University, 1976).

7.   William R. Copeland, *The Uneasy Alliance: Collaboration between the Finnish Opposition and the Russian Underground* (Helsinki: Suomalainen Tiedeakatemia, 1973), 163–65.

8.   *Galai, Liberation Movement in Russia*, 169–75.

9.   A. Tyrkova-Williams, "The Cadet Party," *Russian Review* 12 (1953), no. 3: 173.

10.   Galai, Liberation Movement in Russia, 179.

11.   Ibid., 188.

12.   Terence Emmons, *The Formation of Political Parties and the First*

National Elections in Russia (Cambridge, MA, and London: Harvard University Press, 1983), 31.

13. Galai, *Liberation Movement in Russia*, 188–89.

14. D. Shakhovskoi, "Soiuz osvobozhdeniia," *Zarnitsy* 1909, no. 2, part 2: 112. See also Stephen Jeremy Bensman, "The Constitutional Ideas of the Russian Liberation Movement: The Struggle for Human Rights During The Revolution of 1905" (Ph.D. diss., University of Wisconsin-Madison, 1977), 188–89.

15. Roman Dmowski (1864–1939), shared much of the same intellectual heritage as Lednicki. At gymnasium, he too joined self-education circles, and in the tradition of Warsaw Positivism and the doctrine of "organic work" came to regard the study of Polish language, literature and history as a means of preserving Polish culture and combatting Russification. Also like Lednicki, he rejected Marxist ideology and the doctrine of class warfare. Unlike Lednicki, he rejected the universal humanitarianism preached by Polish democrats in the past. Rather, he embraced a new line of thinking influenced by the Bismarkian model of *realpolitik*, power politics and cultural imperialism. See Glenn Alfred Janus, "The Polish Kolo, the Russian Duma, and the Question of Polish Autonomy" (Ph.D. diss., The Ohio State University, 1971), 19–29. In this regard, Lednicki espoused an "outdated" ideology, for as one scholar notes, "the second half of the 19th century had brought about...the decomposition of patriotic-democratic values, attacked on one side by Marxism, which stressed...class interests over the national consciousness and interests, and on the other side by nationalism, which sharply denied the rights of individual persons and mankind as of equivalent value to those of the nation." See B. Cywinski, "Narodowe i ludzkie w myśli Stanisława Brzozowskiego," in Wokoł myśli Stanisława Brzozowskiego, ed. A. Walicki and R. Zimand (Kraków, 1974), 258, cited by Grzegorz Godlewski, "Polska myśl kulturalna na progu niepodległości: Żeromski, Zdziechowski, Znaniecki," in *Historia i kultura: Studia z dziejów polskiej myśli kulturalnej*, ed. Andrzej Mencwel (Warsaw: Wydawnictwa Uniwersytetu Warszawskego, 1987), 177.

16. Teodor Shanin defines this phenomenon as the "ethnic frontiers of hostility" erected by the National Democrats in their battle against "aliens"—Jews and other non-Poles who were living within the boundaries of the *Rzeczpospolita*. See Teodor Shanin, *The Roots of Otherness: Russia's Turn of Century*, vol. 2, *Russia, 1905–1907: Revolution as a Moment of Truth* (New Haven, London: Yale University Press, 1986), 194–95.

17. Emmons, *Formation of Political Parties*, 457, f.n. 131.

18. W. Lednicki, *Pamiętniki*, 2: 477.

19. GARF, f. 63, op. 24, d. 403, l. 28. Report dated 13 May 1904.

20. Ibid.

21. Galai, *Liberation Movement in Russia*, 118–19, 187. Shakhovskoi's own memoirs are one of the best sources on the Union. See "Soiuz osvobozhdenie," 81–171.

22. W. Lednicki, '*Entente cordiale*', 39.

23. W. Lednicki, *Pamiętniki*, 2: 493.

24. W. Lednicki, '*Entente cordiale*', 34.

25. A. Lednicki, "Z Pamiętnika," *Niepodległość* 7 (1933): 39. Lednicki participated in the third and fourth congresses of the Union of Liberation; he admitted that the fourth and final congress was held at his home in Moscow. See K. F. Shatsillo, "Novoe o 'Soiuze Osvobozhdeniia'," *Istoriia SSSR* (1975), no. 4: 142. See also Lednicki's autobiographical statement, "Avtobiografiia," 102.

26. The attacks on Lednicki by the National Democrats were brutal and vitriolic. Zygmunt Wasilewski went so far as to declare that for his "sins" committed against Poland—at various times Lednicki was described as being a Russian, a half-Jew, or pro-German—"Pan Aleksander Lednicki...did not have the right to enter Polish society without a penitential act." See Wasilewski, *Proces Lednickiego*, 3.

27. Ibid., 321.

28. Ibid.

29. Frolich, *Emergence of Russian Constitutionalism*, 209.

30. Zygmunt Balicki (1858–1916), was a leading figure in the movement that later formed the National Democratic Party. In 1891, he established the Union of Polish Youth (*Związek Młodziesy Polskiej*), a nationalist organization for Polish students in the Kindgom and abroad. He was a leading idealogue within the nationalist movement. In his 1892 book, *National Egoism in Relation to Ethics* (*Egoizm narodowy wobec etyki*), he elevated nationalism to the level of a religion. Racial nationalism, a distinctive trait of National Democracy, later emerged from this line of thinking. See Janus, "Polish Koło," 17–18.

31. A. Lednicki, *Z lat wojny*, 111.

32. Fountain, *Roman Dmowski: Party, Tactics, Ideology*, 75–83; Roman Wapinski, *Narodowa demokracja 1893–1939. Ze studiów nad dziejami myśli nacjonalistycz-nej* (Wrocław: Zakład Narodowy imienia Ossolińskich Wydawnictwo, 1980), 107–08; and Zygmunt Łukawski, "Rosyjskie ugrupowania polityczne wobec sprawy autonomii Królestwa Polskiego w okresie 1905–1917 (W świetle archiwalnych materiałów rosyjskich)," *Zeszyty Naukowe Uniwersytetu Jagiellonskiego. Prace Historyczne* 9 (1962): 147–48. Łukawski contends that the National Democrats tempered their earlier demands for complete independence with the hope that autonomy within the Russian Empire would preserve Polish access to the huge Russian market, thereby benefitting Poland's economy.

33. *Endecja* is a term commonly used to denote the National Democratic Party, whose members are also frequently referred to as "NDs".

34. W. Lednicki, *Pamiętniki*, 2: 524.

35. Lednicki related that he and Balicki remained on good terms until 1906, when their "paths diverged." This probably stemmed from Lednicki's refusal to participate in the Polish Kolo in the First Duma, a move based on fundamental ideological differences regarding the nationalities question: Balicki was concerned only with Poland's fate, while Lednicki fought for the liberation of all

peoples of the empire. See A. Lednicki, *Z lat wojny*, 111–12.

36. See below, 206-7.

37. Tadeusz Piszczkowski, *Odbudowanie polski, 1914–1921. Historia i polityka* (London: Orbis, 1969), 89.

38. Lednicki always seemed one step ahead of Dmowski in his relations with the Russians. Studnicki noted that "in the transition from autonomy to independence, in undertaking action toward the goal of the recognition of this independence by the Provisional Government, Lednicki and his friends outdistanced National Democracy. And this was the main source of its reluctance, even hatred, in regard to Lednicki." Piłsudski Institute, Archiwum Władysława Studnickiego. Teka IV, Teczka 4, p. 5.

39. Piszczkowski, *Odbudowanie polski*, 89. Of particular importance was Lednicki's opposition to Dmowski's proposal for a separate Polish army in Russia. He feared the creation of this army for three reasons: it would be controlled by the NDs, his political opponents; he did not want Poles from Russia fighting Polish forces from the Central Powers; and he was not certain of an Allied victory over the Central Powers. By opposing an independent Polish army, he denied his political opponents an important asset, kept his options open for cooperation with the Polish state established by the Central Powers, and pleased his fellow ministers in the Provisional Government, especially his friend Kerensky, who opposed a separate Polish army in Russia. See M. B. Biskupski, "The Poles, the Root Mission, and the Russian Provisional Government, 1917," *Slavonic and East European Review* 63 (January 1985): 64–65. In his memoirs, Stanislaw Grabski maintained that the Provisional Government strongly believed that Ukrainians, Tatars, and Lithuanians would use the Polish example as an excuse to leave the front. See his *Pamiętniki*, 2 vols., ed. Witold Stankiewicz (Warsaw: Czytelnik, 1989), 2: 11.

40. See Foreign Relations of the United States, suppl. 2, vol. 1: 773–74. This document, regarding a conversation between Dmowski and American representatives in October 1917, is also cited in Wiktor Sukiennicki, *East Central Europe During World War I: From Foreign Domination to National Independence*, 2 vols., ed. Maciej Siekierski, preface Czesław Miłosz (Boulder: East European Monographs, 1984), 1: 451–52. Dmowski regarded all those, like Lednicki, who had dealings with the Council of State (the Polish governing body established by Germany and Austria-Hungary in November 1916) as "masons, Jews, pacifists..." Piłsudski Institute, Records of Komitet Narodowy w Paryż, Roll 95, p. 2. Protocol of meeting in Lausanne, dated 11–12 August 1917. See also Władysław Bułhak, "Kluczowe problemy polityki polskiej w Rosji (marzec-listopad 1917 r.) w działalności Aleksandra Lednickiego," *Przegląd Wschodni* 2 (1992/3), no. 1: 91.

41. Wasilewski, *Proces Lednickiego*, 377, 403.

42. Milukow, "Aleksander Lednicki jako rzecznik," 25.

43. Galai, *Liberation Movement in Russia*, 209–10.

44. Ariadna Tyrkova-Vil'iams, *Na putiakh k svobode* (New York:

Chekhov, 1952), 166; cited by Geifman, *Thou Shalt Kill*, 338

45. Ibid., 176; cited by Geifman, *Thou Shalt Kill*, 338.

46. A. Lednicki, *Z lat wojny*, 71.

47. Galai, *Liberation Movement in Russia*, 207–08.

48. Ibid.; Terence Emmons, "Russia's Banquet Campaign," *California Slavic Studies* 10 (1977): 46–47.

49. Shmuel Galai, "The Impact of War on the Russian Liberals in 1904–5," *Government and Opposition* 1 (1965): 87.

50. In his memoirs, Lednicki's son provided information about contacts between his father and Piłsudski:
"I remember," Wacław recalled, "father's story about his meeting with Piłsudski in Paris. Sometime before the Russo-Japanese War, or during the war, he was travelling with him in a cab, and Piłsudski layed out to him his program of an armed, revolutionary struggle with Russia. Father listened to such inferences with great skepticism. When Piłsudski began to define precisely various details and mention his secret military preparations—father became so irritated that he got out of the cab, saying that Poland had already shed enough of its blood in vain and that it was a sin not only to distract Polish youth from its studies, but to thrust them towards unavoidable imprisonment and exile." W. Lednicki, *Pamiętniki*, 2: 320.

51. Galai, "Impact of War," 89.

52. Ibid., 91.

53. Barbara Petrozolin-Skowrońska, "Z dziejów liberalizmu polskiego. Partie liberalno-demokratyczne inteligencji w Królestwie Polskim, 1905–1907," *Dzieje najnowsze* 3 (1971), no. 3: 3–4. In addition, A. L. Pogodin argued that the Kuznicy wanted closer cooperation with the Russian liberation movement to better promote the cause of autonomy. See "Pis'mo iz Pol'shi. Progressivnyia stremleniia," *Russkaia mysl'* (June 1908): 91.

54. Voskobiynyk, "The Nationalities Question in Russia," 116–17.

55. Wojciech Bułat, "Zjazd polsko-rosyjski w Moskwie 21–22 kwietnia 1905 r.," *Studia z najnowszych dziejów powszechnych* 2 (1962): 189–90.

56. Ibid., 192–93. Więckowski worked closely with Lednicki for the next decade. He founded the left-leaning *Kolko Przyjaciół Niezawisłości Polski* in 1916, which aimed to organize Russian support for Polish independence. Lednicki joined the group after he left the Kadets in disgust over their refusal to recognize Polish independence. See Irena Spustek, *Polacy w Piotrogrodzie 1914–1917* (Warsaw, Państwowe Wydawnictwo Naukowe, 1966), 380–81.

57. Petrozolin-Skowrońska, "Partie liberalno-demokratyczne inteligencji," 3–4.

58. Galai, *Liberation Movement in Russia*, 217. See also K. F. Shatsillo, "Iz istorii osvoboditel'nogo dvizheniia v Rossii v nachale XX veka (O konferentsii liberal'nykh i revoliutsionnykh partii v Parizhe v sentiabre-oktiabre 1904 goda)," *Istoriia SSR* (1982), no. 4: 51–70.

59. According to Miliukov, the Polish question occupied two full days of discussion. See Pawel Milukow, "Aleksander Lednicki jako rzecznik," 27. The nationalities problem was the most contentious issue addressed by delegates. See Wojciech Bułat, "Konferencja partii opozycyjnych i rewolucyjnych Rosji w Paryżu w 1904 r. — kilka uściśleń," *Z pola walki* 18 (1975), no. 1: 168.

60. Paul Miliukov, *Russia and its Crisis*, new forward by Donald W. Treadgold (New York: Collier Books, 1962), 381–82. This book was based on Miliukov's lectures in Chicago in 1903 and at the Lowell Institute in Boston in December 1904, although the author discussed events up to March 1905. Also see Thomas Riha, *A Russian European: Paul Miliukov in Russian Politics* (Notre Dame: University of Notre Dame Press, 1969), 59–60. The resolutions were published in *Listok 'Osvobozhdeniia'* 17 (19 November/2 December 1904): 1–2.

61. Miliukov, *Russia and its Crisis*, 384.

62. Riha pointed out that in *Russia and Its Crisis*, Miliukov devoted only 5 of 600 pages to this matter. See *Russian European*, 61–62.

63. Miliukov, *Russia and Its Crisis*, 381–84; see also Bensman, "Constitutional Ideas," 298–99.

64. *Kurier Polski*, 18 November 1905.

65. At one point, the financially strapped editors turned to Lednicki as a potential buyer. From March to May 1905, Piltz entered into negotiations with a consortium headed by Lednicki, but they failed to reach an agreement. The asking price at the time was 100,000 rubles. See Zenon Kmiecik, *"Kraj" za czasów redaktorstwa Erazma Piltza* (Warsaw: PWN, 1969), 66.

66. *Kurier Polski*, 18 November 1905.

67. Trenam, "Without a Free Poland," 139.

68. For correspondence between Lednicki and Tetmajer, see PIASA, Aleksander Lednicki Collection (006), folders 57–58, 64.

69. *Kurier Polski*, 18 November 1905.

70. Ibid.

71. Ibid.

72. Galai, *Liberation Movement in Russia*, 223.

73. Frolich, *Emergence of Russian Constitutionalism*, 153.

74. Ibid., 197.

75. A. Lednicki, "Avtobiografia," 102.

76. I. V. Gessen, "V dukh vekakh. Zhiznennyi otchet," *Arkhiv russkoi revoliutsii* 22 (1937): 183.

77. A. Lednicki, "Avtobiografia," 102–03.

78. Sanders, "Union of Unions," 205–07.

79. Ibid., 213.

80. Shakhovskoi, "Soiuz osvobozhdeniia," 141–42.

81. Emmons, "Banquet Campaign," 49–50.

82. Emmons, *Formation of Political Parties*, 32.

83. Emmons, "Banquet Campaign," 78.

84. *Listok 'Osvobozhdeniia* 18 (20 November/3 December 1904): 1. The Eleven Theses of the congress are found in Shipov's memoirs, *Vospominaniia i dumy o perezhitom* (Moscow, 1918), 261–65. See also Fischer, *Russian Liberalism*, 182–88.

85. Milukow, "Aleksander Lednicki jako rzecznik," 26.

Chapter Four

RUSSO-POLISH RAPPROCHEMENT, NOVEMBER–DECEMBER 1904

The first Russo-Polish conference took place in Moscow on 12–13 November 1904, a few days after the conclusion of the Second Zemstvo Congress. In reality, the conference consisted of two separate meetings: on the first day, the Polish delegation met with zemstvo activists at the palace of Prince Pavel Dolgorukov. The next day, Lednicki hosted a discussion between the Poles and representatives of the Moscow city council and other non-zemstvo activists.

The Polish delegation did not represent the full spectrum of Polish politics. Aside from Lednicki, it consisted solely of conciliationists (*ugodowcy*) who were not fully committed to the constitutionalist demands voiced by a growing number of Russian oppositionists. Their overriding concern was the oppressive policy of russification which had rendered the Kingdom a mere Russian province. Prior to the November conference, the Poles met first with Lednicki, who helped them formulate their demands. These included the use of the Polish language in all governmental and social institutions in the Kingdom, and legislative and administrative autonomy with a separate sejm in Warsaw.[1]

During the first day of discussions, Lednicki, Stanisław Wydżga, Władysław Żukowski and Ludwik Straszewicz represented Polish interests, while the zemstvoists Prince Dmitrii Shakhovskoi, Prince Pavel Dolgorukov, Ivan Petrunkevich and Fedor Kokoshkin made up the Russian delegation. According to Straszewicz's account, the meeting had an official air. Delivering the opening address for the Poles, Wydżga charged the tsarist bureaucracy with responsibility for all the problems in Poland. The Russians were very sympathetic to this argument, for they too blamed bureaucratic lawlessness for Russia's plight.

Prince Dolgorukov read an article from *Osvobozhdenie* that confirmed that zemstvoists had been discussing the political and national needs of Poland for some time. Petrunkevich did note that the Polish legislative assembly should not be called a *sejm*; that would make many Russians anxious about Polish designs to regain complete independence. Lednicki and Żukowski responded that they regarded terminology as a secondary matter and would not object to a different name.[2]

In one of the few tense moments in the proceedings, Petrunkevich made it clear that the zemstvoists were not seeking help in fighting the government. Rather, they wanted a Polish guarantee that they would not push for the separation of the Kingdom from Russia. Petrunkevich warned that such demands would provide ammunition to those reactionaries who argued that the introduction of a constitution to Russia would lead to the dissolution of the empire.[3]

Petrunkevich's concerns revealed an acute awareness of the divisive nature of the Polish question. The nationalities issue in general, and the matter of Poland in particular, would prove the main stumbling block for a united liberal camp in 1905. Everyone realized that any just resolution to the nationalities problem would necessarily entail a reduction of the prerogatives of the central authorities, but few Russians wanted dismemberment of the empire. Russian reactionaries vehemently opposed such a development, and few liberals would sign on to Lednicki's plan for a new federation of autonomous states. At the November conference, Petrunkevich merely fired another salvo in the ongoing battle to define the acceptable limits of cultural and political autonomy for the borderlands.

Lednicki feared that the next day's discussions with the Moscow activists would not proceed as smoothly as the meeting with the zemstvoists. He regarded this group as "less politically mature" and feared that its unfamiliarity with the Polish issue would hinder an open discussion on the matter of autonomy. Long committed to decentralization of the empire, the zemstvoists were naturally sympathetic to demands for greater freedom from the constraints of the central bureaucracy, even if they balked at the notion of a radical restructuring of the state.[4] Lednicki's concerns proved unwarranted, however, and the meeting with Moscow social activists was also successful.

With Count Adam Krasiński replacing Żukowski, the Polish delegation argued their cause before a distinguished Russian audience of veteran oppositionists: Sergei Muromtsev, Viktor Gol'tsev, Vasilii Skalon, Nikolai Shchepkin, Dimitrii Anuchin and Nikolai Guchkov. Wydżga again spoke first. He described the general state of affairs in the Kingdom, stressing the destructive nature of Russian rule. He voiced the Poles' frustration at tsarist efforts to destroy Polish culture through russification of the schools. Straszewicz continued on this theme, bemoaning the fact that Poles were forced to speak Russian in schools, courts and public areas. He regarded this as the most brutal form of oppression—the eradication of a nation's culture. The Russians were visibly moved. Gol'tsev was driven to tears, and Muromtsev could only add with embarrassment that Russia had treated Poland just as Rome had treated its conquered provinces.[5] Lednicki had assembled a sympathetic audience for the airing of Polish grievances.

Both groups of Russians agreed on the need for more discussions with the Poles. At the urging of Lednicki, the conference also agreed to establish an organizational bureau, with Prince Shakhovskoi at the head. The bureau was assigned the task of making arrangements for a Polish-Russian congress, to be held 23 April 1905. This would be two days before the next scheduled zemstvo congress would convene. The timing was important: Lednicki hoped to ensure the maximum participation of Russian zemstvoists.[6] The Russians and Poles also agreed on the need to 1) get Poles to participate in zemstvo meetings; 2) orient Russian liberal circles to Polish public opinion; and 3) acquaint Russians with the actual political conditions in the Kingdom.[7]

While the November conference did not produce any concrete results, it did serve to make clear Russian attitudes toward Polish autonomy. Essentially, Russian liberals staunchly defended the Polish right to national development and cultural freedoms within the Kingdom. They assigned a crucial role to culture and freely acknowledged the need to end the brutal policy of russification.[8] Yet as

Petrunkevich was quick to note, any Polish demands for political autonomy were destined to encounter strong opposition. The historian Nikolai Kareev was typical of Lednicki's Russian colleagues, for although "as a liberal he recognized the right of the Polish nation to the development of its own culture...as a bourgeois Russian politician he desired the maintenance of the existing boundaries of Russia...."[9]

Elaborate arguments were provided to support this brand of Russian nationalism: Fedor Rodichev wrote in a landmark article on Poland that "the revival of a nation requires the freedom of culture and law, and not an army, diplomacy or customs-house."[10] The Poles were entitled to cultural nationalism, his argument went, but not to political independence. Cultural self-determination would become the rallying cry for Russian liberals who sought to fulfill their sincere desire to satisfy the demands of national minorities, while at the same time remaining true to their nationalistic nature. In a democratic Russia, they believed, everyone's rights would be guaranteed. Therefore, there would be no reason to break up the empire. At the Zemstvo-Municipal Congress in September 1905, A. M. Koliubakin summed up the general sentiment among liberals, when he asked the rhetorical question: "Who will leave a free state, when each region can freely develop its own culture?"[11]

Polish liberals quickly picked up on this argument, and throughout the period of the 1905 revolution they strove primarily for the right to end cultural oppression in the Polish lands.[12] They had discovered in their discussions with Russian liberals in 1904 that they must concentrate on the issue of cultural development, rather than push for full political independence. Forever intent on forcing the *osvobozhdentsy* to recognize Polish political rights as well, however, Lednicki tried to manipulate the argument for cultural self-determination into a defense of political autonomy.

In the months between the November and April gatherings, Lednicki worked tirelessly to achieve this goal. He travelled to Warsaw to familiarize social activists on developments within the Russian opposition. Soon thereafter, representatives of the democratic intelligentsia gathered around the journal *Kuznica* and coalesced into an organized political movement. Led by Andrzej Niemojewski, these men followed Lednicki's lead and established direct contacts with the

Russian constitutionalists. They ratified a platform that corresponded closely to Lednicki's plan of action: Polish unity in the struggle for
liberty; cooperation among national minorities in the fight against
Russian oppression; cooperation with the Russian liberation movement; and a constitution for Russia.[13]

Lednicki's interest in the Warsaw liberal movement reflected his
continued search for a suitable political partner for the Russian constitutionalists. In late 1903, his overtures to the National Democrats
had been rebuffed. The Polish delegation to the Polish-Russian conference in November had consisted entirely of conciliationists gathered around the influential St. Petersburg paper *Kraj*. Like the NDs,
they did not necessarily care what sort of Russian government granted concessions. This hindered fruitful discussions with the liberal
Russians, who were committed constitutionalists. Lednicki himself
firmly believed that only a democratic Russia could resolve the
Russo-Polish dispute equitably. Sharing this belief, the *Kuznicowy*
provided Lednicki with a receptive audience for his preachings on
Russo-Polish cooperation.

At the initiative of the *Kuznicowy*, in December 1904 the *Komitet
Wieców Polskich* was established. This organization served as patron
for a series of meetings, at which autonomy for the Kingdom and
democratic freedoms were discussed. At one such gathering, on 5
December, the activists reiterated their demands for the free use of
Polish in local schools, courts and administration, as well as the call
for local self-rule.[14] Other meetings passed resolutions expressing a
desire to negotiate not with the tsarist government but with the "future
government with Shipov at the head."[15]   These sentiments were
echoed elsewhere in the Warsaw progressive movement. Editors of
two newspapers long associated with Warsaw Positivism and Polish
liberalism, Aleksander Świętochowski, who edited *Prawda*, and
Stanisław Kempner, who edited *Gazeta Handlowa*, made plans to
form a progressive-liberal party devoted to cooperation with the
Russian *ozvobozhdentsy*.[16] Pursuant to this goal, Świętochowski and
his followers wanted to hold talks with Russian liberals. They turned
to Aleksander Lednicki.[17]

In the weeks following the November conference, Lednicki hosted a series of meetings in Moscow between his Russian comrades and

representatives of these progressive circles in Warsaw. The roster of participants reflects Lednicki's drift to the left in his search for suitable political allies. Although Adam Krasiński, Tadeusz Balicki, Włodzimierz Brocholski, Marian Zdziechowski and other moderates took part in these meetings, several future progressive-democratic activists were also present: Stanisław Kempner, Rafal Radziwillicz and Wacław Sieroszewski.[18] These men worked closely with Lednicki, attempting to forge a working relationship between Polish and Russian democrats. A major step toward this goal came in December, when Lednicki, Świętochowski, Kempner and other progressives founded the first liberal party in Poland. As vice-president of the *Związek Postępowej-Demokratyczny* (ZPD)—the Progressive-Democratic Union—Lednicki would from now on represent a well-defined group in his discussions with Russians rather than act merely as an individual.

The inaugural meeting of the ZPD took place at Aleksander Świętochowski's home in Warsaw.[19] The nucleus of the new party was the same group that had attended the recent Polish-Russian meetings. The ZPD was made up of publicists, scholars, literati, lawyers, doctors and other professionals, as well as bankers and wealthy merchants. Many had been close to Świętochowski since their collaboration in the secret literary circles of the 1880s. Two prominent founders of the party, Wacław Sieroszewski and Zygmunt Heryng, were simultaneously members of the PPS.[20] The main ZPD ideologues were Jerzy Kurnatowski and Leon Brunn, who used the pseudonym Leon Gorecki. Gorecki served as Stanisław Kempner's co-editor on *Nowa Gazeta*, and devoted much of his time to exposing the anti-democratic tendencies of the National Democrats.[21]

The ZPD was a tiny party that never numbered more than a hundred members, but because it consisted of the elite of the Polish intelligentsia it wielded significant influence in intellectual circles and among the bourgeoisie in Poland. Assimilated Jews made up about one third of party membership; that may account in part for Dmowski's bitter denunciations of all liberals as non-Polish.[22]

The ZPD sought to be a third force between the *Endecja* and the Socialists. There were three political strands in the party: one rooted in Warsaw Positivism, personified by Świętochowski, the president of the

ZPD; the *Kuznicowy*, who stood slightly to the left of the Positivists; and the group made up of members of the PPS, who would leave the ZPD the following spring as a result of its eventual opposition to the workers' strikes it initially supported.[23] On this issue and others, the right wing of the party came to dominate, although the PPS group played a crucial role in the first months of the party's existence.

Foremost among the members of the PPS who participated in the formation of the ZPD was Wacław Sieroszewski (1858–1945). A long-time opponent of tsarist policies in the Kingdom, Sieroszewski had been exiled to Siberia for political crimes in 1880. A staff writer for *Kuznica*, he evidently became acquainted with Lednicki through his work for the progressive journal. In April 1905 Sieroszewski would attend the First Russo-Polish congress in Moscow. The Russian public first became aware of the ZPD program in an article he wrote for the St. Petersburg daily *Naszi Dni* in January 1905. Sieroszewski, Heryng, and above all Aleksander Więckowski led efforts to publicize the ZPD platform among Petersburg society.[24] In Moscow, Lednicki coordinated all efforts to convince Russian liberals to cooperate with the new party.

The ZPD program called for 1) restoration of the Polish Kingdom to its former boundaries established at the Congress of Vienna in 1815; 2) a constitutional-parliamentary system in Russia, with autonomy for the Kingdom; 3) a separate sejm in Warsaw, elected by universal, secret, equal and direct vote; 4) introduction of the Polish language into schools, courts and administration; 5) a reduction of restrictions connected with social origin and religion; 6) freedom of association, assembly, speech, and strikes, as well as personal immunity; 7) municipal and local self-government based on universal suffrage; 8) recognition of Polish rights in the *Kresy*; and 9) mandatory free elementary education in the Polish language.[25]

As indicated in the first point in its program, the ZPD regarded the Polish matter as an international issue and claimed that the Treaty of Vienna guaranteed the Kingdom's status as a separate political entity. Russian liberals agreed; Struve wrote approvingly of the ZPD program in Osvobozhdenie in the article "Program partii demokraty-cznej."[26] He supported a solution to the Polish question based on the 1815 settlement. Struve hailed the ZPD as an organization which shared the same ideology as the Russian liberals. Kareev also wrote approvingly of the ZPD, and the progressive Russian paper *Rus* called on its readers to support the ZPD rather than the NDs.[27] In his reports on developments in Russia, Max Weber opined that "the emergence and strengthening of the Progressive Democratic Party, whose programmes show an affinity with Russian liberalism," would lead to further Russo-Polish cooperation.[28] Lednicki had succeeded in his efforts to fill the void: the Russian liberals now had a political party with which they could work.

Lednicki, Świętochowski and Kempner dominated the party from the start. Although widely regarded as the dean of the progressive movement, Świętochowski gradually lost political popularity because of his inflexibility. Over time, he came to rely more and more on Lednicki's opinion on many matters.[29] He gradually lost his taste for political life and returned solely to social activism.[30]

Świętochowski's influence among Polish progressives remained great, however, and in October 1906 he founded the *Towarzystwo Kultury Polskiej* (Society of Polish Culture), or TKP. Devoted to the preservation and promotion of Polish culture, the TKP represented a return to Świętochowski's roots. He had always been primarily interested in social and cultural work—the "organic work" which Warsaw Positivism considered the most noble form of patriotic activism. The TKP devoted its resources to establishing schools, reading rooms, libraries, trade unions, hospitals and "people's houses" in which lectures and courses on Polish culture were provided for working-class Poles. ZPD activists played an integral role in the society, for they shared Świętochowski's belief that the universalization of culture and education among wide circles of Polish society was their sacred duty as members of the intelligentsia.[31]

Lednicki was a major supporter of the TKP. He was, of course, a devotee of the precepts of organic work. Under his tutelage, the Roman Catholic Relief Society in Moscow had played a role similar to the TKP. Above all, Lednicki was a cultural nationalist keen on the preservation and dissemination of Polish culture. To further this cause, he and his wife gave generously to the TKP.[32]

The ZPD entered the political fray at a time of great turmoil in the Polish lands. The PPS had launched a campaign to harness the opposition to the war, which continued to grow in intensity as the Russian army suffered a series of defeats in the Far East. On 22 October 1904, anti-war demonstrations reached a fever pitch when the government called up more reserves. The PPS seized the opportunity to try to ignite a general revolution. On 13 November the party organized a large anti-war demonstration of more than a thousand people on Grzybowski Square in Warsaw. Armed PPS militia clashed with tsarist police and Cossack units; twenty seven protestors were wounded and six killed, and six hundred people were arrested. This tragedy, however, did not incite a nation-wide armed rebellion.[33]

Discontent over the war nevertheless continued to grow, for the economy of the Kingdom suffered from the unstable situation. Investment in Polish industries plunged as the financial burden of the war effort increased. As a result, industrial production decreased by about 30–40% in mid-1904. Unemployment rose as workers lost jobs; this precipitated further labor unrest.[34]

The stress of the war also compounded the age-old tension between the Polish population and a tsarist government that regarded the Kingdom as a conquered territory. Chafing under the tsarist yoke, all sectors of society voiced their resentment of russification policies in ever angrier tones. The National Democrats and conciliationists still hoped the tsarist government would grant concessions to give Poles greater cultural autonomy. They petitioned the government for change, including the use of Polish language in schools, the appointment of Poles to administrative posts in the Kingdom, municipal self-government and religious freedom.[35] A memorial of 10 November 1904, signed by twenty-three prominent Poles—including the Lednicki proteges Włodzimierz Spasowicz, Erazm Piltz, Count Krasiński, Ludwik Straszewicz and Stanisław Wydżga—asked for similar reforms. At the same time, these men pledged their support for the Tsar and recognized the need to preserve a unified Russian state.[36] The government rejected the petitions.

The ZPD chose to occupy the middle ground; while it opposed the social revolution sought by the socialists, it also refused to beg the tsarist regime for change from above. Rather, Polish liberals hoped for a political revolution that would bring to power progressive Russians devoted to finding a just solution of the nationalities prob-

lem. They allied themselves with the *osvobozhdentsy* and zemstvoists who sought to replace the autocracy with a constitutional system. Lednicki and his cohorts were confident that if Russia were
granted a constitution, then Poland would receive one, too. Lednicki
was the driving force behind this "entente cordiale" between Russian
and Polish constitutionalists. He charted a difficult route to freedom,
counting on the success of the Russian liberation movement. At the
beginning of 1905, with the old regime apparently on the brink of collapse, this seemed to be a sound policy.

Lednicki's political fortunes were also on the rise. Before the formation of the Progressive-Democratic Union late in December 1904,
Lednicki had not represented any definite Polish political group.
Although he exercised great influence among Russian liberals
because of his enormous personal appeal, the diffuse nature of the
Russian opposition made it difficult for him to pinpoint a specific
audience for his efforts on behalf of Poland. As one scholar has
noted, this situation required "enormous prudence, delicacy, elastici-
ty and above all great political tact" in dealing with potential Russian
and Polish allies. Lednicki justified his apparent "political opportunism"[37] of this period in an open letter to the Polish press on 22
January 1920, in which he professed the belief "that in [political]
actions one should consider a task adjusted to concrete conditions and
possibilities, and not desires and ideals...."[38]

During the revolutionary period, Lednicki deftly gauged the
political attitudes of his Russian friends and fashioned a Polish party
willing to work with the liberation movement. Crucial to any effective relationship was a realistic approach to the problem of Polish
demands: while Lednicki and his fellow Polish progressives all wanted full independence, few Russian liberals were willing to support the
dismemberment of the state. Through their meetings with the Russians,
the Poles had determined to limit their immediate demands to autonomy within a democratic Russian empire. As Wladyslaw Studnicki
commented, "Lednicki played the role of honest broker in Polish-
Russian relations" during the first two decades of this century, using his
considerable skills to mediate an agreement between the two sides.[39]

Lednicki was well suited for this part, for he favored compromise
over conflict. His son, Wacław, recalled that "he always held this

strategy in politics, attempting persuasion and concessions to over-come an obstacle with which...the path of politics is overrun."[40] Lednicki explained in colorful terms his cautious manner in negotiating with Russians, claiming that "just as an alcoholic is afraid to touch a liquor glass, lest it rouse his passion...so we in politics dread reasonings and mutual elucidations based on feeling, and not on real considerations, on mutual, well-understood interests."[41]

Nevertheless, Lednicki's politics had unshakeable ideological foundations: a firm belief in democracy and a passionate defense of the rights of all nationalities. In the fight for freedom, Lednicki and his colleagues regarded the tsarist bureaucracy as the enemy. As Judith Zimmerman has written, "for all Russian liberals, practical politicians and theorists alike, the greatest enemy was *proizvol* (arbitrariness)," for the Russian government could "harass, hinder, humiliate and punish Russian citizens, even respectable, educated citizens like themselves, at will, and it was, thus, an intolerable infringement of human dignity."[42] Lednicki knew well that he and other national minorities were special targets of these discriminatory measures. He lamented that "adopting the motto, *divide et impera*, our bureaucracy strives for the complete disintegration of the social organism, for the pitting of one class of people against another, one nationality against another."[43]

Other leading liberals supported his call for an end to such disruptive policies. The Polish linguist Jan Baudouin de Courtenay preached the politics of inclusion, maintaining that "the government and central institutions of such a state, as Russia...[must] be based not on nationalism, not on aggressive patriotism of one of the nations...but on an all-state solidarity."[44] The liberal politician and specialist on Polish history Nikolai Kareev seconded Lednicki's notion that strained relations between Russia and Poland were created not by the Russian nation but by the tsarist bureaucracy. This view was essentially Slavophile in nature: if only the Russian and Polish peoples were consulted, Russo-Polish tensions would dissipate.[45]

While Lednicki abhorred the arbitrary nature of the tsarist regime and its total disregard for human rights, he was equally repelled by the vulgar chauvinism of the National Democrats. He and other progressive liberals in Poland denounced the *Endecja* for fostering a brand of nationalism that Tadeusz Wróblewski labelled the "poison of hatred" which had "crept into the hearts of the [Polish] nation."[46] Zygmunt Nagórski recalled that "Aleksander Lednicki was not an advocate of the politics, the tactics, nor the philosophy of the national camp...he was too individualistic, too progressive, and...too liberal."[47] Despite the overture to the National Democrats at the Kraków conference, Lednicki himself maintained that he and his political circle "were never advocates of the theory of national egoism....We regarded it as artificially transplanted onto the field of Polish humanism and our particular national desires to universal freedoms...."[48] At the Lednicki-Wasilewski slander trial in 1924, he testified that

> the nationalist ideology, which Pan Dmowski represented...never interested me, I never had anything in common with it and I was never a follower of it....I constructed a vision of a free Poland in the realm of universal freedom and in this ideology of universal freedom is the reason for me belonging to the Kadets. This found support within Polish society at that time, for in Warsaw and beyond...my ideology was understood.[49]

Central to Lednicki's politics was a fundamental belief in the need for cooperation among all social and economic classes and ethnic groups. In a 1922 article, he reiterated his definition of a democracy:

> ...a democratic and parliamentary government excludes both a dictatorship of an individual, and a dictatorship of one part of the nation. In a democratic state there is no place for a dictatorship of nobility nor of capitalists, nor a dictatorship of the worker-peasants. A democratic government must be in a word the will and thoughts of a majority of the nation, taking into consideration the interests and rights of all the groups and classes of the nation. Speaking of the interests and rights of all the groups, we ought to remember that the Polish nation today is an established state, in which not only the Polish nationality lives. Poland today is not merely a nation, as in past years, but—a State, as in former times.

The new Polish state bases its existence not only on social and class justice, but also on *the justice of nationalities*. Respecting the rights of national minorities of our own volition...we will not imitate our former oppressors.[50]

Social solidarity was a keystone of Lednicki's ideology, which was shared by his fellow Polish and Russian liberals. This concept of "solidarism" was integral to the ideologies of the two political parties founded by Lednicki, the ZPD and the Kadets. Both parties called for the cooperation of all citizens in implementing a program of wide reform within the existing social system.[51] The Polish and Russian *intelligentsia* considered it their duty to work for the entire nation and for harmony among the different socio-economic classes. Lednicki's important contribution to liberalism was his application of solidarism to the nationalities problem, calling for all oppressed peoples to unite in a struggle for democratic reform of the Russian empire. He had "a deep conviction...that the struggle with autocracy was indissolubly tied with the national-liberation struggle of all nations oppressed by tsarism, and the Polish question, despite its significance, was only one of its elements."[52]

Lednicki's public speeches and political pronouncements during the revolutionary years 1904–1906 reflected the basic tenets of his politics: the need for Russian-Polish understanding and cooperation in a joint struggle for joint liberty; cooperation with the opposition movement, not the tsarist government, in the drive for true reform in Russia; and a belief in the ultimate victory for Russian democrats and a subsequent just solution of the Polish problem.[53] Another important element was Lednicki's emphasis on the need to link the Polish struggle not only with the Russian liberation movement, but also with the efforts of all national minorities in the empire. He constantly preached that only a united front of all in the empire who chafed under the tsarist yoke could bring about fundamental change. Lednicki's advocacy of an all-Russian liberation movement made good political sense in an empire populated by oppressed peoples. Hopes were high for the full development of a united front at the start of 1905, and Lednicki stood in the vanguard of the drive to mobilize progressive elements throughout the empire in opposition to the tsarist regime.

ENDNOTES

1. W. Lednicki, *Pamiętniki*, 2: 507.
2. *Kurier Polski*, 18 November 1905.
3. Ibid.
4. W. Lednicki, *Pamiętniki*, 2: 508.
5. *Kurier Polski*, 18 November 1905.
6. Bułat, "Zjazd polsko-rosyjski," 195.
7. Smolen, "Działalność polityczne," 64.
8. Emmons, *Formation of Political Parties*, 69; and Zimmerman, "Between Revolution and Reaction," 82.
9. Juliusz Bardach, "Problematyka Polska w liberalnej historiografii rosyjskiej schyłku XIX—początku XX wieku: N. I. Kariejew," in *Polsko-Rosyjskie związki społeczno-kulturalne na przełomie XIX i XX wieku*, ed. Marian Leczyk (Warsaw: Książka i Wiedza, 1980), 140.
10. "K pol'skomu voprosu," *Pravo* 11 (20 March 1905): 798.
11. Quoted in Bensman, "Constitutional Ideas," 750–51.
12. Trenam, "Without a Free Poland," 5.
13. Ibid., 101.
14. Herman Rappaport, ed., *Narastanie rewolucji w Królestwie Polskim w latach 1900–1904* (Warsaw: Państwowe Wydawnictwo Naukowe, 1960), 700–01. Overall there were nearly 40 meetings with an average attendance of 100. See Tadeusz Stegner, *Liberałowie Królestwa Polskiego 1904–1915* (Gdańsk: Studencka Spółdzielnia Pracy "Techno-Service," 1990), 21.
15. Petrozolin-Skowrońska, "Partie liberalno-demokratyczne," 4. Dmitrii Shipov was a prominent zemstvoist who sought concessions from the government. Shipov was not, however, a constitutionalist.
16. *Prawda* and *Gazeta Handlowa* subsequently became the main organs for the ZPD. *Prawda* conducted a sharp dialogue with the PPS-run *Kurier Codzienny*, while *Gazeta Handlowa* (which changed its name to *Nowa Gazeta* in 1905) attacked the ideology and politics of the *Endecja*. See Zenon Kmiecik, *Prasa polska w rewolucji 1905–1907* (Warsaw: Państwowe Wydawnictwo Naukowe, 1980), 101–15.
17. Petrozolin-Skowrońska, "Partie liberalno-demokratyczne,"4.
18. Bułat, "Zjazd polsko-rosyjski," 191.
19. Trenam, "Without a Free Poland," 105. About seventeen people took part in the meeting.
20. Bułat, "Zjazd polsko-rosyjski," 192. See also Tadeusz Stegner, "Postępowa demokracja a inteligencja," in *Inteligencja Polska XIX i XX wieku*, ed. Ryszard Czepulis-Rastenis (Warsaw: Państwowe Wydawnictwo Naukowe, 1985), 4: 279. Zygmunt Heryng (1854–1931), was a workers' advocate and economist from an assimilated Jewish merchant family. Early on he became acquaint-

ed with Aleksander Więckowski in St. Petersburg, and also established close relations with Georgii Plekhanov and the People's Will party. Exiled to Siberia in 1879 for revolutionary activity, he joined the PPS in 1898.

21. Kmiecik, *Prasa polska*, 115.

22. Stegner, "Postępowa demokracja a inteligencja," 279. Elsewhere, Stegner lists the total membership of the ZPD as never exceeding 200. See "Liberałowie Królestwa Polskiego wobec kwestii żydowskiej na początku XX wieku," *Przegląd historyczny* 80 (1989), 70.

23. Petrozolin-Skowrońska, "Partie liberalno-demokratyczne," 6. The idea of progress was central to the ZPD program. Liberals hoped to liquidate social inequalities without social revolution. They wanted a change in the political system that would enable social reforms. The ZPD believed that with the destruction of autocracy in Russia and the creation of a new, progressive, and democratic government, political autonomy for the Polish Kingdom and social justice would become a reality. See Stegner, *Liberałowie Królestwa Polskiego*, 42–67.

24. Bułat, "Zjazd polsko-rosyjski," 192–93.

25. The program of the ZPD was published in December 1904 in a brochure entitled "Związek P-D: Zasady Programu." A copy is located in GARF, f. 579, op. 1, d. 1317, ll. 1–16. The fundamental points of the program are outlined in fond 579, op. 1, d. 1336, l. 14 (ob). Wacław Sieroszewski discussed the party program in his article, "K polskomu voprosu (Pismo iz Warszawy)," *Naszi Dni*, 24 January 1905.

26. *Osvobozhdenie* 3(5/18 March 1905), no. 67: 278–9.

27. *Rus* devoted a great deal of attention to the Polish question at this time. See *Sprawa polska w dzienniku 'Rus'/ Pol'skii vopros v gazete 'Rus'* (St. Petersburg: Tipografia N. P. Sobko, 1905).

28. Max Weber, *The Russian Revolution*, ed. and tr. Gordon C. Wells and Peter Baehr (Ithaca: Cornell University Press, 1985), 55.

29. PIASA, Aleksander Lednicki Collection (006), folder 7. Letters from Świętochowski to Lednicki, dated 8 December 1907; 29 February 1908; and 1 January 1910. In the letter of 8 December 1907, for example, Świętochowski asks Lednicki about party plans for the upcoming electoral campaigns.

30. Petrozolin-Skowrońska, "Partie liberalno-demokratyczne," 7–8. The two men remained on good terms, however, throughout the pre-revolutionary period. See Petrozolin-Skowrońska, "Problem genezy 'Zarania' (W świetle listu Aleksandra Świętochowskiego do Aleksandra Lednickiego z 11 listopada 1907 roku)," *Roczniki dziejów ruchu ludowej* 10 (1968): 516–21. In 1910, Lednicki wrote the introduction to the Russian edition of Świętochowski's treatise on utopian thought. See A. Sventokhovskii, *Istoriia utopii*, tr. E. Zagorskii, intro. Aleksandr Lednitskii (Moscow: V. M. Sablin, 1910).

31. Stegner, "Postępowa demokracja a inteligencja," 286–87.

32. Maria Brykalska, *Aleksander Świętochowski: Biografia*, 2 vols. (Warsaw: Państwowy Instytut Wydawniczy, 1987), 2: 100.

33. Robert E. Blobaum, *Rewolucja: Russian Poland, 1904–1907* (Ithaca and London: Cornell University Press, 1995), 41–51.

34. Ibid., 52.

35. Ibid., 70–71.

36. Rappaport, *Narastanie rewolucji*, 856–64.

37. Smolen, "Działalność polityczna," 56.

38. Wasilewski, *Proces Lednickiego*, 90.

39. Piłsudski Institute. Archiwum Władysława Studnickiego. Teka IV, Teczka 4, p. 2.

40. W. Lednicki, *Pamiętniki*, 2: 171.

41. A. Lednicki, *Mowy polityczne*, 19.

42. Judith E. Zimmerman, "Russsian Liberal Theory, 1900–1917," *Canadian-American Slavic Studies* 14 (Spring 1980): 12.

43. A. Lednicki, *Mowy polityczne*, 21.

44. Prof. I. Boduen-de-Kurtene, "Pol'skii vopros v sviazi s drugimi okrainnymi i inorodcheskimi voprosami," *Pravo* 32 (14 August 1905): 2563. Jan Baudouin de Courtenay (1845–1929), a Pole of French descent, organized the Union of Autonomists-Federalists, which held a congress in St. Petersburg in November 1905. Representatives from Poland, Finland, Ukraine, Belorus, the Baltic region, the Caucasus and Central Asia took part. On de Courtenay's political activities, see Robert A. Rothstein, "The Linguist as Dissenter: Jan Baudouin de Courtenay," in *For Wiktor Weintraub: Essays in Polish Literature, Language, and History Presented on the Occasion of his 65th Birthday*, ed. Victor Erlich, et al (The Hague; Paris: Mouton, 1975), 391-405; and Irena Spustek, "Jan Baudouin de Courtenay a carska cenzura," *Przegląd historyczny* 52 (1961): 112–26.

45. Bardach, "Problematyka Polska w liberalnej historiografii," 141.

46. *Kraj* 18 (1906), 14. Tadeusz Wróblewski (1858–1925), was a lawyer and social activist from Wilno. He was arrested for subversive activities in 1881, and spent two years in Siberian exile. Wróblewski, like Lednicki, was a *Kresy* Pole who defended the rights of non-Poles living in the lands of the former *Rzeczpospolita*.

47. Nagórski, "Aleksander Lednicki," 42.

48. A. Lednicki, *Z lat wojny*, 113.

49. Wasilewski, *Proces Lednickiego*, 383.

50. A. Lednicki, *Zadania chwili* (Warsaw: Zjednoczenie, 1922), 13. Emphasis in original.

51. Stegner, "Postępowa demokracja a inteligencja," 280.

52. Mieczysław Smolen, "DziałalnośćAleksandra Lednickiego w I Dumie Panstwowej," *Studia historyczne* 34 (1991): 416.

53. W. Lednicki, *Pamiętniki*, 2: 522–23..

Chapter Five

JANUARY–MARCH 1905

The "Bloody Sunday" massacre of peaceful protestors on 9 January 1905 was a watershed event. Appalled at the tragedy, Russians of all classes lost faith in the tsarist regime to effect any peaceful changes in the empire. Energized, the opposition movement grew dramatically more radical as the months passed.[1] One analyst later recalled that "in these days...everyone spoke one's mind openly and without fear, like children with all their pent up desires and thoughts springing forth..."[2] Lednicki believed that 1905 marked a turning point in the pursuit of the goal of a constitutional, parliamentary democracy in Russia and Poland.[3]

Developments in the Polish Kingdom kept pace with events in Russia as the various political groups increased their demands. In February, a nationwide boycott of Russian schools was launched. At its peak, some 20,000 students took part. Coordinated by student groups at all levels of education and supported by all major political parties, including the ZPD, the boycott was the strongest manifestation up to that time of the Poles' determination to end Russian cultural hegemony.[4]

Polish schools had become the rallying point for opposition to the policy of russification. The most zealous activists wanted to fully polonize the education system. In an effort to gain concessions from the tsarist regime, Aleksander Świętochowski led a delegation to St. Petersburg, where on 9 March 1905 he presented a petition signed by 30,000 Poles. It demanded the reorganization of Polish schools in the Kingdom, with more local control. Polish was to be reinstated as the language of instruction in public schools, and Polish teachers were to replace Russians. In late April the Russian government granted concessions.[5]

While in Russia, Świętochowski and his entourage met with representatives of the Russian opposition movement. Mediated by Lednicki, the conference proceeded with the participation of other future Kadet leaders. The Poles convinced their Russian counterparts that Poland would remain unsettled unless the government granted concessions. It was becoming increasingly evident to the *osvobozhdentsy* that Poles would not be satisfied with anything less than full autonomy.[6]

As a result of Lednicki's continued pressure on his fellow *osvobozhdentsy*, the Polish question was debated at the Third Congress of the Union of Liberation, held 25–27 March 1905 in Moscow.[7] The programmatic statement contained important clauses dealing with the nationalities question. It repeated Petr Struve's call for equality of all citizens regardless of sex, religion, or nationality. The Congress also resolved that "any estate distinctions and any limitations of the person and property rights of Poles, Jews, and other separate groups of the population must be abolished."[8] *The osvobozhdentsy* also demanded the reform of the state structure, allowing for broad local and regional self-government. Decentralization was gaining acceptance as a solution to the nationalities problem. On this point, too, the Congress' statement mimicked Struve, demanding that a "liberated Russia must consciously and decisively break with the oppression of the borderlands and bureaucratic centralization."[9] Finally, the concluding statement of the Third Congress argued that

> the constitution of Finland, which guarantees its special status, must be entirely restored...the broadest regional self-government must be granted to the regions of the Empire, which are sharply distinguished by their way of life and historical conditions, for example, Poland, Lithuania, Little Russia, or the Transcaucasus. Regarding the nationalities, which are part of Russia, we unconditionally recognize their right to cultural self-determination. The use by all nationalities of the Russian state of their native language in primary schools and in all local institutions must be recognized as necessary in principle.[10]

This sort of categorization of the various non-Russian peoples of the empire was common within the liberation movement. In a March

1905 article, S. N. Uzhakov made this same distinction between the different "types" of nationalities. He divided them into two basic groups: those living in lands populated primarily by ethnic Russians, and those living in their own territories, in some cases as the majority. In the first group, Uzhakov placed Jews, Tatars, Kalmyks, Bashkirs and other "little minorities."[11] The author advocated granting equal rights, including the right to vote and cultural self-determination, to these peoples. This was an easy matter, he determined, for there could be no question of territorial autonomy.[12] Those nationalities who lived in well-defined homelands posed a different problem. For these peoples—Poles, Georgians, Armenians, etc.—he proposed political autonomy including separate legislatures. Uzhakov argued that local rule would facilitate the solution of local problems in a more timely and equitable fashion than if matters remained in the hands of the central government.[13]

While the Third Congress of the Union of Liberation went further than the Union's constitution in its advocacy of the nationalities' struggle for equal rights and autonomy, it still gave preference to the Finns. Petr Struve took exception, equating the Polish and Finnish problems. In both cases, he argued, historical legal rights had been denied. In general, Russian liberals willingly recognized that Finland's constitution had been illegally revoked by the tsarist regime, but were loathe to grant the same consideration for the Polish case. Struve, however, was one of the most outspoken supporters of Polish autonomy in 1905.

Struve agreed with Lednicki's contention that Poland's autonomy, which had been sanctioned by the Treaty of Vienna in 1815, had been illegally, unilaterally revoked by Russia. Lednicki and the ZPD demanded a return to the situation established by the Treaty of Vienna. Struve wrote in "The Democratic Party and Its Program" that

> the relations between Russia and the Kingdom must be reformed on the basis of the recognition in principle of the constitution granted to Poland by Alexander I in 1815. The governmental and legal relations of the empire and Poland must be regulated by an agreement between the constituent assembly of the Russian Empire and the constituent sejm of the Kingdom of Poland.[14]

Struve pointed out that this was identical to the ZPD program. Over time, Lednicki convinced other Russians to accept this view. The April Russo-Polish Congress would provide his first opportunity to convert large numbers of Russian liberals to this idea.

Interestingly, while Struve openly supported Polish autonomy, and was sympathetic to the free national development of Jews, Estonians, Latvians, Georgians and Armenians, he refused to grant the same consideration for Belorussians or Ukrainians. Professor N. A. Gredeskul' later decried this inconsistency and called for uniformity in Struve's—and that of the Russian liberal community in general—attitude toward the nationality question. Gredeskul' argued that Struve felt threatened by the national awakening of the Belorussian and Ukrainian nations, seeing in it a danger to "an all-Russian cultural development."[15] This was but an euphemism for Russian cultural hegemony. Struve and other nationalistic liberals still regarded these peoples as essentially Russian and refused to recognize the existence of their distinct ethno-linguistic identities. These attitudes hindered Lednicki's efforts to convince representatives of other nationalities to join him in supporting the Russian liberals.

By the spring of 1905 the liberal Russian press had begun to routinely propagandize the Polish cause. The legal weekly *Pravo* took a leading role in this effort to convince the Russian public that Poland must be granted reforms. Lednicki, who had connections with *Pravo* and other leading liberal journals, spurred this development. In a seminal article on the Polish issue, Fedor Rodichev argued that liberalization was needed throughout the empire. He maintained that Poland and other national minorities ought to be tied to Russia not through oppression but through bonds of friendship. Rodichev tried to reassure his fellow *osvobozhdentsy* that a just solution to the nationalities problem entailed not the dismemberment of the Russian state but rather guarantees for the free cultural development of all peoples. He argued that

> We live not in the 18th, but the 20th century, and the idea of a national dominion and state system is fading away: [it] is becoming merely a slogan of the oppressor. The revival of a nation requires the freedom of culture and law, and not of army, diplomacy and customs-house.[16]

Rodichev believed that in order to keep the empire intact, reform was needed for all of Russia. It was his contention that "old Poland will find itself and its rights only in a free Russia."[17]

Fedor Rodichev (1856–1933), Lednicki's indefatigable coworker in the struggle for Polish autonomy, was widely hailed by contemporaries as a champion of Polish rights.[18] As Paul Miliukov noted, "in the nationality question he [Rodichev] was an inveterate defender of Polish interests."[19] In fact, Rodichev was well-disposed to the Polish cause long before he met Lednicki. In his student days he associated with the Polish group of students at St. Petersburg University and the Polish colony in that city.[20] In his youth he was greatly influenced by the writings of Alexander Herzen, with whom he shared a concern for Polish rights.[21] As Rodichev's interest in the Polish issue grew over the years, it was perhaps inevitable that he would become Lednicki's staunchest ally and closest personal friend within the Russian liberation movement.

In a series of autobiographical letters to Lednicki shortly before his death, Rodichev recalled how the two men met:

> In the winter of 1903 or 1904 a Polish deputation under the leadership of Sventokhovskii [Swietochowski] came to Petersburg. The Poles were very worried...about Russian legal opinions on the Polish question. At the invitation of I. V. Gessen I wrote an article in *Pravo*. I received two precious salutations: from you in Moscow and from Spasovich [Spasowicz] in Warsaw. After that I was a devoted participant in the Polish-Russian conferences at your home. In this matter I never swayed, because here for me was an unshakable foundation: the rights...of the individual and of a nationality.[22]

Vasilii Maklakov later recounted the special relationship between Lednicki and Rodichev. He believed that their friendship was not based on "personal sympathies" but rather "stemmed from political agreement and from common work on the same problem."[23] The two shared Miliukov's belief that the main enemy of the liberation movement in 1905 was on the right; others shared the sentiments of their friend and fellow *osvobozhdenets* Maklakov, who feared the revolutionary wrath of the radical left.[24] While Lednicki was a committed democrat, however, Rodichev continued to believe in the efficacy of a constitutional monarchy.[25]

The two friends and comrades also differed in their attitudes to the Polish question on one key point. Lednicki regarded autonomy for the Kingdom as a temporary solution to the Polish problem; eventually, Poland would regain its independence. Autonomy, therefore, was a minimum program for Lednicki and many other Poles. For Rodichev and other Russian liberals sympathetic to the Polish cause, Polish autonomy was a maximum demand: he never believed in the separation of Poland from Russia. As Maklakov pointed out, Rodichev was a sincere patriot of a "Great Russia" and an imperialist. He believed, however, that the huge multinational Russian empire could only thrive if the nationalities matter was settled peacefully.[26] Rodichev's thinking was strongly influenced by his legal training. As "a liberal and a legalist," he "felt that the law must be uniform for all, regardless of estate, creed or nationality."[27] Above all, Rodichev realized that "the Polish problem, which the Russian public...poorly understood, required a judicious solution."[28]

The Lednicki-Rodichev relationship, and each man's attitude to the Polish problem, is best summed up by recounting an event remembered by Lednicki during testimony before the Provisional Government in 1917. He described Rodichev's appearance in "1912 or 1913" at the annual celebration in Kraków of the Polish victory over the Germans at the Battle of Grunwald in 1410:

> After the conclusion of the speeches of the president and others, someone shouted: "Among us is a member of the State Duma—Rodichev." And in response to this the huge crowd standing in the square shouted: "Let him speak!" Rodichev stood and replied in Russian, saying that he was not able, that he did not know how to speak Polish. In answer to this a general cry rang out: "Let him speak in Russian!" And this greeting was issued in Kraków almost one year before the war, one year before the formation of the Galician Legions...directed subsequently against Russia...his

speech in Russian was greeted with extraordinary enthusiasm, which was expressed in a continuous ovation.[29]

For Lednicki, the reception given his Russian friend was telling. It indicated that Poles were not hostile to Russians; they wanted independence but did not hate the Russian people. This validated Lednicki's fundamental belief in the Slavic brotherhood between Poles and Russians and confirmed his view that the oppression suffered by both peoples at the hands of the tsarist bureaucracy was the only stumbling block on the path toward rapprochement.

While Lednicki—and other Poles in attendance at the Krakow celebration, too—viewed the warm welcome given Rodichev as an expression of Slavic solidarity and Russian goodwill, Rodichev definitely did not intend to raise the hopes of those Poles clamoring for independence. Rodichev's speech was in fact especially pro-Polish, stressing that "the Polish nation is in the front rank with Russia in the struggle for liberty."[30] At a banquet later that same day, Lednicki's friend and co-founder of the ZPD, Wacław Sieroszewski, turned to Rodichev with an exhuberant toast: "Teodorze Izmaijlowicz! Fighting for the separation of Poland from Russia, we fight for the freedom of the Russian nation."[31] Startled by such a reaction to his speech and fearful of a grave misunderstanding, Rodichev later sent a letter to the editor of the Polish daily *Nowa Reforma* stressing that he would always defend the Kingdom's right to autonomy but would never advocate the separation of Poland from Russia.[32]

For Lednicki, limiting Polish demands to autonomy within a liberal Russian state was merely a tactical move. He always wanted full independence for the Polish Kingdom, but in 1905 he realized this was impossible. As the Lithuanian statesman Augustinas Valdemaras wrote of the nationalities movements in the Russian empire at this time:

To strive for complete separation from Russia in 1905 would have been madness. Nobody in Russia would have made such demands, not even the Poles, even though a Polish Problem was recognized. Such demands can only be made in the cataclysm of a general war.[33]

Many Russians suspected Polish duplicity in limiting their demands in 1905 to autonomy, and opponents to Polish autonomy charged Lednicki and his fellow Poles with harboring greater ambitions. Even Lednicki's friend and ally, Miliukov, later admitted that he "could not but realize that the Poles' refusal to have their independence restored was only temporary and conditional." He was convinced that Poles continued to dream of a Poland with pre-partition borders, stretching from "sea to sea."

Unlike Rodichev, who never wavered in his opposition to Polish independence, Miliukov seemed incapable of consistency on this most difficult issue. Miliukov regarded the Polish matter as particularly thorny, since it involved "the old tradition of a lost state, the mysticism of national dreams, and complicated international relations." He noted that "it was precisely this awareness that led [him] to be extremely cautious" when dealing with Poles. Miliukov stated late in life that

> I myself wanted their [Poles'] independence restored, as did a few Russian Slavophiles; but I also knew that Poland could only be restored as a whole, that is, as a result of a general European agreement after a European conflict.[34]

In fact, Poland was resurrected as an independent state only after the cataclysm of World War I drastically altered the international scene.

Although Miliukov would work closely with Lednicki on the nationalities question, the two men had fundamentally different outlooks on the Polish matter. Despite his affection for Miliukov, Lednicki believed that

> Pavel Nikolaevich found himself, in his views on the nationality question, under the influence of prejudiced ideas about state structure which were deeply imbedded in his mind. He was therefore prone toward largely unitary and unionistic tendencies in the solution of the national problem and paid little attention to existing historical· preconditions and to national feelings based on national instincts.[35]

These statements highlight the political differences that dogged relations between Russian and Polish liberals throughout the pre-revolutionary period. While the Russian statist Miliukov spoke of "the old tradition of a lost state," and "the mysticism of national dreams," Lednicki the Polish patriot demanded consideration for "existing historical preconditions" and "national feelings based on national instincts." The refusal of Miliukov and the Kadets to recognize the legitimacy of Polish demands for independence during World War I, even after the Central Powers established a rump Polish state in November 1916, induced Lednicki to leave the party and search for Russian allies on the left.[36]

But in the heady atmosphere of revolution in 1905, Polish autonomy—and eventual independence—seemed to be within reach. At long last, the Polish question was being addressed by Russian society, and the issue of autonomy for the Kingdom assumed a prominent place in political debate. At this time a series of congresses of various professional unions issued statements concerning the fate of national minorities. They called for greater autonomy for the borderlands, on the condition that the integrity of the Russian state be preserved.[37]

One of the most important gatherings of professionals in early 1905 was the First Congress of the Union of Lawyers. Lednicki helped organize the gathering; consequently, he made certain that the nationalities question would be on the agenda. At a large gathering of about 280 Moscow lawyers on 13 March, he pushed for a resolution on this matter. Approved by the assembly, the declaration stated that

> all Russian citizens, without distinction of sex, origin, religion and nationality, must be guaranteed the following rights: inviolability of person and dwelling, freedom of speech, press, religion, freedom of travel, assembly, association, strikes and equality of all national languages.[38]

Delegates to the upcoming Lawyers' Congress were also chosen at this meeting. Lednicki, Vasilii Maklakov and Sergei Muromtsev were among the 18 full delegates and 7 alternates selected.[39]

Lednicki made certain that his Russian comrades would have to pay special attention to Poland by arranging for the participation of a

Polish delegation. Poles in the Kingdom held a special pre-congress meeting in March, at which the 150 lawyers in attendance chose 12 men—8 from Warsaw and 4 from the provinces—to represent their interests at the Lawyers' Congress. They were instructed to inform the Russians of their position: 1) Polish lawyers must remain a separate entity, and could not join the Russian union; 2) the Kingdom should have full internal legal-administrative autonomy, based on the universal, equal, secret [and direct?] vote of all citizens of the Kingdom; 3) the Poles were in sympathy with the Russian constitutional movement; and 4) representatives would take part in the work of the Congress, with the condition that the need for autonomy of the Polish Kingdom be recognized.[40] In addition to the 12 Poles from the Kingdom, 20 Polish lawyers from Moscow, Petersburg and the *Kresy* took part in the Congress.[41]

The gathering convened at the Free Economic Society in Petersburg from 28-30 March 1905. There were 178 delegates in attendance, including 44 from St. Petersburg, 38 from Moscow, 25 from Kiev, 12 each from Warsaw and Tiflis, and 6 from Wilno.[42] Immediately after opening ceremonies, the Polish issue took center stage. Lawyers from the Kingdom promptly informed their Russian colleagues of the conditions under which they would participate in the proceedings. They told their counterparts they must recognize the complete equality between the Polish and Russian bars. Essentially, they demanded that the Lawyers' Union assume a federative form. Also, the Poles relayed the key element to the resolutions they had approved earlier in March: unless the Russian lawyers endorsed the call for legal-administrative autonomy for the Kingdom, then the Poles would leave in protest.[43] As Vasilii Maklakov later recalled, the Poles were "well-prepared" to argue their cause.[44]

Luckily for the Poles, Fedor Rodichev had been chosen to preside over the deliberations.[45] Together, he and Lednicki swayed the Congress, pushing through acceptance of the Polish proposals.[46] Rodichev was able to soothe the hostile audience by appealing to the delegates' idealism.[47] He spoke about Poles' long-standing devotion to the cause of liberty, professing his belief that wherever there was a struggle for freedom, Poles were sure to be there. Therefore, he argued, it was only right to accept Polish demands.[48] He and Lednicki convinced the Russians to accept Polish demands for a federated union, and the demand for Polish autonomy was approved without opposition. In addition, the Congress supported the Union of Liberation's call for cultural self-determination for all national minorities. Lednicki personally drafted the resolution on the nationalities issue.[49] Due in large part to Lednicki's influence, the Lawyers' Congress was one of the first professional gatherings to specifically call for Polish legal and administrative autonomy.[50]

While lawyers in Russia were forced to address the issue of Polish autonomy, other professional unions tried to avoid taking a stand on this volatile issue. Frequently, their congresses passed resolutions of a more general nature, without any specific reference to Poland. At the First Congress of the All-Russian Union of Journalists (5–8 April 1905), for example, delegates did not embrace Polish demands. The journalists approved a moderate resolution reflecting the prevailing sentiment among Russian liberal activists. National minorities should be guaranteed the right to cultural development and limited autonomy, but on the condition that the Russian state remain intact.[51]

Polish activists thus learned that they had to strive constantly to introduce the Polish matter into the daily order of business at the various all-Russian congresses, in order to make their Russian comrades in the liberation movement fully aware of their demands. Aleksander Lednicki took this line of reasoning a step further: he organized the First Russo-Polish Congress, held at his home in Moscow from 7–9 April 1905. He resolved that only through direct talks between Russians and Poles, devoted solely to the issue of Polish autonomy, could Russian *osvobozhdentsy* be persuaded to take a stand on this issue. As Miliukov noted in his memoirs, thanks to Lednicki's persistence, "we were forced to touch upon the nationalities question, in connection with the strivings of the Poles for autonomy."[52] Lednicki would have two tasks at the April gathering: to persuade the Polish delegation to agree with his views, and to convince the Russians of the need for Polish autonomy.[53]

ENDNOTES

1. On the events surrounding this catastrophe, see Walter Sablinsky, *The Road to Bloody Sunday: Father Gapon and the St. Petersburg Massacre of 1905* (Princeton: Princeton University Press, 1976).

2. M. A. Slavinskii, "Russkaia intelligentsiia i natsional'nyi vopros," in *Intelligentsiia v Rossii. Sbornik statei*, ed. K. K. Arsen'ev, et al. (St. Petersburg: Knigoizdatel'stvo 'Zemlia,' 1910), 230.

3. Alexandre Lednicki, *L'idee nationale et son evolution. A l'occasion du XXVIeme Congres International de la Paix reuni a Varsovie le 25 juin 1928* (Warsaw: Messenger Polonais, 1928), 8.

4. Blobaum, *Rewolucja*, 169.

5. Brykalska, *Aleksander Świętochowski*, 2: 60.

6. Ibid., 60–61. Russians present included Prince Dmitrii Shakhovskoi, Nikolai Kareev, Nikolai Annenski and Fedor Rodichev.

7. This was the first Union congress attended by Lednicki. See Shatsillo, "Novoe o 'Soiuze Osvobozhdeniia,'" 142.

8. Bensman, "Constitutional Ideas," 494.

9. Ibid., 497.

10. Ibid., 498.

11. S. N. Uzhakov, "Polityka," *Russkoe bogatstvo* (March 1905), no. 3: 162.

12. Ibid., 163.

13. Ibid.

14. Bensman, "Constitutional Ideas," 489–90.

15. Professor N. A. Gredeskul', "Prof. N. A. Gredeskul' ob otnoshenii russkago obshchestva k natsional'nomy voprosy," *Ukrainskaia zhizn'* 5 (1916), no. 4–5: 116.

16. Fedor Rodichev, "K pol'skomu voprosu," *Pravo* 11 (20 March 1905): 798.

17. Ibid.

18. PIASA, Aleksander Lednicki Collection (006), folder 59. Letter from Stanisław Posner to Lednicki, dated 18 February 1911.

19. Paul Miliukov, *Political Memoirs: 1905–1917*, ed. Arthur P. Mendel, trans. Carl Goldberg (Ann Arbor: The University of Michigan Press, 1967), 166.

20. W. Lednicki, *Pamiętniki*, 2: 512–13.

21. Kermit McKenzie, "The Political Faith of Fedor Rodichev," in *Essays on Russian Liberalism*, ed. Charles E. Timberlake (Columbia: University of Missouri Press, 1972), 55.

22. Fedor Ismailovich Rodichev, *Vospominaniia i ocherki o russkom liberalizme*, ed., annotated and intro. Kermit E. McKenzie (Newtonville, MA: Oriental Research Partners, 1983), 161. Rodichev here makes a chronological error; the Swietochowski delegation came to Russia in the spring of 1905. In

another letter to Lednicki, Rodichev gets the date correct, noting that "in 1904-1905 the Petersburg journal "Pravo" was very [closely] tied to the Union of Liberation. The editors asked me to write an article on Poland." See PIASA, Aleksander Lednicki Collection (006), folder 5, p. 5.

23.   W. A. Maklakow, "Lednicki, Rodiczew i sprawa polska," *Wiadomości literackie* 17 (1936): 14–15. A Russian-language version of the article appeared under the title "F. I. Rodichev i A. R. Lednitskii," in *Novyi zhurnal* 16 (1947): 240–51.

24.   McKenzie, "Fedor Rodichev," 58.

25.   Kadet leader Ariadna Tyrkova-Vil'iams noted that while "among the Kadets there were republicans... Rodichev always remained a constitutional monarchist." See her article "F. I. Rodichev (1854–1933)," *Novyi zhurnal* 38 (1954): 219.

26.   Maklakow, "Lednicki, Rodiczew," 14–15.

27.   Tyrkova-Vil'iams, "F. I. Rodichev," 215.

28.   Ibid., 216.

29.   A. Lednicki, "Pokazaniia A. R. Lednitskogo, 27 sentiabria 1917," in *Padenie tsarskogo rezhima. Stenograficheskie otchety doprosov i pokazanii, dannykh v 1917 v Chrezvychainoi Sledstvennoi Komissii Vremennogo Pravitel'stva*, vol. 7, ed. P. E. Shchegolev (Moscow and Leningrad: Gosudarstvennoe Izdatel'stvo, 1927), 235–36.

30.   Antoni Giza, *Neoslawizm i Polacy 1906–1910* (Szczecin: Wydawnictwa Naukowe Wyzszej Szkoly Pedagogicznej, 1984), 209.

31.   Ibid.

32.   Ibid.

33.   Augustinas Valdemaras, *La Lithuanie et ses problemes* (Lille: Mercure universelle, 1933), 182. Cited by George Urbaniak, "White Eagle, White Knight. The Polish-Lithuanian Dispute, 1918–1920" (Ph.D. diss., University of Toronto, 1985), 30.

34.   P. N. Miliukov, *Political Memoirs*, 214.

35.   A. Lednitskii, "P. N. Miliukov i pol'skii vopros," in *P. N. Miliukov: Sbornik materialov po chestvovaniiu ego semidesiatiletiia, 1859–1929* (Paris, 1929), 214; translation by Thomas Riha, *A Russian European*, 61. For the most recent study on Miliukov, see Melissa Kirschke Stockdale, *Paul Miliukov and the Quest for a Liberal Russia, 1880–1918* (Ithaca and London: Cornell University Press, 1996).

36.   GARF, f. 102 (00), op. 1916, d. 149. Reports dated 4 January 1916; 20 July 1916; and 2 August 1916. Although under intense pressure from Lednicki and the left wing of the Kadet Central Committee, the majority of party leaders — including Lednicki's friends and allies Kokoshkin and Miliukov — would not give up Russia's exclusive right to determine the internal structure of Poland. The Kadets stubbornly stuck to their original 1906 plan for limited Polish autonomy. See also Spustek, *Polacy w Piotrogrodzie*, 375–81.

37. Sanders, "Union of Unions," 585. One such congress was the First All-Russian Congress of Professors and Teachers in Institutions of Higher Education, which met in St. Petersburg from 25–28 March and was attended by 200 delegates. Resolutions called for the full equality of all citizens and the recognition of the right of self-determination for all nationalities in the empire.

38. *Pravo* 11 (20 March 1905): 828.

39. Ibid., 829.

40. W. Lednicki, *'Entente cordiale'*, 57–58.

41. Ibid., 58.

42. GARF, f. 63, op. 25, d. 814, ll. 1–4 (ob). For a complete list of participants, see *Nasha zhizn'*, 13/26 September 1905.

43. I. V. Gessen, *Istoriia russkoi advokatury*, vol. 1, *Advokatura, obshchestvo i gosudarstvo 1864 20/XI 1914* (Moscow: Izdanie Sovetov Prisiazhnykh Poverennykh, 1914), 417–18.

44. V. Maklakov, *Vlast' i obshchestvennost' na zakate staroi Rossii. (Vospominaniia sovremennika)* (Paris, 1928), 362.

45. On Rodichev's recollections of the congress, see his correspondence to Lednicki in PIASA, Aleksander Lednicki Collection (006), folder 5.

46. GARF, f. 63, op. 25, d. 814, ll. 1–4 (ob).

47. V. Maklakov, *Vlast' i obshchestvennost'*, 363.

48. Halina Kiepurska, *Warszawa w rewolucji 1905–1907* (Warsaw: Wiedza Powszechna, 1974), 152.

49. GARF, f. 63, op. 25, d. 814, ll. 1–4 (ob).

50. Acceptance of Polish demands at the Lawyers' Congress paved the way for the formation of a Polish lawyers' union. In June 1905 Polish lawyers convened their own congress in Warsaw. Lednicki attended, and helped create the Union of Polish Lawyers, which sought to promote Polish autonomy. See Zdzisław Krzemiński, ed., *Zarys historii adwokatury polskiej* (Warsaw: Państwowe Wydawnictwo Naukowe, 1980), 117.

51. Voskobiynyk, "Nationalities Question in Russia," 141–42.

52. Paul Miliukov, *Political Memoirs*, 17.

53. W. Lednicki, *'Entente cordiale'*, 79.

Chapter Six

THE FIRST RUSSO-POLISH CONGRESS, APRIL 1905

The Russo-Polish Congress of April 1905 heralded an intensification of discussion on the issue of Polish autonomy in Russian political circles and in the Russian press.[1] It had been planned since the previous November, when Poles and Russians first met to discuss Polish autonomy as an issue of mutual interest. At that time, an organizational bureau was established, headed by Prince Dmitrii Shakhovskoi. Before the April gathering, Shakhovskoi, Prince Dolgorukov and Fedor Rodichev travelled to Poland to gauge Polish concerns.[2] As a result of these discussions, the organizational bureau developed a list of tasks for the upcoming congress, including the creation of a permanent union between Russians and Poles and the promulgation of a joint Polish-Russian statement.[3] A change of heart among the Russians was also evident: at the November conference, they specifically stated that they were not seeking Polish help, while at the April congress they welcomed the opportunity to forge an alliance with progressive elements in Poland. Prince Shakhovskoi regarded the Russo-Polish Congress as part of an ongoing "search for a concrete basis for the possibility of an agreement" between Russians and Poles.[4]

The period before the April congress was a difficult one for Polish deputies, who had to agree on a common platform. They realized that a united front would strengthen their position in discussions with the Russians. Representatives of the ZPD and PPS agreed on the goal of autonomy for the Kingdom, with a separate constituent assembly in Warsaw. The National Democrats in the delegation, however, proposed a more modest plan that did not call for a separate constituent assembly. In a last-ditch effort to achieve unity before the journey to Moscow, the Polish delegation met in Warsaw and approved the following joint resolution, sponsored by the ZPD:

> Recognizing the integrity of the central state authority, and namely the form of government; commonality of foreign affairs and all international, political and trade treaties; the integrity of the army and navy; the all-state budget and debts—we demand for the Polish Kingdom an autonomous legal-political organization, based on its own constitution enacted in Warsaw by a Polish constituent assembly, chosen by a universal, secret, equal and direct vote.[5]

After their arrival in Moscow, however, the Poles decided to allow each representative to deliver his own party's resolution. Instigated by the *Endecja*, this decision broke up the unity of the delegation and allowed the National Democrats to promote their own agenda.[6]

The three-day congress, coined the "Polish Days" by one journalist,[7] opened on 7 April at Lednicki's spacious home on the Arbat. By now, Lednicki's house was so well-known as the site of important political meetings in Moscow that his street, Krywonikolski, was dubbed "Krywopolski" or "Krywolednicki" street.[8] Over 100 persons participated, including over 40 Poles from the Kingdom and the *Kresy*. D. N. Anuchin presided over the first day's discussions, while Marian Zdziechowski oversaw the next day's proceedings. The Russian delegation included leading representatives of Russian liberalism.[9] The Polish delegation was far more representative than at the November conference, with socialists, liberals and nationalists all present.[10]

The congress opened with flowery professions of affection and understanding. Rodichev gave a long talk about the mutual fate of nations and the Poles' traditional role as fighters for liberty throughout the world. Anuchin cited the friendship of Mickiewicz and Pushkin as an example of Russian and Polish cooperation in the past. Shakhovskoi greeted the Poles in their own tongue. Wacław Sieroszewski reciprocated in Russian, finishing his speech with a rousing call for "the motto of both nations...to be indentical—For your freedom and ours!"[11] After this exchange of pleasantries, the congress turned to the debate on Polish autonomy.

The Poles informed their Russian counterparts about conditions in the Kingdom, hoping to make clear the need for self-rule. Zygmunt Balicki, an ideologue for the *Endecja*, spoke first. He criticized sharply the tsarist government's policies that had destroyed public life in the Kingdom after the January Insurrection of 1863. Worse of all, he argued, these policies had led to the class warfare then raging in Poland.[12] Alojzy Wierzchleyski, a ZPD delegate and Lednicki ally, argued that the demands of Polish workers and their party, the PPS, were not necessarily at odds with those of the bourgeoisie. For example, the PPS shared the ZPD demand for a local legislature. But he warned that the Socialists were conducting "a struggle under the banner of complete political independence."[13]

The *endeks* Harusewicz and Paderewski reminded the Russians that Poles in the Kingdom were fighting for the introduction of the Polish language in local assemblies and schools, a move that they believed would restore Polish character to these institutions. Stanisław Kempner, a founding member of the ZPD and the last Pole to speak that day, emphasized the universal desire among Poles for autonomy. If Russians did not recognize this sentiment, he warned, Poles would not support any Russian government. In general, the National Democrats stressed the narrow national question, while ZPD speakers placed the national question within a broader socio-political context.[14]

Russian speakers focused on two issues: the character and extent of Polish autonomy, and the possibility of tying Polish demands for autonomy to the program of the Russian *osvobozhdentsy*. The vast majority of Russians present regarded the Polish resolution as going too far; it was too risky for Russian liberals to support full autonomy in the face of growing ultra-nationalism in Russia. They wanted well-defined limits for any autonomous Kingdom, but they also realized that merely extending the zemstvo system into Poland would not satisfy Polish demands. Many delegates also urged Poles to renounce the call for a separate sejm in Warsaw.[15]

Fedor Rodichev was one of the first Russians to speak, explaining that he and his countrymen did not represent any party, but rather constituted a group of individuals interested in the Polish question. Therefore, Polish demands could not be incorporated into any party program, especially since the Russian liberal camp was divided on this contentious issue. N. Shchepkin added that the imprecise nature of the Polish plan for autonomy made it "impossible to accept."[16] It was clear that most Russians present regarded Polish demands as excessive.

Some did accept the Polish resolutions, including the call for an independent sejm, and wanted to tie Polish demands to those of the Russian liberation movement. M. Mandelshtam, a Moscow lawyer, dismissed the concerns of Rodichev and Shchepkin. He felt Polish demands ought to be included in the liberals' own platform. Viktor Gol'tsev, Lednicki's friend and a long-time advocate of Polish rights, also supported the Polish position.[17] Still others, like Fedor Kokoshkin, accepted the notion of Polish autonomy, but expressed tactical objections to a separate sejm in Warsaw. He believed this would weaken both Russian and Polish liberation movements. Kokoshkin argued that a unified movement, with joint participation in one common empire-wide duma, was the only way to effectively pressure the tsarist government for reform.[18]

Rodichev agreed, adding that any attempt by a radical Russian party to attach Polish autonomy with a separate sejm to its program would cause moderate allies, whom he regarded as a majority in Russian society, to embrace the government. He also noted that these same Russian moderates would probably control any future Russian parliament. Poles could ill afford to alienate any elements in Russian society, especially those sympathetic to their plight but unwilling to allow the disintegration of the empire. Rodichev concluded that Poles ought to move forward "arm in arm" with the Russian opposition, and not push purely national demands.[19]

The Poles refused to buckle under the pressure, however, and doggedly pursued their goal of Russian recognition of their right to autonomy. Wacław Sieroszewski tried to allay Russian fears of Polish separatism. He maintained that if Poles and Russians struggled separately for different goals, it would not weaken the liberation movement. W. Żukowski was more belligerent, reiterating that, without an acceptance of the demand for autonomy, there could be no understanding.[20]

The Russians added another wrinkle to the debate, one that would haunt Poles throughout the rest of the tsarist period: if Poles were granted autonomy, what would be the fate of non-Russians in the Kingdom? Essentially, Russian liberals were concerned about anti-semitism, and whether Poles would persecute Jews.[21] One Pole in the delegation tried to disarm those who doubted Polish intentions regarding non-Poles, professing that he was "a Polish Jew, or more precisely...a Pole of Jewish extraction," and was not concerned about his safety.[22] The debate grew heated as Sieroszewski "protested energetically" against this charge, lamenting that Russians were treating Poles like children who needed protection and guidance. He argued that the Poles needed a constitution to protect their rights, not Russian advice.[23] Considering the maltreatment of Jews by the Russian government, the Russians' whole argument seemed to the Poles—and the modern scholar—quite specious.

Tempers were beginning to boil over, when Aleksander Lednicki stepped in to play the role of mediator. It was readily apparent that Russians were particularly sensitive to the issue of an independent sejm in Warsaw. Therefore, he refrained from commenting on this issue in his pronouncements at the congress, letting others—like Sieroszewski—push for controversial concessions. Lednicki in turn stressed the common ties and shared goals of both groups. Above all, he wanted to facilitate some sort of agreement.

Lednicki tried to persuade Poles to moderate their demands, arguing that they should be realistic. Poles had succumbed to flights of fancy before, he reminded his countrymen, producing only intensified russification and further restrictions on Polish autonomy. Lednicki urged caution; although he clearly addressed this plea for calm to his fellow Poles, Lednicki must have sensed that the struggle with the temptation to act hastily and push for independence was something of a personal battle. Lednicki's romantic spirit, impetuosity and devotion to the Polish cause had to be harnessed to gain short-term concessions from Russians who feared any plan that hinted at the disintegration of the state.

Aware of his Russian colleagues' insistence on preserving the integrity of the state, Lednicki took pains to ease their concerns about Polish aims. Later accused of being duplicitous and "selling out" to

the Russians, Lednicki was in reality practicing politics as it is done
in a pluralistic society: he realized that compromise was the corner-
stone of a democratic system. He therefore limited his demands to
autonomy, assuaging doubts among the Russians concerning Polish
separatism. In addition, he made it clear that Poles had neither pretensions to Russian territory nor secret plans to resurrect the old
Rzeczpospolita:

> Above all, I ought to state, that as unanimous is the desire
> for an autonomous government in the Polish Kingdom, so
> also is the unanimity in an awareness of the indispensabili-
> ty of the maintenance of state unity with Russia and also the
> unanimity in the definition of boundaries of the Polish
> Kingdom within the limits of the existing territory of the ten
> provinces, occupied practically everwhere by an equal mass
> of Polish people. There is not a thought, nor a word, about
> the boundaries of former Poland. There is only talk of the
> ethnographic boundaries and the expressed desire of an
> autonomous structure referring only to this territory.[24]

Lednicki also addressed Russian concerns for non-Poles living in
these Polish lands. National self-determination and the right to unfettered development of one's culture were fundamental tenets of
Lednicki's political philosophy; he had no difficulty, therefore, in
promising Russians that the rights of minorities in an autonomous
Poland would be guaranteed by a "declaration of the rights of man."
No one in Poland, he assured his Russian colleagues, would oppose
this pledge.[25]

Lednicki was not a toady for his fellow *ozvobozhdentsy*, however, and he informed the Russian delegation that the fate of Poland was
not theirs to decide. He stated that even though he was eager to work
with them in seeking a solution to the Polish problem, in reality the
"Polish question is not a question of internal politics of Russia, it is
entirely an international matter."[26] Lednicki would continually voice
this interpretation of the Polish question, one which was also part of
the ZPD party program. Basically, Lednicki and his fellow Polish
progressives argued that an autonomous Kingdom had been created

as a result of the Treaty of Vienna in 1815, and therefore was guaranteed by international agreement. All actions taken by the tsarist regime to curtail Polish rights since that settlement were therefore in violation of international law. Moreover, Polish lands were occupied by three empires, and thus Russia could not pretend to hold the key to solving such a complex international problem.[27]

Lednicki expressed great concern for the fate of Polish culture. For him, the russification of the Kingdom and the *Kresy* was a greater crime against the Polish nation than the revocation of Polish political sovereignty. He even averred that self-government was not an end unto itself, but was merely a means to ensure Poland's free cultural and national development.[28] Cultural freedom was more important to Poles than political independence, he argued, noting that

> Poles are...more individualists, than collectivists, or admirers of statism [*panstwowosc*]. In the past they did not organize a strong state and today do not desire a politically strong state, but security and the free development of their national and cultural vocation.[29]

The tsarist regime's practice of stripping conquered peoples of not only their political independence, but also their cultural heritage was particularly galling to Lednicki. He did not blame the Russian people, however, but assailed the tsarist bureaucracy:

> adopting the motto: *divide et impera*, our [Russian] bureaucracy strives for the complete disintegration of the social organism, for the pitting of one class of people against another, one nationality against another. All social institutions and organizations have been destroyed...for example, even in the field of education, private initiative has been hindered....[30]

Lednicki's outrage at the atomization of Polish society under Russian rule illustrated his ideological grounding in solidarism, which called for the preservation of a nation's organic unity. For Lednicki, the integrity of the "social organism" and the harmonious coexistence of all classes and peoples of Polish society was more important than the sanctity of the Russian state, which concerned most of his Russian colleagues, or the primacy of an ethnically pure Polish nation, which Dmowski raised to the level of a cult. Fundamental to Lednicki's politics was a belief that societal concerns, including those of all peoples and all classes, far outweighed the considerations of any government, be it Russian or Polish.

Lednicki lectured the congress about the evils of a bureaucratic state, recounting the cultural crimes committed by Russian authorities in the Kingdom. He lamented the closing of Polish-language schools and noted in disgust that even criminal cases were tried in Russian.[31] For this reason, his son recalled, Lednicki refused to take cases tried in the Kingdom, sickened by the thought of speaking Russian in a Polish court. Lednicki argued that this cultural war was entering a new phase: Orthodox churches were being built in Warsaw not for the "teaching of love and brotherhood, but with the aim of exacerbating political passions."[32] Lednicki supported religious freedom in principle but took exception to what he regarded as another step in the ongoing process of state-sponsored russification in Polish lands.

In fact, the Russian government did try to weaken the hold of Polish culture on the populace. Tsarist officials realized that Polish culture was the glue that had held the Polish nation together since the partitions. Worse still, in the eyes of Russian nationalists, Polish culture predominated among non-Poles in the *Kresy*. Although populated primarily by Belorussians, Ukrainians, Jews and Lithuanians, the *Kresy* was generally regarded as a battleground between the the two great cultures of the region: Polish and Russian. As Miliukov noted, "this was a struggle between the two centers of emulation and already in the 17th century it took very violent forms that have been retained until the present."[33]

The Russian government, and even Russian liberals, were very concerned about the perceived "Polish threat" to Russian hegemony over the so-called Western Territory. This threat had several sources, including the ties between Russian Poles and Poles in the lands incorporated by Germany and Austria-Hungary. Of greatest concern, however, was the cultural strength of the Poles, combined with their glorious past: Poland was the only "historical nation" on Russia's western border whose possible great-state pretensions the tsarist government continued to fear.[34]

Emerging Belorussian nationalism complicated the Russo-Polish dispute over the *Kresy*. In 1903 A. Burbis founded Hramada, the Belorussian socialist party. It demanded "territorial independence," which later at the party's second congress in January 1906 was reduced to "territorial autonomy." The revised program called for regional autonomy with a diet in Wilno. Both Polish and Russian participants at the April Congress were aware of the Belorussian national movement; the Hramada had taken part in the Paris Conference in November 1904.[35]

Despite these complications, Lednicki believed that Polish culture would prevail in the *Kresy*. Tsarist russification policies were doomed to failure, he maintained, because "the goal of the denationalization of a people is unrealizable, a matter contradictory to nature."[36] At the April Russo-Polish Congress he contended that the goal of the Russian bureaucracy, "russification and creation of a unified state with [one] language and belief, is unrealizable."[37] Lednicki's faith in the appeal of Polish culture explains why he did not demand autonomy for his beloved *Kresy*. He believed that if the playing field was level, Polish culture would continue to flourish in the region. As a guide to the First Duma noted, Lednicki "championed the abolition of all the restrictions and all the privileges with the exception of one privilege, that of cultural competition."[38] He hoped that a democratic Russia would guarantee this free cultural competition.

Regarding the Kingdom, however, Lednicki tied his demand for cultural rights to a call for political autonomy. He justified his request by explaining that

> the cultural creativeness of a nation manifests itself not only
> in the arrangements of local life, but also in the creation of
> legal norms...that is why...it is essential to include the right
> of legislative initiative and authority.[39]

He argued that an autonomous Polish sejm should have jurisdication over issues affecting Polish courts and administration. It had to have the right to tax and rule on local economic matters, and to determine all questions concerning the education system. Matters not strictly Polish in nature, but affecting the whole empire—declarations of war, control over the army, general finances, tariffs, trade agreements and diplomatic relations—should remain under the control of the central government.[40]

Lednicki was not surprised that many Russian liberals balked at Polish proposals for political autonomy. He was well aware of their fears that moderate constitutionalists would break away from the liberation movement if the sanctity of the state was threatened. He did not sympathize with these fears; he maintained that chauvinism and ethnic hatred were alien to the Russian soul, "a characteristic feature of...[which] was tolerance."[41] Lednicki blamed Russian society's negative attitude toward Poland on the distorted news reports fed the reading public by the conservative press. He resolved to conduct his own public relations campaign—at congresses, in private gatherings, and in the liberal press—to present a different interpretation of events in the Kingdom and make it clear that Polish demands did not include separation from Russia.[42] He hailed recent discussions at the Slavic Club in Krakow and the efforts of *Russkaia mysl'* to disseminate Polish literature in Russian society as steps in the right direction.[43]

Lednicki thus concluded his address to the Russo-Polish Congress on a positive note. Several themes in his speech would appear time and again throughout the period leading up to the elections for the First Duma: 1) Poles sought autonomy, not the destruction of the Russian state; 2) there would be no move to redraw the borders of an autonomous Poland along the boundaries of the former *Rzeczpospolita*—rather, he assured Russians that an autonomous Poland would be restricted to ethnographic boundaries; 3) the rights of national minorities living within an autonomous Poland would be guaranteed; and 4) the Russian nation was not the enemy of the Polish people. The Russian and Polish nations should work together to fight the crippling policies of the tsarist bureaucracy.[44]

But the *Endecja* had already undermined Lednicki's efforts to mediate a resolution on autonomy for the Kingdom. On their arrival in Russia, Zygmunt Balicki and other National Democrats at the congress issued a revised proposal that was less far-reaching than the common platform all delegates had agreed on before leaving Warsaw. Balicki's seven-point program called for an end to russification, restoration of language rights, autonomy of the Catholic Church, and more Polish control over local government and administration. However, the most crucial demand—political autonomy—was omitted.[45]

This rift in the Polish delegation forced the Poles to settle on a resolution that did not fully decide the issue:

> Recognizing the need of an autonomous structure of the Polish Kingdom with the preservation of state unity and representation in a Russian parliament, but with a separate sejm elected on the basis of an universal, equal, direct and secret vote without distinction of nationality and confession—the congress considers it necessary to postpone the specific definition of the boundaries and limits of the autonomy to the time of a universal elaboration of this question.[46]

The congress also addressed the fate of *Kresy* Poles, demanding that

> in provinces where Poles make up one of the nationalities living there, thus in Lithuania, Belorussia and Ukraine, they must be granted an extension of their political and national rights without any sort of legal or administrative restrictions, and with a legal-state guarantee of liberty and national-cultural development.[47]

Miliukov introduced these resolutions to the congress, which "after long and stormy debate" were accepted by the vast majority of the delegates.[48]

This tentative acceptance of the Polish demand for autonomy was difficult for those Russian participants who believed that such a move would divide the liberation movement. Their fears were realized just five months later at the September Zemstvo Congress, when a small minority refused to approve a resolution on Polish autonomy. In October, the Kadet founders were still struggling with the issue. Miliukov later noted that the position formulated at the April Russo-Polish Congress induced the Kadets to introduce Polish autonomy to their program, even though the party realized "it risked...the loss of a part of its followers in the future electoral struggle."[49]

Some published reports about the April Russo-Polish Congress criticized participants for pretending to speak for the entire Polish nation when in fact not all political parties were represented. The PPS organ *"Przedświt"* (Pre-Dawn) denounced the absence in both the Russian and Polish delegations of representatives from the working classes. Only these men, *Przedświt* argued, had the right and authority to govern their nations after the fall of the tsarist regime.[50] The paper correctly noted that while the participants at the congress did actively oppose absolutism, it "was not a meeting of revolutionists."[51] The Socialists were particularly critical of the National Democrats, who were so willing to compromise on the key issue of autonomy.[52]

Despite his failure to gain the cooperation of the National Democrats, the Russo-Polish Congress was a considerable personal success for Lednicki. Its resolutions, although not as far-reaching as hoped, did force the Russian liberals to acknowledge support for Polish autonomy as a prerequisite to forging a working relationship with their counterparts in Poland. Lednicki was not particularly disturbed by the misgivings of some *osvobozhdentsy*, for he regarded their concerns about the possible separation of Poland from Russia to be a manifestation of the "fundamental feature of Russian nature: a careful, vigilant, even in revolutionary conditions inseparable care for the integrity of the state."[53] After the Congress Lednicki launched a propaganda campaign to reorient Russian public opinion and spread the word that even full Polish autonomy would not compromise Russian national interests.

Among those assisting him in this effort was Nikolai Kareev, who published his thoughts on the Polish question in *Pravo* in April 1905. Kareev wrote that most Poles had rejected the romantic notion of regaining political independence through the use of force, embracing instead the doctrine of Warsaw Positivism. He reassured his readers that "organic work," not armed insurrection, was the rallying cry for modern Poles. Kareev maintained that

> this is the point of view not only of conservatives, but also many progressive elements of Polish society, for which... cultural development in the wide sense of the word appears more important and desirable than the possibility of having

its own diplomacy and its own army, its own flag and its own orders, its own gendarmes and own prisons.[54]

Kareev called for an understanding between the progressive forces in Russia and Poland. He argued that liberal Russians commited to maintaining the integrity of the state did not have to deal solely with the Conciliationists, who were not devoted to ridding Russia of the tsarist yoke.[55] Rather, they should come to an agreement with the ZPD. Heartened by Lednicki's statements at the Russo-Polish Congress, Kareev emphasized that Polish progressives did not call for an independent Polish state within the extended boundaries of the old Republic, but rather autonomy within ethnographic borders with a guarantee of the free development of Polish culture.[56]

Kareev professed his belief that a union of the two nations should be based on democratic principles rather than national egoism.[57] He asserted that, if only Russians would recognize the fundamental Polish need for autonomy within a Russian empire, with the right to freely develop their way of life, then the Poles would not try to rend asunder the ties between the two peoples. This relationship, Kareev argued, was vital to Polish security: "The German *Drang nach Osten* frightens Poles, and the political advantage is for them to be in a union with Russia."[58] Besides, he pointed out, a union with Russia would benefit Polish industries, since the Russian market held greater potential than the German.[59]

Kareev touched on an aspect of the Polish question that Lednicki would repeatedly address over the years: confronted with the constant threat of German aggression, the survival of the Poles required unity with their Slavic brethren to the east. Lednicki preached a doctrine of Slavic brotherhood, and with some success: the specter of encroaching German economic power and cultural influence convinced Russian liberals of the wisdom of pacifying Poland by granting it limited autonomy. Better an autonomous but happy neighbor to the west to serve as a buffer against Germany, than a disgruntled, embittered colony.

It was appropriate that the Russo-Polish Congress had been convened in the Slavophile stronghold of Moscow. Like Lednicki,

Moscow liberals drew a sharp distinction between the Russian state and the Russian nation. Therefore, they could in good conscience agree to changes that would end the tsarist drive to destroy Polish culture and atomize society. For them, Poles were Slavic brothers whose homeland shared the same fate as the Russian nation; its organic wholeness had been fractured by the arbitrary policies of Petersburg bureaucrats. They only asked that Poles in turn not work to upset a harmonious Slavic union by clamoring for separation from Russia.

Moscow was the natural focal point for resentment against the decrees from St. Petersburg. The second city in a centralized empire, it became the center for local self-government advocates. Moscow thus served as the site for the emergence of many independent societal groups promoting the development of a civil society: the zemstvo congresses, the Moscow Juridical Society, and the Moscow Circle of Public Defenders.[60] In Lednicki's political philosophy, we see a convergence of the Slavophile notions of societal independence from the state and the preservation of society's organic wholeness, with the modern liberal commitment to civil society. He made a sharp distinction between the good Russian nation versus the evil, artificial, and bureaucratic tsarist state. He deeply resented attempts to russify the Kingdom, yet he and other Poles believed that cooperation with the Russian nation in the fight against the Russian government made perfect sense. And they were in no small measure influenced by the fear that the "might of Prus" would, if given the chance, totally destroy Polish culture.

Like Lednicki, the *Endecja* leader Roman Dmowski was driven by a fear of Germany to seek Russo-Polish conciliation and eventual Polish autonomy within a Russian framework. A major distinction between the two men, however, was in their concern for the fate of the Russian nation. Dmowski wanted freedom for Poles, but this was not linked to "any feelings of solidarity—or indeed, of concern—with the Russian nation."[61] He sought Russian help solely because he feared German aggression and the annihilation of Polish culture. Dmowski felt no compunction to fight for Russian freedom. But for Lednicki, whose motto was "For your freedom and ours," a primary goal of the revolution was the liberation of all peoples, including the Russian nation, from the tsarist yoke. Fully engrossed in Russian political and cultural developments, Lednicki was not only a fighter for Polish freedom but also a leader in the Russian liberation movement. In reconciling these two aspects of his political life, he sought an underlying ideological basis. This he found in the Panslavist notion of the spiritual and cultural kinship of the two peoples, Poles and Russians, who together faced the incessant threats of German aggression and western duplicity. For Lednicki and many other progressive Poles and Russians, liberalism and Panslavism dovetailed nicely in the matter of Polish autonomy.

Indeed, a brand of liberal Panslavism known as "neoslavism" was promoted by Russian *osvobozhdentsy* as a new movement for Slavic unity. Russians stressed that their belief was different from nineteenth century Panslavism because it was not political in nature and did not call for Russian domination of fellow Slavs. Rather, they claimed, it was based on cultural equality and mutual economic solidarity.[62] Essentially, it was the Russian liberals' answer to government-sponsored Slavophilism. In Moscow, this movement became embodied in the Society of Slavic Culture, which was established on 29 March 1908. Lednicki played a major role in the society, which closely followed his line of thinking.[63]

A sister organization, the *Klub Słowianski* (Slavic Club), had already come into existence in Kraków in December 1901 and represented the same line of thinking. The *Klub Słowianski* never had a large membership. It reached its peak in 1902 with forty-five members, but many leading Poles took part in its proceedings; in 1905–6, Lednicki twice spoke on political developments in Russia.[64] The club published the monthly, *Świat Słowianski*, which became the main Polish organ of Neoslavist orientation, constantly emphasizing the historic role of Poland for Slavdom. From its first issue *Świat Słowianski* advocated a Polish-Russian agreement on the basis of Polish autonomy.[65] The journal's most important contributor was Marian Zdziechowski, who was close to Lednicki.[66]

Neoslavism certainly contained an element of anti-Germanism. Many critics of Germany denounced the negative influence of its culture among Slavic peoples. Rodichev, for example, denounced Austria for introducing the idea of a police state into Slavdom.[67] Evgenii Trubeckii was more explicit, calling for the "solidarity of

Slavic culture and mutual support of Slavic nations against the rising wave of Germanism."[68] Rodichev and Trubeckii were but two voices in a growing chorus of Russian liberals who insisted that Slavic unity necessitated a resolution of the Polish problem.

Aleksander Lednicki subscribed to the neoslavist school of thought, at least until mid–1916, when the Central Powers began to seriously consider establishing a Polish state. While Lednicki's son, Wacław, adamantly maintained that his father "never had any tendencies toward the Slavophile fancies but from the beginning to the end of his life remained faithful to his European orientation,"[69] his statements reveal a belief in a lasting Slavic kinship. In a speech to the Moscow Slavic Club in 1911 in honor of the historian V. O. Kliuchevskii, Lednicki noted that the society was "not making an idol out of this or that nation" but rather aimed at the "familiarization of Russian society with the national creations of Slavic peoples."[70] The society's main function, Lednicki added, was the propagation of the Neoslavist doctrine of "one general Slavic root of kindred origin" and the "many mutual interests and tasks" of Slavic peoples.[71]

The events of World War I naturally inflamed Lednicki's anti-Germanism, eliciting further calls for Slavic unity. He wrote in 1915:

> Today it is a clear thing, that Russia has two paths: either with the Germans against Poland, or with Poland against the Germans. *Tertium non datur.* And for Poland from the start of the war it was clear, that only on a three-sided agreement, only on the victory of Russia and its allies, only on the defeat of German might is it possible to base the hope of a free tomorrow.[72]

Lednicki once again voiced concerns about the German threat in an article written in January 1916. He mourned the fate of Serbia, whose occupation by Austrian forces he regarded as "a tragedy for the entire Slavic world."[73] He maintained that "the divergence of Slavic peoples has brought about the present state of affairs in the Balkans," singling out Russian-Polish discord for allowing the emergence of "the might of Prus."[74]

ENDNOTES

1. See L. Panteleev, "Vremiia prishlo: K voprosu ob avtonomiia Tsarstva Pol'skago," *Nasha zhizn'*, 18 April/1 May 1906.

2. Lednicki, *Pamiętniki*, 2: 515. Fedor Kokoshkin was also a member of the delegation but was unable to participate because of illness.

3. Ibid., 517–18.

4. Shakhovskoi, "Soiuz ozvobozhdeniia," 158.

5. Wojciech Bułat, "Zjazd polsko-rosyjski w Moskwie 21–22 kwietnia 1905 r.," *Studia z najnowszych dziejów powszechnych* 2 (1962): 195–96.

6. Ibid., 196; Stegner, *Liberałowie Królestwa Polskiego*, 136–37.

7. *Rus'*, 12/26 April 1905.

8. A. Lednicki, *Pamiętniki*, 183.

9. W. Lednicki, *'Entente cordiale'*, 79; also see Bułat, "Zjazd polsko rosyjski," 196. The Russian delegation included Prince Dmitrii Shakhovskoi, Sergei Muromtsev, N. Shchepkin, Princes E. N. and S. Trubecki, Fedor Kokoshkin, the Dolgorukov twins, Vladimir Nabokov, Pavel Miliukov, Fedor Rodichev and Viktor Gol'tsev.

10. Ibid. Most notable among those members of the *Endecja* present were Zygmunt Balicki, J. Harusewicz, Paderewski, Radziszewski and Zygmunt Makowiecki. ZPD delegates included Lednicki, Alojzy Wierzchleyski, Stanisław Kempner, Wacław Sieroszewski and Zygmunt Heryng. Also present were P. Podhorski, Count W. Grocholski, F. Nowodworski, R. Radziwillowicz and W. Zukowski.

11. W. Lednicki, *'Entente cordiale'*, 79.

12. Bułat, "Zjazd polsko-rosyjski," 196.

13. Ibid.

14. Ibid., 197.

15. Ibid., 199.

16. Ibid.

17. Ibid., 201–02.

18. *Polski-rosyjski zjazd w Moskowie* (Kraków: Wydawnictwo Redakcyi "Przedświtu," 1905), 10.

19. Ibid., 11.

20. Ibid.; Bułat, "Zjazd polsko-rosyjski," 202.

21. *Polski-rosyjski zjazd,"* 11–12.

22. Ibid., 13.

23. Ibid., 12.

24. A. Lednicki, *Mowy polityczne*, 20. Lednicki's speech also appeared in the Russian press. See Aleksandr Lednitskii, "Pol'skii vopros," *Russkaia mysl'* 26 (July 1905): 128–36.

25. A. Lednicki, *Mowy polityczne*, 20.

26. Ibid.

27. Ibid.

28. Ibid., 24.

29. Ibid., 20–21.

30. Ibid., 21–22.

31. Ibid., 22.

32. Ibid.

33. Zaprudnik, "Political Struggle for Byelorussia," 34; citing P. N. Miliukov, *Natsional'nyi vopros: Proiskhozhdenie natsional'nosti i natsional'nyie voprosy v Rossii* (Prague: "Svobodnaia Rossiia," 1925), 154.

34. Theodore R. Weeks, "Defining Us and Them: Poles and Russians in the 'Western Provinces,' 1863–1914," *Slavic Review* 53 (1994): 29. Also see Weeks' "The National World of Imperial Rusia: Policy in the Kingdom of Poland and Western Provinces, 1894–1914" (Ph.D. diss., University of California, Berkeley, 1992).

35. Zaprudnik, "Political Struggle for Byelorussia," 65–66. Hramada delegates also took part in the founding Congress of the Union of Federalist Autonomists, held in St. Petersburg from 19–21 November 1905 under the leadership of Jan Baudouin de Courtenay.

36. A. Lednicki, *Mowy polityczne*, 23.

37. Ibid., 24.

38. Zaprudnik, "Political Struggle for Byelorussia," 98; citing *Pervaia Gosudarstvennaia Duma. Alfavitnyi spisok podrobniia biografii i kharakteristiki chlenov Gosudarstvennoi Dumy* (Moscow: I. D. Sytin, 1906), 107.

39. A. Lednicki, *Mowy polityczne*, 25.

40. Ibid.

41. Ibid.

42. Ibid., 26.

43. Ibid., 28.

44. W. Lednicki, *'Entente cordiale'*, 80–81.

45. Bułat, "Zjazd polsko-rosyjski," 204.

46. Ibid., 205.

47. Ibid.

48. A. Lednitskii, "P. N. Miliukov i pol'skii vopros," 213.

49. Pawel Milukow, "Aleksander Lednicki jako rzecznik," 32.

50. *Polski-Rosyjski Zjazd*, 3.

51. Ibid., 6.

52. Ibid., 4.

53. Smolen, "Działalność polityczna," 92.

54. Nikolai Kareev, "Pol'skaia natsional'nost' v russkoi gosudarstvennosti," *Pravo* 14 (10 April 1905): 1071.

55. Ibid., 1072.

56. Nikolai Kareev, "Novaia pol'skaia partiia," *Pravo* 15 (15 April 1905): 1175–81.

57. Kareev, "Pol'skaia natsional'nost'," 1074.

58. Ibid.

59. Ibid.

60. David A. Davies, "V. A. Maklakov and the Westernizer Tradition in Russia," in Charles E. Timberlake, ed., *Essays on Russian Liberalism* (Columbia: University of Missouri Press, 1972), 85–86.

61. Fountain, *Roman Dmowski: Party, Tactics, Ideology*, 83.

62. Miroslaw Wierzchowski, "Problematyka polska w rosyjskiej prasie liberalnej w latach 1907–1912," *Studia z dziejów ZSRR i Europy Środkowej* 1 (1965): 167–68.

63. Pawel Piotr Wieczorkiewicz, "Udział Polaków w ruchu neosławianskim a stosunki polityczne polsko-rosyjskie (1908–1910)," *Pamiętnik słowiański* 28 (1978): 133–38.

64. Zbigniew Solak, "Marian Zdziechowski i Klub Słowianski," *Studia historyczne* 30 (1987), no. 2: 220–25.

65. Giza, *Neoslawizm i Polacy*, 32–33; and Wieczorkiewicz, "Udzia_ Polakow," 140. The society published Lednicki's first two books.

66. Marian Zdziechowski (1861–1938) was present at the April Russo-Polish Congress. A *Kresy* Pole born in Minsk, he was devoted to the ideals and traditions of the *Rzeczpospolita*. Like Lednicki, he defended the rights of Lithuanians, Belorussians and other nationalities living in the Kresy. He regarded nationalism as "the same sort of plague that in the 16th and 17th centuries was religious fanaticism...leading to mass insanity and the spread of savagery." See Juliusz Bardach, "O świadomości narodowej Polakow na Litwie i Białorusi w XIX–XX w." In *Polska myśl polityczna XIX i XX wieku*, ed. Wojciech Wrzesinski, vol. 6, *Miedzy Polska etniczna a historyczna* (Wrocław: Zakład Narodowy imienia Ossolińskich Wydawnictwo Polskiej Akademii Nauk, 1988): 245. For more on Zdziechowski's relationship with Lednicki, see Zbigniew Opacki, *W kregu Polski, Rosji i slowianszczyzny. Myśl i Działalnośćspoleczno-polityczna Mariana Zdziechowskiego do 1914 roku* (Gdańsk: Wydawnictwo Uniwersytetu Gdańskego, 1996), 145–70.

67. *Riech'*, 30 November 1908; cited in Wierzchowski, "Problematyka polska," 169–70.

68. *Moskovskii ezhenedelnik*, 3 February 1908; also cited in Wierzchowski, "Problematyka polska," 169–70.

69. W. Lednicki, "Panslavism," in *European Ideologies: A Survey of 20th Century Political Ideas*, ed. Feliks Gross, with an Introduction by Robert M. MacIver (New York: Philosophical Library, 1948), 902.

70. A. R. Lednitskii, "V. O. Kliuchevskii kak istorik slavianin," *Izvestiia slavianskoi kultury* (1911): 3.

71. Ibid.

72. A. Lednicki, *Z lat wojny*, 11.

73. Ibid., 35.

74. Ibid.

Chapter Seven

THE POLISH QUESTION AND THE FORMATION OF THE CONSTITUTIONAL-DEMOCRATIC PARTY, MAY–OCTOBER 1905

In spring and summer 1905, the situation in the Polish Kingdom grew increasingly unstable. Opposition to tsarist rule soared, sparked by Russian defeats in the Far East and the attempt to mobilize Polish reserves. Reliable Russian troops were often needed to suppress rioters and striking workers; the bloodiest fighting took place in Łódź from 9–11 June. Center of light industry in Russian Poland, the "Polish Manchester's" textile mills produced mainly for the Russian market. Government forces suppressed the "Łódź Uprising" with hundreds of casualties.[1]

In response to the disturbances, St. Petersburg vacillated between the policies of suppression and concession. On 17 April, the government issued the Edict of Toleration, which promised that persecution of non-Orthodox Christians would cease. The edict allowed Catholic priests to oversee the religious education of youths in the Kingdom, using Polish as the language of instruction. New regulations also allowed for the construction, renewal or repair of non-Orthodox churches.[2] An *ukaz* of 1 May allowed Poles in the nine western provinces to rent, lease, and buy landed estates without specific restrictions. At the same time, however, the regime reiterated its belief that the *Kresy* had been "Russian from time immemorial," the native population "Russian in origin."[3] A decree of 6 June granted further cultural rights to Poles, permitting instruction in Polish grammar to be conducted in that language.[4] In the end, however, the tsarist regime resorted to brute force, enacting martial law in Poland's largest cities in mid-June. In November, all of the Kingdom came under military rule. The initiation of martial law served to heighten Polish anger and induce greater sympathy for the Polish cause among liberals in Moscow and St. Petersburg.

The widespread disturbances, and the subsequent use of force by the government to keep order, made Polish autonomy an urgent issue for Russian *osvobozhdentsy*. Throughout 1905 oppositionists routinely addressed the nationalities question; by the end of April, the Polish matter held center stage in these debates. At the first meeting of the Union for Women's Equality, held in Moscow from 7–10 May, a resolution "recognizing the rights of the nationalities...to political autonomy and national-cultural self-determination" was approved at the urging of Polish, Belorussian and Jewish delegates.[5] Members of the Union of Unions began deliberations at their first gathering on 8 May with a statement condemning the government's bloody suppression of a May Day demonstration in Warsaw that left 150 workers dead.[6]

Buoyed by the outcome of the Russo-Polish Congress in April, Lednicki launched an intensive propaganda campaign for Polish-Russian rapprochement in Moscow, St. Petersburg, the Kingdom and the *Kresy*. His main theme was the need for—and possibility of—a joint Polish-Russian understanding. Also central to his vision was the notion of a united front of all nationalities waging war against the tsarist regime. As the revolutionary mood intensified in Poland and Russia during the summer, Lednicki became bolder in his actions and more explicit in his political pronouncements. In this manner, he laid the groundwork for debates on Polish autonomy at zemstvo meetings in September and November, and at the Kadet founding congress in October.[7]

On 13 June, Poles from the Kingdom, the *Kresy* and Russia took part in a gathering of the Polish Lawyers' Union in Warsaw. Lednicki had played an integral role in organizing the March All-Russian Congress of Lawyers, and he also helped bring about this meeting, at which he and his fellow ZPD activists—along with a socialist contingent—made up the progressive wing.[8] At the conclusion of the proceedings, a banquet was held at Konstantin, near Warsaw. It was here that Lednicki gave his first political speech on Polish soil.

In an address full of poetic imagery, Lednicki outlined the history of Poland's many struggles for freedom. He compared Poland to a white acacia bush, with Warsaw at its head. Just as the gardener prunes the acacia every fall, so had Poland's rebellions ended in defeat; but like the acacia bush, which erupts with a brilliant display of flowers each spring, "again widely and radiantly spreading its branches," so does Poland repeatedly rise from defeat.[9] Lednicki promised that despite tsarist repression, Poland would continue the fight for freedom: "With steadfast strength, with redoubled energy we stand for the struggle...for the freedom of the nation."[10]

Lednicki asserted that although Poles had lost much in previous attempts to gain freedom, this time they would be successful. In 1905, he argued, the Poles would not be fighting alone. Rather, they would be joined by their Russian friends, "because today this nation, like our own, desires to shake off the fetters of an age-old bondage and to strive for the long-desired liberty with quick, conscious, sure steps."[11] He reminded his audience that the Russian people had also suffered for centuries under tsarist oppression and were willing to fight for their freedom. He argued that he and his fellow Poles living in Russia must lead the way in bringing the two peoples together in a joint struggle, by convincing Russians of the justness of the Polish liberation movement. Poles in Russia, he proclaimed, were "*ipso facto* representatives of the Fatherland...in effect consuls for the Polish cause."[12]

Lednicki called for an alliance between progressive forces in the two nations based on their common desire to overthrow the autocracy. He painted a vivid picture of the state of affairs in Russia at that time, noting that the nation was now divided into two great opposing camps:

In one—the final efforts of despotism, in the other—a struggle, perhaps excessively, a desire for the hitherto untasted freedom...In one—the lust for authority, egoism and exploitation, in the other—a belief in the great ideal of humanity...In one prevails a hatred for the struggling slaves, in the other—a mutual love and sincere sympathy for comrades of adversity, regardless of racial differences. And we Poles ought to take advantage of this great historical moment.[13]

This call for a united front was not merely tactical. Despite his protestations at the April congress that politicans should always base their actions on sober decisions arrived at through reason, his politics invariably was imbued with the spirit of his own peculiar ideology. Evident in this call for Russo-Polish cooperation was a strong element of Slavophilism, colored by a fear of German imperialism. Lednicki called on the two great Slavic nations to oppose this threat by forming "a bulwark between the German onslaught and the East....And if a friendly Slavic hand is stretched out to us, honestly and sincerely, then we ought to also accept it in a friendly manner."[14]

Following the lawyers' meeting, Lednicki travelled to the *Kresy*, where he delivered a speech at a reception in Wilno hosted by Count Władysław Tyszkiewicz. The occasion was the first performance of the Warsaw Variety Theater in Wilno since the 1863 January Insurrection, after which tsarist authorities suppressed Polish cultural activities throughout the *Kresy*. Lednicki viewed the event as an important step in the reemergence of Polish culture in the borderlands. In a vivid demonstration of his cultural nationalism, he argued that *Kresy* Poles must bear "a torch of culture, an emblem of justice and mutual understanding—never hostile or imposed, but always kind and friendly."[15]

Lednicki called on Poles to carry out their historic mission among the various peoples of the *Kresy*, by spreading education and "culture"—that is, by polonizing the region. He consistently argued for unfettered cultural competition, believing firmly in the vitality of Polish socio-cultural influence in the *Kresy*. He also believed that Poles had a special responsibility:

Thus, do not expect so much national activities for us, but social-cultural...here we [Poles] have no privileges—but only unfulfilled duties...we are only able to strengthen ourselves jointly, through our historic union with Lithuania based on free will...only at that time will we be able to think and speak about the permanence of political significance for us—Poles in this country. Liberty and equality ought to be the motto for all those who want to act politically here....[16]

While Lednicki was stirring up trouble in Poland, other national minorities in the empire also began to call for reform. On 15 June, for example, the Kutaisi city duma submitted a plan for Georgian autonomy to the Council of Ministers.[17] But it was not just the non-Russian borderlands that clamored for self-determination in 1905. Indeed, Siberian demands for wide self-rule were probably most disturbing to Russian nationalists. Siberian separatism was in part responsible for the vehement opposition of some liberals to any resolutions on the delicate matter of decentralization. It was one thing to consider limited autonomy for historical nations that had been absorbed by the Empire, but no *osvobozhdenets* was willing to sanction the loss of "Russian" lands.[18] In the long run, the plethora of demands for territorial autonomy hurt the Polish cause: if Poland received self-determination, opponents argued, then every *oblast'* in the empire would seek the same right.

While Lednicki was abroad preaching the gospel of cooperation with the Russian liberation movement, his fellow *osvobozhdentsy* and zemstvo activists were stepping up their organizational campaigns. In June, an assembly of municipal representatives resolved to merge with the zemstvo movement, with a joint gathering planned for July. The two groups established an organizational bureau of 35 men from both camps. The organizational bureau presented the July congress with a draft constitution, prepared under the direction of Sergei Muromtsev. Known as the "Muromtsev constitution," the document was read to the assembly on 7 July by Fedor Kokoshkin. Although it did not specifically support autonomy for the Kingdom, it contained several provisions pertinent to the Polish question: more local self-government; the equality of citizens, regardless of ethnic origin, religion or estate; and the guarantee of freedom of religion.[19]

Debate concerning the constitution focused on the issue of minority rights. An ultra-rightist from Kursk, Prince N. F. Kasatkin-Rostovskii, argued that although the "alien races (*inorodtsy*) have equal rights here with the Russians...we know that they aspire to separate themselves from the Empire. We will be beaten by the alien races we have conquered."[20] I. L. Shrag, a Ukrainian activist from Chernigov, undoubtedly was referring to his native land when he countered that whole regions had joined the Russian state voluntarily.

He called on the assembly to support the principles of autonomy and federalism. Pavel Dolgorukov also supported the national minorities' cause, adding that all members of the organizational bureau knew that Russia could not progress without the proper development of the borderlands.[21]

Immediately after the conclusion of this first joint assembly of zemstvoists and municipal activists, the Zemstvo-Constitutionalists met for the fifth time on 9–10 July. Galvanized by the government's announcement of the Bulygin reforms, which included plans for a national duma, this group made the first move to establish a constitutionalist party by apppointing an organizational bureau to begin laying the foundations.[22]

The zemstvoists' decision to create a constitutionalist party prodded the *osvobozhdentsy*, who followed suit at the fourth and final gathering of the Union of Liberation. Held from 23–24 August, this "conspiratorial congress of a secret society"[23] was hosted by Lednicki at his home in Moscow. Fifty people attended the gathering; one-third were zemstvoists or municipal duma deputies, while the rest were members of the professional intelligentsia that now dominated the Union.[24]

Debate at the congress centered on whether the Union should join the zemstvoists in the drive to form a political party. After long discussion, those gathered decided to sanction the creation of the Constitutional-Democratic Party.[25] A vast majority of delegates voted in favor of participating in upcoming Duma elections, with the hope of converting that body into a genuine parliament chosen on the basis of the four-tail vote.[26] The assembly concluded its deliberations by choosing forty men to serve as an organizational bureau, which was instructed to negotiate with other political groups—in particular the zemstvoists—to gain support for the nascent Constitutional-Democratic Party.[27]

These two groups melded together well; more than a dozen representatives of the Union of Liberation were also Zemstvo-Constitutionalists.[28] Lednicki was a member of this enlarged organizational bureau, which also included many of his friends who were the "flower of zemstvo liberalism:" Prince Dimitrii Shakhovskoi, Princes Pavel and Petr Dolgorukov, Pavel Miliukov, Fedor Kokoshkin,

Sergei Muromtsev, and Vasilii Maklakov.[29] These liberal activists were entrusted with the task of completing preparations for the founding congress of the Constitutional-Democratic Party, which was scheduled to be held in October.

Moderates within the organizational bureau like Maklakov and Muromtsev opposed the creation of a party with a well-defined program. They believed that a central electoral bureau could nominate candidates for the upcoming elections. This group wanted to consolidate its popularity with the liberal-conservative wing of the liberation movement, and did not seek any expansion of the limited electorate enfranchised by the decree of 6 August, which had provided for the so-called Bulygin Duma.[30]

Opposing this policy, the radical democrats in the organizational bureau advocated creation of a permanent political party with a detailed program including socioeconomic reforms. In this manner, they hoped to appeal to a broader audience, addressing not only the demands of the intelligentsia but also those of workers, peasants and embittered non-Russians. Essentially, the radical wing wanted the new party to model its platform after the program of the Union of Liberation.[31] Lednicki allied himself with Miliukov and the left in the struggle to create a party ideologically akin to the Polish ZPD. Miliukov recalled in his memoirs that a compromise was hammered out between the zemstvoists and *osvobozhdentsy*: the former accepted the Union's March program, while the latter agreed to cease their underground activities and adopt "the tactics of an open political party in the European sense of the word."[32]

Before the new party convened for the first time, the zemstvoists met once again at the Second Congress of Zemstvo and Municipal Activists, held in Moscow from 12–15 September 1905. While this assembly accepted the Bulygin Duma, deputies still regarded a true, democratically-elected parliament as the ultimate goal of the liberation movement. In general, the assembly moved to the left.[33]   The gathering had been eagerly anticipated in Russia and abroad, and correspondents from major newspapers in Moscow and St. Petersburg attended, as well as reporters from France and Britain. Nearly 200 delegates, representing not only zemstvo assemblies and municipal dumas but also non-zemstvo provinces, took part in the proceedings.

The *Kresy* was especially well-represented.[34] Miliukov was released from jail in time to take part; he and the academician Maksim Kovalevskii were coopted into the organizational bureau, contributing to its leftward shift.[35]

But moderates launched a frontal assault to counter the radicalization of the liberation movement. It was at this congress that the future Octobrist leader, Aleksander Guchkov, achieved national prominence. He led a conservative clique of about thirty delegates, mainly municipal duma deputies, in a drive to put a brake on what he later termed a "growing revolutionary mood in the zemstvo milieu."[36] The most heated debates focused on proposals of the organizational bureau concerning the nationalities matter and decentralization. Disagreement on these issues—which had proven contentious throughout the year—would drive a wedge between the future Octobrists and Kadets. The organizational bureau had been authorized by the July zemstvo-municipal meeting to draft a report on these matters. In addition, it arranged for the participation of delegates from the borderlands at the September gathering.[37]

Once again, Lednicki played a crucial role in coordinating contact between Poles and Russians. He convinced several members of the organizational bureau to travel to Warsaw, and in July the *osvobozhdentsy* Fedor Rodichev, Prince Dmitrii Shakhovskoi and Prince Dolgorukov went there and held talks with ZPD and ND representatives.[38] The Russians assured the Poles that at the upcoming gathering zemstvo activists would discuss the Polish matter, and pledged to promote Polish autonomy. Their promises that a democratic Russia would grant autonomy to the Kingdom, with the caveat that the integrity of the Russian state must remain intact, evidently induced some Poles to establish in Warsaw a branch of the emerging Constitutional-Democratic Party.[39]

Soon after these talks, *Pedecja*[40] and *Endecja* representatives travelled to Russia to discuss in detail Polish participation at the September meeting of zemstvoists and municipal representatives. Fifteen Polish leaders met for two days with members of the organizational bureau. They attempted to elicit the Russian attitude toward Polish demands and to learn whether the September congress would promulgate a program with provisions for Polish autonomy. But the zemstvoists could only promise that their colleagues would probably accept the general outlines of Polish autonomy—autonomy with an independent sejm, on the condition that state unity not be jeopardized—which had been discussed widely since Lednicki's first Russo-Polish conference in November 1904.[41] The Poles also voiced concern that the *Kresy* be represented by some of the twenty-six Polish delegates allowed to attend the upcoming congress. Anyway, they noted, no Pole was eager to be part of a "Russian" conference that would not issue a pro-Polish pronouncement—it would be bad politics.[42]

The Poles refused to sanction any sort of bilateral agreement with the Russians, lest the assembly of zemstvoists and municipal representatives fail to produce any tangible results. They did not want to be regarded as representatives of any Polish party in the discussions, but as private citizens they were willing to express their personal opinions on the question of autonomy. In their opinion, a statement on Polish autonomy should have read:

Upon the condition of the preservation of state unity with the other parts of the Empire, the Kingdom of Poland must have an autonomous structure with an independent sejm which has jursdiction over the legislation of the country, and with its own autonomous administration.[43]

Both the Progressive Democrats and National Democrats agreed on this resolution. In addition, each party added their own, differently worded, endorsements of the four-tail vote.[44]

The Poles also offered several suggestions for improvement of the Muromtsev constitution. They called for greater local control over education by each nationality, and also for the right to use their native languages in local courts, schools and administration.[45] Most importantly, the Polish delegation demanded the introduction of a special section on the autonomy of the Kingdom of Poland:

Article I. The Kingdom of Poland is united with the Empire through the monarch as Emperor and King, through an autonomous constitution with a separate sejm, and

through the participation of deputies of the Kingdom of
Poland in an all-state representative body.

Article II.   Excluded from the competence of the
autonomous institutions of the Kingdom of Poland and sub-
ordinated to the all-state institutions are:

1) the civil list;

2) foreign affairs, political and commercial treaties;

3) monetary policy;

4) the army, strategic communications and installa-
tions;

5) legislation concerning customs and excise taxes, the
railway, postal, telegraph, and telephone systems. Note: The
administration of the aforesaid subjects within the borders of
the Kingdom of Poland belongs to its government.[46]

All other matters not mentioned in Article II were to be under the
jurisdiction of the Polish sejm. The proposal also called for the extension of civil rights to the Kingdom, with the possibility of the sejm
expanding these liberties.[47]

The Russians reiterated the old concerns for the fate of minorities
living in the Kingdom. They warned that the boundaries of the
Kingdom might have to be altered to reduce the number of Lithuanians
and Ukrainians living there. The Poles countered that their suggested
additions to the Muromtsev constitution would protect minority
rights. They added, however, that in order to put the Russians' minds
at ease they would consider border changes that would give the
Kingdom a more homogenous population.[48]

Despite the latent hostility that surfaced at this conference, Poles
were invited to send delegates to the next zemstvoist gathering. The
September congress was the first to welcome representatives from
non-zemstvo provinces.[49] Lednicki attended the congress as a representative of the "party of Warsaw progressives,"[50] and the delegation
also included two other leading Polish activists from the *Kresy*:
Lednicki's close political ally Hieronim Drucki-Lubecki, who represented the Minsk Agricultural Society; and Tadeusz Wróblewski from
Kowno.[51] Hoping to ensure a smooth debate on the issue of Polish
autonomy, on the eve of the congress Lednicki hosted a final meeting

of Poles from the Kingdom and the *Kresy* with members of the congress' organizational bureau.[52]

The Second Congress of Zemstvo and Municipal Activists convened on 12 September at the home of Prince Shcherbatov, and was presided over by Iu. A. Novosil'tsev. About two hundred representatives attended, including delegates from non-zemstvo regions: the *Kresy*, the Baltic territories, the Polish Kingdom, the Don *oblast'* and Siberia.[53] Debates went on for four days; a great deal of time on three of those days was spent on the nationalities question in general, with special emphasis on the Polish matter. Lednicki later recalled that as a result of debates at the September and November zemstvo assemblies, as well as the inclusion of a demand for autonomy in the Kadet party platform, the fate of Poland became a major political issue in the latter half of 1905. Indeed, the September congress was the first all-Russian gathering at which "the equality of rights for nationalities appeared as one of the urgent slogans of the liberation struggle."[54]

Debate centered on the presentation of the organizational bureau's report, which had several sections. The section entitled "On the Participation of Social Activists in the Upcoming Elections to the State Duma" was read by P. S. Iakushkin. He paved the way for discussion of the nationalities question, informing the congress that the bureau regarded local autonomy and equal rights for all nationalities to be an important aspect of the legislative program for the future Duma.[55]

Deliberations began on the most volatile issues—the rights of nationalities and decentralization—on the evening of 13 September. Fedor Kokoshkin, who had "so carefully and painstakingly worked out"[56] these sections of the organizational bureau's report, delivered his findings in a lengthy presentation entitled "On the Rights of Nationalities and the Decentralization of the Administration and Legislature."[57] This document took into account concerns voiced by Poles in their recent discussions with members of the organizational bureau. Kokoshkin noted that the groundwork for a Polish-Russian understanding had been laid at the November 1904 Polish-Russian conference, and continued at the April Russo-Polish Congress.[58] Essentially, the report reflected an extension of the basic zemstvo tenet of decentralization, applying it to the nationalities problem.[59]

Judging by its far-reaching recommendations, the organizational bureau undoubtedly aimed at gaining the support of the national minorities who were present at a zemstvoist gathering in large numbers for the first time.

Kokoshkin was a natural choice to present the bureau's findings. From the first years of the century until the proclamation of Polish independence by the Provisional Government in March 1917, he and Lednicki worked closely together on formulating a solution to the Polish problem.[60] Already, at the first gathering of the Union of Liberation in January 1904, Kokoshkin had advocated Polish autonomy and an independent sejm.[61] His fellow liberals regarded him as a specialist on the nationalities question; the widow of Kadet leader Maksim Vinaver recalled that "[i]n the opinion of my husband, Kokoshkin was the only man in a position to cope with this problem. The question of nationality rights, and the question of autonomy were worked out by Kokoshkin with unusual talent."[62] In addition, Kokoshkin was a gifted orator, despite his peculiar lisp,[63] and was "able to mesmorize an auditorium...through his complete understanding of a given topic, his clarity of thought and forceful argumentation."[64]

Kokoshkin defined the nature of the problem and the difficulties it posed for any constitutional regime that might emerge in Russia. He noted, that

> [t]he centralizing and Russianizing policy of the bureaucratic government, setting itself the task of fusing this diversity [of the empire] into one whole with the aid of compulsory measures, not only has not achieved its goal but, on the contrary, has aggravated national discord and intensified centrifugal aspirations. Therefore, along with a general political movement encompassing the population of the empire, there has manifested itself in the borderlands a clearly defined tendency, which, while sharing the aspiration for civil and political freedom, is not satisfied, however, by a liberal-democratic program and demands that the future constitutional system safeguard both national and local independence through the establishment of regional autono-

my. It is necessary to consider seriously these demands in all proposals concerning the future political structure of Russia. The enforced subordination of any part of the population of the state to a political order, not conforming to its needs and aspirations, is not only unjust but almost always disadvantageous. And a policy of such a nature is especially dangerous for a constitutional state, since it undermines the very foundations of political freedom. Thus, in Russia the question about a radical reform of the entire state system is inevitably complicated by the regional and national questions.[65]

Kokoshkin pointed out that the organizational bureau had received several proposals regarding the nationalities problem. In addition to the Polish demands for amendments to the Muromtsev Constitution discussed in late July at the Polish-Russian conference, Georgian and Ukrainian national groups had bombarded the bureau with similar requests. Kokoshkin stressed that these petitions could not yet be fully analyzed or debated. Besides, he added, national minorities were still under-represented at the zemstvo assembly, making any debate on the matter strictly one-sided. This is why, he continued, the organizational bureau had couched its report in general terms.[66]

The organizational bureau made an important distinction, however, between the national and regional matters. It maintained that while both issues were tied to the problem of decentralization, they were not identical. Only in the Polish Kingdom were the issues closely entwined, for it was a well-defined geographical area with a generally homogenous population. The organizational bureau believed regional autonomy much more problematic in other areas, where the ethnic mix was more jumbled and the potential for ethnic strife far greater.[67]

In his report to the congress, Kokoshkin therefore discussed the matter of national minorities separately from the debate on the decentralization of state authority. He pointed out that every petition presented to the organizational bureau contained the three main demands made by all national minorities:

1) the equality of all citizens regardless of nationality;
2) the elimination of all obstacles to the preservation and free development of the language, literature, and culture of each nationality; and
3) the equality of the languages of the various nationalities in local state and social institutions and in schools.[68]

Kokoshkin explained that the first point had been addressed by the zemstvo congress of November 1904, and subsequently the second demand had received widespread acceptance within the liberation movement. Regarding the third point, he maintained that Russian should remain the language of the central government and the military, while local courts and administration should use local languages to ensure justice. Local officials should be appointed from among the local population to facilitate this reform.[69]

The report next addressed the issue of decentralization. Reform in this area was needed not only because of ethnic diversity but also because the geographic, economic and social peculiarities of the empire's many regions made it desirable. The organizational bureau cited three different ways to reconcile local autonomy with state unity: administrative decentralization, political decentralization, or a combination of the two. It added that in the borderlands the aspirations of the various ethnic groups within one region, and in many cases their recollections of former political independence, complicated the matter enormously. Simply granting autonomy on a geographic basis was not feasible in most areas.[70]

Despite these reservations, the organizational bureau rebuked those who argued against autonomy:

Objections against the idea of autonomy, deriving from misgivings about state unity, are refuted by the political experience of the West, by the example of such federative states as Switzerland, Germany, and the United States, or of such states as the British Empire, which, although not federative, broadly decentralizes legislation. These examples show that even a federative structure, which involves in the individual parts of the state the existence of not only local legislative assemblies but also governments that are independent from the central authority, does not at all undermine the unity of the state and does not hinder the dev:lopment of its power.[71]

It was the organizational bureau's belief that in such a large, multinational state as Russia, any attempt to establish a constitutonal regime required both administrative and legislative decentralization.[72]

Kokoshkin proceeded to apply these stated principles to Poland, which he and his colleagues regarded as a special case. Since the Kingdom was a distinct territorial unit inhabited mainly by ethnic Poles, there would be no need for any artificial administrative divisions. Further, Poles were united in their wish for autonomy: Kokoshkin and the organizational bureau had been reassured of this time and again by Lednicki and his fellow Polish liberals. Kokoshkin was quick to point out that he had no personal preference regarding the matter, but the case of Poland was far less complex than those of other regions. Coupled with the singular historical significance of the Polish problem for Russia, the congress was presented with a logical starting point for debate on the matter of decentralization. Kokoshkin did add, however, that the fate of Poles living outside the Kingdom, as well as non-Poles living within the Kingdom, were potential sticking points.[73]

Moreover, the organizational bureau clearly believed that any consideration of demands for autonomy could not be addressed fully until after the success of the Russian liberation movement and the formation of a new democratic government. Its report read:

> First of all, one ought to agree that *the question of regional autonomy cannot be finally settled before the general political liberation*....But as soon as the fundamental goal is achieved, as soon as the rights of civil liberty are guaranteed and a democratic popular representative body with constitutional rights is established for the entire empire, *a legal route must be opened immediately for the formation of autonomous regions, in accordance with the clarification of their natural boundaries and the needs of the local population*....

> There is no need for the introduction of regional auton-
> omy throughout the entire empire in the immediate future.
> It can be introduced *gradually by way of promulgating each
> time a special all-empire law on the formation of this or that
> autonomous region....*[74]

Despite these reservations, the organizational bureau proposed resolutions that addressed the thorny nationalities problem, as well as the
divisive issue of decentralization. They called for the "right of free cultural self-determination," including educational instruction in one's
native language, and local control over administrative affairs.[75] The
fate of Poland merited special reference; this section of the report elicited the greatest opposition. In the end, disagreement on the following
proposal for Polish autonomy tore the zemstvo movement apart:

> Having in view that the greater part of the Kingdom of
> Poland represents an entity that is completely uniform in
> national-cultural-social relations and is a body sharply dis-
> tinguished from the other parts of the empire, we recognize
> it as necessary to assign immediately, after the establishment
> of an all-empire democratic popular representative body
> with constitutional rights, the Kingdom of Poland as a spe-
> cial autonomous unit with a sejm, elected on the basis of a
> universal, direct, equal, and secret vote, with the preserva-
> tion of the state unity of the empire and with the possibility
> for the rectification of the boundaries between the Kingdom
> of Poland and the adjacent provinces, on either side, by
> mutual agreement in accordance with the ethnic composi-
> tion and desires of the local population.[76]

On 14 September, delegates began discussing the nationalities
question and the matter of decentralization in earnest. Count Geiden,
a moderate, immediately called for a moratorium on discussion of
these complex issues, since the congress lacked time to thoroughly
address them. A heated debate took place, during which Rodichev
argued that while the general matter of a federated structure for
Russia was indeed an academic one without urgency, the Polish ques-

tion demanded the congress' immediate attention. He pushed for immediate discussion of this issue; if time allowed, the congress could consider the matter of federation after a resolution had been reached on the Polish question.[77] Delegates approved Rodichev's proposal, and the battle was joined.

Tadeusz Wróblewski, responding to those who objected to the mere discussion of federalism, reassured the congress that the Polish delegates merely sought autonomy and not separation from Russia. Some delegates refused to believe this. V. M. Kashkarov, from Kaluga, argued that Poles really wanted independence; interestingly, he emphatically pledged his support to any such demands.[78]

Most of those who doubted Polish intentions, however, were primarily concerned with preserving the unity of the empire. Many delegates wondered whether granting Polish demands—and those of the Finns, Georgians, and others—would lead to the disintegration of the state. G. Dmitriev posed the question that was on everyone's mind: "Is this separatism, or a striving for a better form of state structure? The question is too difficult."[79]

A. M. Nemirovskii expressed the greatest fears of those Russian moderates who advocated a change in the regime but did not want to alter the structure of the state. He argued that if Poland were to receive autonomous status, not only the borderlands but regions in the heart of Russia would want the same treatment. This would eventually result in the dissolution of the empire.[80] Many also believed that embracing a program that seemed anti-Russian would serve to strengthen the ultra-nationalists at the polls. Maksim Kovalevskii countered this argument, pointing out that while broader self-rule, rather than wide autonomy, was an acceptable system for "internal provinces," others—specifically Poland, Finland and "Little Russia" (Ukraine)—had a strong "historical right" to autonomy.[81]

But ardent nationalists refused to cave in on this point, and just "as the agrarian question incited a bitter class struggle, so did the nationalities question in its new formulation provoke a nationalistic protest."[82] Aleksander Guchkov, a member of the Moscow city duma, emerged as the leader of the nationalist wing within the congress. He went further than Nemirovskii, throwing down the gauntlet for those who would grant Polish autonomy:

If we only disagree on this one question, we are political enemies; if we agree, we are allies. It is said that our state must become federal, a union, but we are not told where the limit will be set on the number of federal regions, what will remain for the central authority, to which regions and nationalities this applies. No wonder, then, that many cities now remember their liberties; Novgorod, Pskov and Tver' will be dragged after them—and very likely the business will reach Moscow. It is unknown how far the business of fragmenting the state will go. When we, standing for the reform of the existing order, place before the voters a party program of hidden federalism, then undoubtedly our powerful opponents will appear as a party that defends the present regime and the most reactionary measures. Then one cannot doubt to which party the people will give preference, and the former arbitrary rule will remain in reformed Russia.[83]

Guchkov maintained that the borderlands, including Poland, would be satisfied with extensive local self-government, without real autonomy and without turning Russia into a federated state.[84]

Kokoshkin immediately rose to defend his report, arguing that "Poland, the Caucasus, [and] the Northwestern area will support the program of the bureau, but they will not support another."[85] A. M. Koliubakin took a different tack in his defense of Polish rights. He reassured those gathered that "without a doubt the state is not at all diminished by regional autonomy."[86] He dismissed Guchkov's argument concerning the imminent dissolution of Russia, pointing out that "there is no aspiration for secession among the borderlands."[87]

Regarding Poland, Koliubakin maintained that it served Poland's best interests to remain tied to Russia:

[I]f Poland will aspire to secede, then Germany will swallow her. The awareness of the advantage of living in a lawful state, where there is no place for arbitrary rule, will always restrain the borderlands from secession...Who will leave a free state, when each locality can freely develop its own culture? On the contrary, separatism arises from centralization,

> from oppression of the local organs....A great state can be
> created where freedom and justice attain full supremacy.
> Without regional federation the realizaiton of this is impos-
> sible.[88]

Koliubakin here echoed the key themes of Lednicki's politics: Poland wishes only for autonomy within a democratic Russian empire populated by peoples free to develop their own cultures and protected from foreign aggression.

Rodichev picked up on this argument, pointing out that an autonomous Poland would remain on friendly terms with Russia, serving as "a bulwark against imperialism, against our enemy, who will be turned against Russia."[89] Only a unified Slavdom, he argued, would be able to thwart German advances to the east. But this did not require Poland's total subservience to Russia. Rodichev regarded Polish autonomy as "the first step along that road—toward the federation of Slavdom and the pacification of Europe."[90] Perhaps with his friend Lednicki in mind, Rodichev concluded that "[w]e must create a situation, by which a Russian Pole would become a Russian patriot and be proud of it."[91]

At the conclusion of the September zemstvo gathering, Prince Pavel Dolgorukov hosted a meeting of the liberal discussion group, *Beseda*, at his home in Moscow.[92] Dolgorukov personally placed the whole debate about Poland on a different plane, confessing that for him "the Polish question is neither a political question, nor an economic one, but is exclusively a moral problem and a question of conscience for the Russian nation."[93] In addition to participants at the congress, outside observers interested in Russian politics were invited to the banquet. Among them was William T. Stead, an eminent British journalist and founder of *Review of Reviews*.

Stead spoke to the gathering about the merits of tsarist reform efforts. He applauded the edict of 19 August, which promised the "Bulygin Duma," a largely advisory body with limited powers. He argued that the Russian opposition should be satisfied with that sort of arrangement because Russian society was not mature enough to handle a constitutional system.[94] Obviously ignorant of the real nature of Russian politics, Stead was convinced that Nicholas II wanted reforms, but was thwarted by conservative forces opposing change, notably the grand dukes, the Church and the bureaucracy.[95] On 9 September Stead had had a long conversation with the tsar, who encouraged him to talk to the zemstvoists on the topic of the duma. Determined to preserve the autocracy, Nicholas evidently hoped that an outsider could convince the liberal leaders to accept the Bulygin Duma in lieu of a true parliament.[96] Stead also met with A. F. Trepov; he asked the head of police to work for Miliukov's release from prison. In fact, the liberal activist was freed on 13 September, in time to participate at the zemstvo congress. This move reassured Stead that "the Tsar and his officials were evidently going to behave like sensible men."[97]

While Miliukov and many other Russian opposition leaders were present at the Dolgorukov banquet, it was the Pole Lednicki who responded most vociferously to Stead's plea for moderation. Angered by the misguided interference, Lednicki seized the opportunity to denounce the Poles' historic reliance on the West in their struggles for freedom. He also argued that Russians hoping for sympathy in the reform efforts should not look westward either. Because of the success at the zemstvo congress, where Polish demands for autonomy were approved by the vast majority of the delegates, Lednicki was increasingly influenced by notions of "Slavic brotherhood." He also believed that only a truly democratic regime would emancipate the Poles. Thus, he took deep offense at Stead's remarks and launched into an assault on the West. He asserted that Great Britain did not want to see a successful reform of the bankrupt system in Russia, for it hoped to create another "sick man," like Turkey, in Europe. The Poles, not the West, were the true allies of Russians in the struggle against tsarist bureaucratic rule.[98]

Lednicki charged that the West had long tried to

convince us that Poles are the enemies of the Russians, and the Russians—enemies of the Poles, but now all has changed. The scales of deceit and lies have fallen from our eyes. Everyone understands, that only through the joint efforts...of all nations living in Russia, will we be able to conquer the common enemy.[99]

The "common enemy" was autocracy, and he called on all peoples of the empire—"Russians and Poles, Jews and Georgians, Latvians and Estonians"—to join in a united struggle for liberty.[100]

For Lednicki, the upheaval in Russia was no longer a movement to merely squeeze reforms from the tsarist regime. He now believed that he and his fellow *osvobozhdentsy* had a mission to free all oppressed peoples from tyranny. He warned Stead that

> as the French Revolution brought to the world the great ideas of the rights of nationalities, freedom and equality, likewise the Russian revolutionary movement is a proclamation that the end of the triumph of lawlessness and all anarchy will be possible.[101]

Lednicki painted a picture of a free union of Slavic peoples, forged by a rejuvenated Russia. This union would be so strong, he believed, that "neither the iron fist of the Teuton, nor anyone's [British?] diplomacy" would be able to rend it asunder.[102] While "other enslaved Slavic nations remember, that here is hidden the source of strength...Mr. Stead finds the center of the nightmare, which oppresses his country."[103] Lednicki had come to view the British as leaders in a concerted effort to keep Russia, Poland and the rest of Slavdom in a backward state. He warned that a victory of democratic forces in Russia would herald a new era in Slavic history, and that "we [Slavs] will settle old reckonings with Europe, but not with blood, but with culture and progress."[104] Apparently, Lednicki's commitment to pacifism was as strong as his Panslavist sentiments.

Debate on the issue of Polish autonomy in September marked the beginning of the end for unity within the constitutionalist movement. Radical democrats, like Lednicki and his cohorts, who were also committed to a just solution to the nationalities question, clearly carried the day. But, as the political activist N. I. Astrov later recalled, Guchkov had "introduced a sharply defined split, and facilitated a new and more precise exposition of political ideas and the division of the congress's participants into political parties."[105]

The split, however, did not occur on the issue of a constitution, for Guchkov and other moderates were firmly in favor of this. The minority (a bloc of 37 out of 200) voted against the majority on two major issues only: direct elections (they accepted the other three elements to the "four-tail vote"), and the organizational bureau's pronouncements on decentralization and national minorities.[106] Interestingly, Guchkov's biographer concedes that, while his "passion for empire or, rather, his pasionate dislike for the concept of a federated state structure, was sincere and deeply felt," his opposition to Polish autonomy was due to a bias against Poles.[107] In any event, it was the Poles' relentless pursuit of a resolution on decentralization that effectively divided the constitutionalist camp into two parties, Kadets and Octobrists.

The outcome of the September congress also incited Poles to continue pressuring the government for concessions. At the beginning of the month, the autonomy of universities had been restored. These institutions quickly became centers of revolutionary activity, with national minorities being particularly radical and vocal in their calls for change. At St. Petersburg University, the nationalities movement was led by a Polish scholar of linguistics, Professor Jan Baudouin De Courtenay. Like Lednicki, he preached solidarity among all national minorities, spreading his message among the student body and the local intelligentsia.[108]

De Courtenay's efforts to mobilize forces for the liberation movement were successful, and on 20 September students at the university met to establish the "Union of Radical Polish Youth." They demanded autonomy for the Kingdom, with a sejm in Warsaw. Their program called for instruction in the Polish language for Polish students, and equal rights for Poles living outside the Kingdom.[109] Other non-Russian students in the capital also mobilized. On 28 September, Ukrainian students gathered to debate the issue of Ukrainian autonomy. They formulated a demand for Ukrainian autonomy on a wide democratic-federal basis; their plan provided for an independent *rada*, and ensured equal rights for all non-Ukrainians living in Ukraine.[110]

Meanwhile, those in Russia who staunchly defended the integrity of the state quickly responded to the zemstvoists' resolutions on the issues of decentralization and Polish autonomy. Although Guchkov could not muster much support among zemstvoists at the September gathering to oppose Polish demands, it appears that the mood among provincial leaders was distinctly hostile to the concept of federalism. Landowners and peasants in Konstantinograd met on 4 October to discuss the upcoming elections to the state duma. They attacked the outcome of the September congress, and vehemently opposed any reforms that might lead to federalism. The foundation of the Russian state, they asserted, must not be weakened by caving in to Polish demands. Two participants at the zemstvo gathering, Sheidman and Grinevich, were also present at the Konstantinograd meeting; confronted by the irate assembly, they renounced their allegiance to the September resolutions.[111]   Local zemstvo leaders in Novokhopersk and Bugul'm also protested the resolution on Polish autonomy and expressed "approval and gratitude" to Guchkov for his defense of Russian interests.[112]

The September zemstvo congress precipitated the formation of political parties, all of which took a stand on the issues of decentralization and nationality rights. At the founding meeting of the Progressive-Constitutional Party, held 7 October in Petersburg, these matters were debated once again. The Pole Tadeusz Wroblewski, who had been a vocal advocate of Polish autonomy at the zemstvo gathering in September, pushed for the equitable treatment of all non-Russians. He seconded Lednicki's pledge, that "we Poles demand the right of national self-determination not only for ourselves, but for the Little-Russians, Belorussians and other nationalities."[113]

Other parties vehemently opposed this viewpoint. The Party of Legal Order was established in St. Petersburg on 15 October, in direct response to the outcome of the September congress. Terrified at the prospect of Polish autonomy, this party regarded the "unity and indivisibility of Russia" as the "most important point" in its program.[114] For many Russian nationalists, state unity seems to have been more important than the preservation of the autocracy.[115]

Lednicki worked hard to counter this backlash to the zemstvoists' resolutions on Polish autonomy, and continued his political campaign to bring all the peoples of Russia together in one united liberation movement. After the congress he traveled to Warsaw, which "boiled over with meetings everywhere," to inform Poles that Russian society was at last accepting the idea of autonomy for the Kingdom.[116] No

sooner had he arrived there, however, than he was summoned home
to Moscow: his wife was begging him to return immediately, since the
city "was about to erupt like a volcano."[117] Almost daily the
osvobozhdentsy held secret meetings, in which Lednicki frequently
took part.[118] Lawyers' groups continued their vocal opposition to
tsarist rule; Lednicki presided over meetings of Moscow lawyers on
20 September and 2 October, which condemned the general bureaucratic license displayed by the government. In particular, the lawyers
chafed at the "illegal" disruption of political meetings by the police.
They also denounced the government-sponsored terror of the Black
Hundreds, which would soon become a personal concern for
Lednicki.[119]

The rampages of Black Hundreds gave fearsome testimony to the
social and political instability that plagued Russia in the fall of 1905.
In October, the nation was effectively brought to a standstill by a
nation-wide strike. A railway strike that began in Moscow on 7
October engulfed all of Russia within a week. The entire nation was
crippled, compelling the tsar to give in to revolutionary demands. On
17 October, he issued a manifesto that extended the concessions of 9
August, which had promised the formation of the so-called "Bulygin
Duma." The October Manifesto provided for a more powerful institution, conceding full legislative powers to the Duma. It also extended the vote and granted more personal freedoms.

Liberationist demands were not met fully, however, and the
nature of the duma was not totally altered. Its members would still be
chosen on the basis of indirect elections. There would be four separate curia, for different sections of society: large and medium
landowners, urban residents, peasants, and workers. Eligible voters in
each curia would elect delegates to provincial and urban assemblies,
which in turn chose deputies to the Duma. There was no universal
suffrage, and the high requirements of property ownership disquali-
fied many urban professionals and workers.[120]

While the manifesto failed to address the nationalities question,
there is evidence that instability in the borderlands—especially the
Polish Kingdom—was a matter of growing concern for the government. Count Witte, in particular, seemed to understand that only fundamental changes in the state system would satisfy the opposition. In

a note to the tsar, dated 9 October, Witte stated that Russia had three major problems confronting it: the labor and agrarian movements, and the drive for autonomy in the borderlands. As a solution to the nationalities' matter, Witte proposed that a form of limited autonomy—broadened local self-government, really—would satisfy the opposition without stripping the central government of its powers.[121] Witte's "Most Humble Report" of 17 October, published simultaneously with the tsar's manifesto, contained provisions similar to those in the 9 October note. Hoping to prevent the dismemberment of the empire, Witte called on the Duma to promote the "equalization of the rights of all Russians subjects, regardless of their religion and nationality."[122]

In the midst of the October strike, the first liberal party in Russia came into being. The constituent congress of the Constitutional Democrats (Kadets) convened from 12–18 October in the Dolgorukov palace in Moscow. More than one-hundred fifty people were invited, but many were unable to attend. The railroad strike paralyzed travel across Russia, preventing Kadets from the provinces, and also the radical contingent from St. Petersburg, from making the journey.[123] Lednicki and many other future party leaders—mostly from Moscow—were present: Pavel Miliukov, Fedor Kokoshkin, the Dolgorukov twins, Vasilii Maklakov, Sergei Muromtsev, Ivan Petrunkevich and Prince Dmitrii Shakhovskoi. In all, eighty-one men were present, thirty-six of whom were from Moscow. The original organizational bureau was well represented: twenty-four out of forty members were present.[124]

This rump congress realized it could only be considered a provisional body, and therefore refrained from making new pronouncements on any matter. As a result, the initial party program simply incorporated elements contained in the March program of the Union of Liberation, as well as resolutions approved by zemstvoists in September.[125] Unable to ignore the tumultuous events unfolding around them, however, the delegates voiced their support for the strikers' demands of political amnesty and a constituent assembly elected by a four-tail vote. The Kadets rejected the October Manifesto, which did not meet the demands of the strikers and in addition failed to mention a constitution.[126]

Despite its self-imposed provisional status, the Kadet gathering did address the nationalities problem and the issue of decentralization. These sections of the party program were virtually identical to the resolutions of the zemstvoists. Miliukov and Kokoshkin introduced into the program a call for the autonomy of the Kingdom; the motion was approved with only one dissenting vote.[127] The Kadet program attracted national minorities to the ranks of the new party: many Estonians, Latvians, Lithuanians, Poles, Ukrainians, Armenians and Tatars would join.[128] National minorities would also be well-represented on the party's central committee.[129]

Shortly after the Kadets' first congress ended, Lednicki organized one of the first local chapters of the new party. At 1 p.m. on 23 October 1905, the first meeting of the Moscow group of Kadets met at his home on the Arbat.[130] Members of the group included many of his close associates.[131] While it was never a party that appealed to the masses, the Kadets soon numbered 50,000–60,000—membership figures similar to those of the socialist parties.[132]

Lednicki and his fellow radical democrats were clearly in the ascendancy within the opposition movement. At the final zemstvo congress in November, they gained more support for their policies, especially the demand for Polish autonomy. While nationalist forces and moderate zemstvoists voiced their opposition, it seemed as if Polish patriots had at last found reliable Russian allies in the Kadets. In the last months of 1905 and the first months of 1906, Lednicki sought to cement this alliance, continuing his drive to meld the Russian and Polish liberationists into one united front opposed to tsarism.

Unknown to Lednicki, the final zemstvo gathering and the election campaign to the Duma would represent the zenith of this movement. The First Duma, although controlled by the Kadets, failed to push for concessions on the nationalities question. By the last days of the Duma, Lednicki was becoming aware that his fellow Kadets would always regard Polish autonomy an issue too risky to fully embrace in the broad national political arena.

ENDNOTES

1. Blobaum, *Rewolucja*, 95–98.

2. Ibid., 172; also Zaprudnik, "Political Struggle for Byelorussia," 48–49.

3. Zaprudnik, "Political Struggle for Byelorussia," 50.

4. Blobaum, *Rewolucja*, 173.

5. Sanders, "Union of Unions," 672–73.

6. Ibid., 850–51.

7. W. Lednicki, *Pamiętniki*, 2: 522; W. Lednicki, '*Entente cordiale*', 83; and Smolen, "Działalność polityczne," 100.

8. Zenowiusz Ponarski, "Aleksander Lednicki (1866–1934)," in *Biblioteka palestry. Szkice z dziejów adwokatury polskiej*, 2d series, ed. Roman Lyczywka (Warsaw: Wydawnictwo Prawnicze, 1978), 74; and Kiepurska, *Warsawa w Rewolucji*, 154–55.

9. A. Lednicki, *Mowy polityczne*, 4.

10. Ibid.

11. Ibid., 5.

12. Ibid., 4.

13. Ibid., 6.

14. Ibid., 7.

15. Ibid., 13.

16. Ibid.

17. *Russkii viestnik* 300 (November 1905): 327–28. The Georgian plan closely resembled Polish plans for autonomy, providing for: 1) the free national-cultural development of Georgia, with the decentralization of the administration; 2) wide political self-rule—that is, autonomy with the preservation of state unity; 3) an assembly in Tiflis with deputies chosen on the basis of the four-tail vote; 4) equal rights for all minorities in Georgia, which was to consist of the Tiflis (Tbilisi) and Kutaisi provinces, the Zakatal'skii and Sukhumskii okrugs and the Batumskii oblast'. Georgian autonomy was to be contingent on the approval of an All-Russian parliament.

18. GARF, f. 518. Soiuz soiuzov. op. 1, d. 39, ll. 13–14.

19. Bensman, "Constitutional Ideas," 444–54.

20. Ibid., 472; *Osvobozhdenie* 76 (2/15), 452.

21. Ibid., 472–73; *Osvobozhdenie* 76 (2/15), 452–3.

22. Emmons, *Formation of Political Parties*, 39.

23. Shakhovskoi, "Soiuz Osvobozhdeniia," 165.

24. Ibid., 164–65.

25. Ibid., 167–69.

26. Bensman, "Constitutional Ideas," 694–98.

27. Emmons, *Formation of Political Parties*, 39.

28. Ibid.

29. E. D. Chermenskii, *Burzhuaziia i tsarizm v pervoi russkoi revoliutsii*,

2d ed. (Moscow: Izdatel'stvo "Mysl'," 1970), 123–24. Other members included M. M. Vinaver, A. A. Kornilov, N. V. Teslenko, M. L. Mandel'shtam, E. I. Kedrin, A. A. Savel'ev, A. M. Aleksandrov, G. A. Fal'bork, A. M. Koliubakin, V. E. Iakushkin, M. V. Chelnokov, M. G. Komissarov, M. Ia. Gertsenshtein, N. A. Kablukov, and A. F. Fortunatov.

30   Ibid., 124–25.

31. Ibid.

32. Emmons, *Formation of Political Parties*, 39.

33. Abraham Ascher, *The Revolution of 1905*, vol. 1: *Russia in Disarray* (Stanford: Stanford University Press, 1988), 181. The congress proposed alienation of public lands, and private estates—if the need arose—with compensation. Tax reforms, the right to form unions and strike, and other labor legislation were also approved.

34. Bensman, "Constitutional Ideas," 700–01.

35. Ibid., 701.

36. *Aleksandr Ivanovich Guchkov rasskazyvaet...Vospominaniia predsedateliia Gosudarstvennoi Dumy i voennogo ministra Vremennogo Pravitel'stva*, ed. V. I. Startsev, et al. (Moscow: "Voprosy Istorii," 1993), 33.

37. Bensman, "Constitutional Ideas," 713–14.

38. Fedor Kokoshkin also intended to make the trip, but was unable due to illness. See PIASA, Aleksander Lednicki Collection (006), folder 5. Undated letter from Rodichev to Lednicki.

39. GARF, f. 523, op. 1, d. 174, l. 6; also see W. Lednicki, *Pamiętniki*, 2: 515.

40. This term was a popular name for the Związek Posępowe-Demokratyczny (ZPD), just as *Endecja* referred to the National Democratic Party.

41. "Doklad organizatsionnago biuro s"ezdy zemskikh i gorodskikh deiatelei po voprosy o pravakh natsional'nostei i o detsentralizatsii upravleniia i zakonodatel'stva," *Pravo* 40 (9 October 1905): 3323–24; also Bensman, 715–18, citing "Zemskii s"ezd i poliaki: doklad biuro zemskogo s"ezda, sdelannyi ego upolnomochennymi 26–27 iiulia," *Osvobozhdenie* 77 (13/26 September 1905): 472–73.

42. *Osvobozhdenie* 77 (13/26 September 1905), 472–3.

43. Ibid.; Bensman, "Constitutional Ideas," 717.

44. *Osvobozhdenie* 77 (13/26 September 1905), 472–73.

45. Ibid.

46. Ibid, 473; Bensman, "Constitutional Ideas," 717.

47. *Osvobozhdenie* 77 (13/26 September 1905), 473.

48. Ibid.

49. *Pravo* 37 (18 September 1905): 3044.

50. *Kraj* 38 (1905), 6.

51. A. A. Bashmakov, ed. *Spravochnaia kniga izbiratelia v Gosudarstvennuiu*

Dumu (St. Petersburg: Slovo, 1906), 292.

52. *Kraj* 38 (1905), 6.

53. *Pravo* 37 (18 September 1905): 3043–44. See also Bashmakov, *Spravochnaia kniga*, 290. He cited 126 zemstvoists and 71 municipal representatives in attendance. A recent account gives different figures: 130 delegates from zemstva and 63 from towns. See N. G. Koroleva, *Zemstvo na perelome (1905–1907 gg.)* (Moscow: Institut Rossiiskoi Istorii, 1995), 151.

54. A. Lednicki, "Natsional'nyi vopros v gosudarstvennoi dume," 154.

55. *Pravo* 37 (18 September 1905): 3050.

56. Miliukov, *Political Memoirs*, 45.

57. This report was published as *O pravakh natsional'nostei i o detsentralizatsii. Doklad biuro s"ezdy zemskikh i gorodskikh deiatelei. 12–15 sent. 1905 goda i postanovleniia s"ezda* (Moscow: O. L. Somovoi, 1905).

58. *Russkii viestnik* 300 (November 1905): 326.

59. Bensman, "Constitutional Ideas," 721.

60. W. Lednicki recalled that "already before the Duma, but particularly in the period between 1906 and 1917 Kokoshkin together with his wife was a frequent guest at our home, constantly called on my father, was imprisoned with him in 1908, and during the war took an active part in Russian-Polish meetings and conferences, which then took place at my father's." See *Pamiętniki*, 2: 495.

61. Bensman, "Constitutional Ideas," 191–92.

62. R. G. Vinaver, "Vozhdi kadetskoi partii (Iz vospominanii)," *Novyi zhurnal* 10 (1945): 254. Vinaver's high regard for Kokoshkin's ability is echoed in the memoirs of Kokoshkin's son. See Vladimir Fedorovich Kokoshkin, "F. F. Kokoshkin," ed. V. F. Kokoshkin and I. Iu. Guadanin, *Novyi zhurnal* 74 (1963): 218.

63. On Kokoshkin's impediment, noted by other contemporaries, see V. A. Obolenskii, *Moia zhizn'. Moi sovremenniki* (Paris: YMCA-Press, 1988), 367.

64. A. Kizevetter, "Pervyia zhertvy. Fedor Fedorovich Kokoshkin," in *Pamiati pogibshikh*, ed. N. I. Astrov, V. F. Zeeler, et al. (Paris: Knizhnoe Delo "Rodnik," 1929), 18.

65. *Pravo* 40 (9 October 1905): 3322; Bensman, "Constitutional Ideas," 721–22.

66. *Pravo 40* (9 October 1905): 3329–41.

67. Ibid., 3330.

68. Ibid., 3332; Bensman, "Constitutional Ideas," 726.

69. *Pravo 40* (9 October 1905): 3331–34.

70. Ibid., 3335–37.

71. Ibid., 3337; Bensman, "Constitutional Ideas," 737.

72. *Pravo 40* (9 October 1905): 3337–38.

73. Ibid., 3338–42.

74. Ibid., 3339–40; Bensman, "Constitutional Ideas," 739.

75. *Pravo* 37 (18 September 1905): 3063.

76. Ibid., 3064; Bensman, "Constitutional Ideas," 744–45.

77. *Pravo* 37 (18 September 1905): 3060–61.

78. Bensman, "Constitutional Ideas," 746–47. Ivan Petrunkevich later recalled that Wroblewski's address was "a splendid speech, eloquent in form, deep in content. It made a huge impression on the gathering..." See I. I. Petrunkevich, "Iz zapisok obshchestvennago deiatelia. Vospominaniia," ed. A. A. Kizevetter, *Arkhiv russkoi revoliutsii* 21 (1934): 390.

79. *Pravo* 38 (25 September 1905): 3170

80. "If oppression from the center is frightful," he argued, "then is not separatism also frightful? Is it really impossible to expect that independent states can be formed in the borderlands and that Russia will descend to nothing? With such decentralization it would be necessary, as in olden times, to go to the Volga and the Kama in order to conquer these regions again, not to mention the remote borderlands..." See Bensman, "Constitutional Ideas," 747–48.

81. *Pravo* 38 (25 September 1905): 3170.

82. A. Lednicki, "Natsional'nyi vopros v gosudarstvennoi dume," 154.

83. *Pravo* 38 (25 September 1905): 3172; Bensman, "Constitutional Ideas," 748. Ivan Petrunkevich later evaluated Guchkov's speech, which, "constructed on patriotic feelings, perhaps, might have made an impression on a few of the members of the Congress, if its patriotic pathos had carried a less provocative character." See I. I. Petrunkevich, "Vospominaniia," 390

84. *Pravo* 38 (25 September 1905): 3172.

85. Ibid., 3174–75.

86. Ibid., 3175.

87. Ibid.

88. Ibid.; Bensman, "Constitutional Ideas," 750–51.

89. Ibid., 3176.

90. Ibid.

91. Ibid.

92. *Russkiia vedomosti*, 16 September 1905.

93. W. Lednicki, '*Entente cordiale*', 39.

94. A. Lednicki, *Mowy polityczne*, 33.

95. Frederic Whyte, *The Life of W. T. Stead* (London: J. Cape, Limited; New York & Boston: Houghton Mifflin Company, 1925), vol. 2: 274.

96. Ibid., 275.

97. Ibid., 276.

98. A. Lednicki, *Mowy polityczne*, 34. For excerpts from speeches of others present at the banquet, see *Russkiia vedomosti*, 17 September 1905 and 18 September 1905.

99. A. Lednicki, *Mowy polityczne*, 35.

100. Ibid.

101. Ibid.

102. Ibid., 36.

103.   Ibid.

104.   Ibid.

105.   N. I. Astrov, *Vospominaniia* (Paris, 1940), 314; also cited by Emmons, *Formation of Political Parties*, 105.

106.   Emmons, *Formation of Political Parties*, 105.

107.   William Gleason, *Alexander Guchkov and the End of the Russian Empire* (Philadelphia: The American Philosophical Society, 1983), 15.

108.   Voskobiynyk, "The Nationalities Question in Russia," 156.

109.   *Russkii viestnik* 300 (November 1905): 325.

110.   Ibid., 325–28.

111.   Ibid., 310.

112.   Ibid.

113.   Ibid., 324.

114.   Bashmakov, *Spravochnaia kniga*, 354.

115.   Emmons, *Formation of Political Parties*, 139–40.

116.   A. Lednicki, "Z pamiętnika," 29.

117.   Ibid., 30.

118.   Ibid. Lednicki recalled two constant demands at these secret meetings: an end to tsarism, and the introduction of a constitution.

119.   "Postanovlenie moskovskikh prisiazhnykh poverennykh," *Pravo* 42 (31 October 1905): 3486–87. It is not certain whether Lednicki participated in the Second Congress of the All-Russian Lawyers' Union, which was held 5–6 October in Moscow. Sixty representatives from 24 chapters participated in the deliberations. See "Vtoroi s"ezd vserossiiskago soiuza advokatov," *Pravo* 40 (9 October 1905): 3364–66; for the resolutions, which did not include any mention of Poland, see "Rezoliutsii 2 s"ezda soiuza advokatov 5–6 oktiabria 1905 g. v Moskve," *Pravo* 43 (8 November 1905): 3538–41.

120.   Galai, *Liberation Movement in Russia*, 263; and Janus, "The Polish Kolo," 55.

121.   Voskobiynyk, "Nationalities Question in Russia," 164.

122.   Ibid., 169–70.

123.   Zimmerman, "Between Revolution and Reaction," 43–44; also see Bensman, "Constitutional Ideas," 763–64.

124.   Bensman, "Constitutional Ideas," 763.

125.   Emmons, *Formation of Political Parties*, 41–42; also see Bensman, "Constitutional Ideas," 764.

126.   Ascher, *Revolution of 1905*, 1: 263.

127.   *Russkiia vedomosti*, 20 October 1905; also see Bensman, "Constitutional Ideas," 789.

128.   C. Jay Smith, Jr., "Miljukov and the Russian National Question," *Harvard Slavic Studies* 4 (1957): 399.

129.   In addition to Lednicki, who joined the committee in April 1906, there were Leon Petrażicki, his fellow Pole; Ia. Chakste, a Latvian; Ia. Ia. Tennison

from Estonia; M. M. Topchibashev, later president of Azerbaijan; the Ukrainian activists I. Iu. Shrag and I. V. Luchitskii; and the Armenian M. S. Adzhemov. See A. Lednitskii, "P. N. Miliukov i pol'skii vopros," 213. For a detailed analysis of the Central Committee, see Emmons, *Formation of Political Parties*, 63–64. For a concise description of the party, see N. G. Dumova and V. V. Shelokhaev, "Oppozitsiia Ego Velichestva: Kadety," in *Istoriia politicheskikh partii Rossii*, ed. A. I. Zevelev (Moscow: Vysshaia Shkola, 1994): 111–43.

130. *Protokoly tsentral'nogo komiteta i zagranichniykh grupp konstitutsion-no-demokraticheskoi partii*, ed. Shmuel Galai, et al., vol. 1, *Protokoly tsentral'nogo komiteta konstitutsionno-demokraticheskoi partii: 1905–1911* (Moscow: Progress-akademiia, 1994), 33–34.

131. Among them were Prince Pavel Dolgorukov, A. A. Kizevetter, V. A. Maklakov, M. L. Mandel'shtam, Prince P. I. Novgorodtsev, and N. V. Teslenko. In all, twenty-six men originally belonged to the local party cell. In time, over 1,000 students at institutions of higher learning in Moscow organized their own separate chapter. See *Pravo* 43 (8 November 1905): 3555–56.

132. Dumova and Shelokhaev, "Kadety," 113. By 1914, however, the Kadets' popularity had declined, and party membership had fallen to about 10,000.

Chapter Eight

THE POLISH QUESTION AND THE FINAL ZEMSTVO CONGRESS, NOVEMBER 1905

After publication of the October Manifesto, many Poles were hopeful that real change was in store, and mass pro-government demonstrations took place in late October throughout the Kingdom. Roman Dmowski and his fellow National Democrats were especially pleased at the prospect of further concessions, and he led a delegation to St. Petersburg to try to persuade Count Witte that autonomy for the Kingdom would undermine those forces promoting revolution.[1]

The manifesto encouraged the *Endecja* but did little to assuage the ire of radicals. The PPS continued to demand political autonomy, an end to censorship, political amnesty, and an end to martial law, which was in place in Warsaw and Łódź.[2] On 20 October, about 4,000 delegates representing the major political parties gathered in Warsaw to discuss the meaning of the manifesto. National Democrats, who supported the manifesto, were quickly ousted from the rally, which fell under radical control. Socialist representatives pushed for a boycott of the upcoming elections, demanding autonomy and an end to autocracy, with all power to be vested in a constituent assembly. *Pedecja* representatives tried to find a middle position: they argued for participation in the elections, but promised they would walk out if the Duma did not support Polish autonomy, a general political amnesty and an end to martial law in Warsaw and Łódź. The Socialists prevailed, however, and the gathering resolved to boycott the forthcoming elections.[3]

The ZPD, faced with a political dilemma, waffled on the election issue until late in the year. By the time party leaders launched an election campaign, they were well behind the *Endecja* in the struggle to popularize their platform. The liberals were forced to forge an alliance with Jewish leaders, a move which would isolate them still further: the Socialists denounced them for taking part in the elections, while their alliance with the Jews precipitated the anti-semitism of the *Endecja* electoral campaign.[4]

Fearful of continued unrest in the Kingdom and the increasingly strident rhetoric of the Socialists, Roman Dmowski allied himself with tsarist authorities after the announcement of the October Manifesto. Also encouraged by the restoration of Finnish autonomy on 22 October, which seemed to foreshadow similar treatment for the Kingdom, Dmowski led a delegation to St. Petersburg in an effort to persuade the government to grant concessions to Poland. He hoped to convince Count Witte that Poles would be appeased, and the Kingdom quieted, if autonomy were granted. Before the group could meet with the minister, however, martial law was imposed throughout Poland. Despite the generally calm political activities in the Kingdom in the days following the announcement of the Manifesto, provincial authorities were pushing the central government to impose martial law. Robert Blobaum has convincingly argued that the Warsaw Governor-General, Georgii Skalon, was responsible for the "steady stream of exaggerated reports" of anarchy, terrorism and imminent revolt that induced the government to implement martial law throughout the Kingdom on 28 October.[5] Temporarily lifted three weeks later after the uprising failed to materialize, martial law was reinstated in all parts of the Kingdom by mid-December and remained in effect until 1909.[6]

While the rest of the delegation refused to meet with Witte so long as martial law was enforced in the Kingdom, Dmowski decided to consult privately with the minister. He pushed Witte to grant the Kingdom autonomy; in return, he promised to use the National Democrats to halt the revolution. In effect, he pledged support for the tsarist regime. Convinced the situation was too volatile, Witte refused to budge. He argued that the granting of autonomy would unleash the wrath of Russian nationalists, especially those in the government.[7] This whole affair typified Dmowski's attitude to the revolution: he wanted concessions for Poland, and could not have cared less about the Russian liberation movement. As Glen Janus concluded, the "proposal to Witte...reflected the political opportunism of the *Endecja* and the willingness on the part of Dmowski to collaborate with the Tsarist regime in order to achieve autonomy."[8]

Like Dmowski, Lednicki was waging a battle for Polish autonomy on two fronts. Immediately after the Kadet congress concluded on 18 October, he travelled to the Kingdom in preparation for an upcoming ZPD gathering. Unlike Dmowski, however, he was a true *osvobozhdenets*, committed to the Russian struggle to end autocracy. He therefore pursued a policy dependent on the mutual cooperation of Polish and Russian liberationists, forever convinced that a just resolution of the Polish problem could be reached only when the tsarist regime was replaced by a liberal democracy. While Dmowski was planning a mission to offer his services to the Russian autocracy, Lednicki was in Warsaw fomenting continued resistance to tsarist rule.

At ZPD rallies in Warsaw, Miliukov later noted, Lednicki "was able to express himself with greater freedom than in Moscow."[9] It is clear that Lednicki had a primary political goal in his campaign in Poland: to fortify the political center. As he reminded his audience at a political gathering, "we [the ZPD] do not want anarchy, but are not afraid of revolution."[10] He was willing to take risks in his pursuit of the elusive middle ground, between radical social revolution and bureaucratic reaction, and he bore the brunt of considerable criticism. Miliukov recalled that members of the ZPD accused Lednicki of turning down the road of "conciliation," of wanting to be in the Duma, of wanting to make concessions to zemstvoists.[11]

These charges ring true, for Lednicki did seek through compromise with progressive elements in Russian society to bring about a peaceful resolution of the Polish problem. An integral part of this solution, he believed, would be Polish participation in an all-Russian Duma that would, in turn, sanction the autonomous status of the Kingdom. While conciliation and compromise with the *osvobozhdentsy* in Moscow and St. Petersburg remained bitter pills too difficult for many Poles to swallow, Lednicki believed that this treatment was the only way to heal the deep wounds Russians and Poles had inflicted on each other over the centuries.

In a speech delivered at a ZPD rally in Warsaw in late October, Lednicki reminded Poles that they should not regard all Russians as their enemies. He posed the questions: "Who is our enemy anyway? Who is our Ally? With whom do we go arm in arm to the final battle? These are the questions," he continued, "to which we must here give answers."[12] Lednicki provided a solution, asserting that the enemy of Polish freedom was not the Russian nation, but the "Russian magnates' bureaucracy, based on absolutism, which for the past forty years has held us by the throat with an iron grip, so that the blood has almost entirely flowed from the face of the Polish nation...."[13] He offered hope, however, contending that despotism had capitulated by granting the October Manifesto.[14]

Lednicki went on to suggest to his audience those Russians with whom the *Pedecja* should cooperate, informing the delegates of each political party's stand on the nationalities issue. In a move calculated to gain the support of the left wing of the ZPD, consisting of men who were also active in the PPS, Lednicki praised the Russian radical parties above all others. He explained that

> social democracy in Russia is a faction of a universal social democracy, which is united under the motto of Marx and Engels: 'Proletariat of all countries unite!' As a result of this position, social democracy is interested in the international question: it is an international party, aiming for the creation of a proletariat state within a state. It is not possible to say, that it is a predisposed enemy to any particular nationality, that it openly denies the nationality factor.[15]

He added that the platform of the Social Democrats (SDs) called for the right of self-determination for every nationality. While he noted that it was unclear whether this meant only political self-determination, or also cultural freedom, he still was "deeply convinced, that the Social-Democratic Party is not able to have anything in common with national oppression."[16]

Lednicki heaped even greater praise on the populist Socialist-Revolutionaries (SRs). He hailed their platform for having a well-defined position regarding the nationalities matter. He noted approvingly that a SR party manifesto in 1900 had denounced the Russian autocracy for oppressing other nations, for "propagating mutual hatred, [and] pitting one against another."[17] He lauded the SRs for standing "on a federative position, on a position of free unions of free peoples."[18] In an overture to leftists within the ZPD, and Socialists in general, Lednicki boldly asserted that Poles should regard the SDs and SRs as "our truest allies."[19]

Lednicki reminded his audience, however, that liberal leaders in Russia were also progressive thinkers. He contended that beginning with the historic zemstvo congress of November 1904, a majority of zemstvoists had clearly supported the demand for a constitution in Russia. Lednicki regarded this congress as the beginning of the liberation movement. From this point on, he added, Russian constitutionalists prevailed at all zemstvo congresses.[20] While admitting that some zemstvoists were initially reticent about granting Poland autonomy, Lednicki reassured his fellow Poles that they were not latent chauvinists. They simply feared that Russian society would be unprepared for such a novel idea as autonomy for the Kingdom. Lednicki expressed his fervent belief that the Russian constitutionalists were "completely removed from aggressive nationalism," and that "Russian public opinion...with few exceptions, generally has recognized [the need] to grant us autonomy."[21]

Denouncing conservative groups for "their nationalistic fanaticism," Lednicki emphasized that "only the left parties, together with the constitutionalists who march beneath the motto of progress, will be our allies."[22] He continued:

> Only in a joint struggle with Russian liberationists are we able to win our own freedom. Not with the government, but against the government. With the Russian nation, with all those who raise high the banner of a struggle for freedom... We do not want anarchy and we regret bloodshed, but with all the strength of our being we strive for the downfall of brute force and oppression....[23]

In conclusion, Lednicki repeated his plea for Poles to join a united front, made up of all peoples who sought the end of tsarist rule. In addition to progressive Russians, he maintained,

> [w]e [Poles] have also in Russia still other very strong and very true allies...all oppressed peoples—our brothers in misery—Ukrainians, Armenians, Georgians, Lithuanians, Latvians, Estonians and Jews. To them we extend a fraternal helping hand. And we know well, that from there comes so strong a solidarity of interests, that we, united with those who are most noble in the Russian nation, will alter this struggle on the triumphal march towards equal rights for all peoples.[24]

This speech represented a sort of political testament, for in it Lednicki clearly elucidated his hope that the revolutionary turmoil engulfing the Russian empire in 1905 would bring about the fulfillment of his dream of a "free union of free peoples."[25]

Lednicki defended this political vision and his tactics at another ZPD rally held on 25 October in Warsaw. Representatives from other political parties attended and voiced opposition to the liberals' platform. Lednicki rose to counter the attacks from both right and left. He denounced the vitriolic nationalism of the *Endecja*, maintaining that "we do not demand a monopoly on patriotism for ourselves, but also do not grant it to others."[26] He also countered zealous Socialists who advocated a boycott of the Duma elections. In another call for Slavic unity, he argued for a moderate course of action:

> We judge, that this [boycott] is a risky and dangerous thing for us. We, acting not in the realm of ideology, but of real facts, are not able to forget...if the East does not support us, then the West will shatter and overwhelm us; that not entering the Russian constituent assembly we would make difficult the situation of our Russian allies, who without us might find themselves in a minority and the Russian liberation movement might be once again annihilated....There, in the general Russian constituent assembly, we will win our autonomy; we will fight for it without concessions, without any kind of compromise.[27]

Lednicki tried to make clear his attitude to the revolution, drawing a distinction between the ZPD position and those of the radical Socialists and the National Democrats. Expressing concern that revolutionary excesses might provide fertile ground for the emergence of a dictator, he insisted that "we [*Pedecja*] do not dread the revolution! It is only anxiety that the revolution not dissipate into anarchy. We remember that, as the Jacobins destroyed the Girondists, then after the Jacobins came Napoleon."[28]

Concluding, Lednicki swore to his political opponents that "we [*Pedecja*] would rather die than transgress our convictions. But we will not die, because on our standard is written the great word: Progress!"[29] He stressed that he and his fellow liberals shared a staunch "belief in the evolution...in the progress of mankind."[30] Pledging that "this torch of progress will never go out," Lednicki cautioned that he and other members of the ZPD would fight any form of despotism: "that which we have come to hate, with which we struggle today, or any other! Our motto is Liberty, Liberty, and Liberty!"[31]

He ended his tour of the Kingdom shortly after this meeting, hastening back to Moscow for the Congress of Zemstvoists and Municipal Activists, which was scheduled to begin on 6 November. His stay in Warsaw had been a success, and there is evidence that he was gaining converts to his way of thinking. On 1 November, the Warsaw bar resolved that cooperation with the Russian *osvobozhdentsy* was the best way to gain support for Polish autonomy. Echoing the sentiments of Lednicki, the lawyers called for Slavic unity against the German threat, proclaiming the motto "Our freedom is your freedom."[32]

After his return to Russia, Lednicki aimed to inform his fellow *osvobozhdentsy* of political developments in the Kingdom. His first opportunity came on 4 November, at a huge Russo-Polish rally in St. Petersburg. More than 2,000 people gathered at the Tenishev Lyceum for the event, which featured speeches by many of the most prominent Russian liberals: Petr Struve, Fedor Rodichev, Nikolai Kareev, and Maksim Vinaver were among those who appeared. The event was sponsored by the Union of Unions, and presided over by N. F. Annenskii, the radical *osvobozhdenets* and editor of *Russkoe bogatstvo*.[33] He opened the meeting with a brief speech, declaring the imposition of martial law in Poland an act of repression aimed not only at Poland but also at the Russian liberation movement. Annenskii harangued the government, declaring that "the blood of Warsaw workers has been mixed with the blood of Russian workers to create a hard cement, which at the present moment strengthens the new edifice of liberty in Russia." The champion of Polish rights, Rodichev, spoke out in favor of granting the Kingdom an autonomous status. Polish and Russian freedom must be found together, warning that "either in a free Russia there will be a free Poland, or there will not be a Russia at all."[34]

In a passionate address, Lednicki warned his Russian colleagues that the tsarist regime aimed to "drown your freedom in our [Poles'] blood."[35] He argued that developments in the Kingdom had been peaceful, and that the local bureaucracy was to blame for any unrest. While in Poland, he said, he had

> penetrated the thicket of national life. I held my hand on the pulse of its life and felt its beat. I thus saw well, which path was taken by the...bureaucracy in Warsaw, wanting to provoke an open rebellion, to sever the bonds of mutual solidarity between the Polish and Russian nations, which with such difficulty they have barely managed to forge.[36]

Lednicki called the declaration of martial law "one of the trump cards" played by the absolutist Russian government in the same old game it had played for centuries: "divide and conquer."[37]

Lednicki enumerated the "tricks" played by the government to convince the general public that Poles wished to separate from Russia. He charged tsarist agents with forging a false declaration of the PPS, which called for an armed uprising. He claimed the government was desperately trying to incite a rebellion in order to bring about a rupture in relations between the Russian and Polish liberationists. Thus far, Lednicki gleefully noted, government attempts had failed. He did warn, however, that gangs of ultra-nationalists had recently launched incursions into the Kingdom with the aim of fomenting pogroms. Lednicki added with pride that their attempts had proven unsuccessful.[38]

Lednicki reiterated his usual call for a joint Russo-Polish struggle for "a free Russia—an organic union of nations."[39] He reassured his comrades that Poles were loyal to the empire, that "an enthusiastic Polish nation, hungering not for separation from Russia but for autonomy in its own national life, wanted to believe, was prepared to believe, at last believes, that autonomy is the only question of the day."[40] He promised the crowd that, contrary to government charges, Poles "struggle today for autonomy, not political independence; at all rallies [in Poland] there were only speeches about this, and despite the government efforts today we preserve peace and stability...."[41] Lednicki once again emphasized the need for Slavic unity against the German threat, maintaining that Poles believed the only way to avoid the "embrace of Prussia" was "in a free union with the great Russian nation."[42] He concluded on a rousing patriotic note in a bid to win the hearts of the Russian public:

> From the depths of my heart, with a growing hatred for those who try to crush us into the abyss of slavery, from the depths of my soul, full of love for those freedom fighters who boldly crush the chains of slavery, I cry—Long live a free Russia, long live a free Russian nation![43]

Another featured speaker, Petr Struve, was making his first public appearance since returning to Russia from Germany on 26 October. Long critical of the government's Polish policy, Struve now condemned martial law as "a senseless crime," drawing thunderous applause from the crowd.[44] During the proceedings a telegram came from the Polish-Ukrainian writer Włodzimierz Korolenko, who echoed Lednicki's sentiments in his appeal for unity and joint tactics. Without an end to the oppression of all peoples living in the empire, he argued, Russia itself could not find liberty. Like Lednicki, Korolenko believed that if they joined together, Poles and Russians would each find their freedom.[45] Speaking on the traditional Polish-Russian cooperation in their struggles for freedom, Kareev seconded this notion.[46] Inspired by such rhetoric, those gathered at the rally passed a resolution on Polish autonomy:

We know that the Polish nation does not desire to separate
from Russia...but only autonomy, indispensible for a nation
possessing its own language and culture...With a full voice,
we declare that we unanimously accept the Polish demand
for autonomy as the only means of solving the Polish question, and as an indispensable condition for a lasting freedom
in all of Russia.[47]

On 6 November, two days after the Russo-Polish rally in
Petersburg, the Sixth Zemstvo-Municipal Congress convened in the
Moscow home of the Dolgorukovs. By unanimous vote, Ivan Petrunkevich was proclaimed president.[48] A large Polish delegation was present, and its members were prepared to make sure that this assembly
did not retreat from earlier zemstvoist resolutions on Poland.[49]

On 8 November, Franciszek Nowodworski was the first Pole to
speak on the issue of autonomy. He described the situation in Poland
under martial law, painting a picture of government-sponsored violence. Despite government oppression, he argued, Poles only wanted
autonomy, adding emphatically that "not one party in the Polish
Kingdom aims at separation, for the separation of Poland from
Russia."[50] In support of his fellow Pole, Lednicki added that

the representatives of the Polish Kingdom consider here not
a Polish question, but a Russian, a state-wide question. The
measures taken here seem important, not only from the
point of view of Poles, but also from an all-Russian point of
view. This speaker has just returned from Poland, having
gone around the entire country, and is able to attest that all
political parties there steadfastly speak out for unity with
Russia. Not only representatives of the national party...but
even all extreme parties, the Social Democratic and
Socialist Revolutionary, stand for the unity of the state.
Representatives of all parties, beginning with the extreme
right and ending with the extreme left, arrive at the unanimous conclusion that at the present time it is not possible to
speak about the creation of a true state. In Poland there is a
liberation movement, as in Russia. This movment is not

only all-Russian, but universal....The politics of the government is clear: it says, that the Polish nation did not deserve its trust, that...the autocracy considers itself the source of all authority and order. In the last session of the Council of Ministers it was even directly stated, that the Polish Kingdom will not receive autonomy. To receive or not—this is not to be decided by the present government, but by the constituent assembly of the people....The representatives of Poland appeal to the Russian people, to Russian society.[51]

Lednicki later repeated his standard argument that no Polish party was actively fomenting an armed uprising. He defended all Polish parties from these charges, including the Socialists and the National Democrats. But Lednicki was most heated in his defense of the ZPD platform, stating that his party stood for "social reform, progress and democracy" and clearly saw "the future of Poland in a free union with Russia, in union with all the other nationalities of the Russian state."[52] Martial law was simply not needed, he protested, for Poles contemplated neither rebellion nor separation from Russia.[53]

In reality, Lednicki asserted, Poles anxiously sought to renew and strengthen their ties to Russia. Only in a relationship with Russia, he maintained, could Poles find refuge from German aggression. He argued that

only the strong and free hand of the Russian nation is able to support us and to conquer those, who are our national enemies...Surely today there is not a Pole who does not understand that the main danger for the country is not this nation which lifts itself from bondage, which in its possession already has vast territories, but that...which must clear a path for itself to the right and left with its elbows, in order to preserve and improve its position...."[54]

Lednicki was also concerned that the tsarist regime would use this German threat to its advantage. Indeed, he and others at the congress accused the government—in particular, Warsaw Governor-General Skalon—of spreading rumors of a German invasion, thereby providing a pretext for applying martial law.[55] Lednicki feared that the Russian public would believe government propaganda, and support the continuation of martial law in the Kingdom.[56] Ironically, it was Dmowski who instigated these rumors of a German attack: he feared that Poles would eventually give up on efforts to gain autonomy from the unyielding tsarist regime and turn to Germany for help.

While the Polish issue had provoked considerable discussion at the zemstvo gathering, nothing yet had been said about the fate of other nationalities. On 9 November, the fourth day of the proceedings, other non-Russian representatives complained about the "preferential treatment" Poles were receiving. Delegate Abramov from Stavropol' wondered aloud: "Why does the resolution speak only about the lifting of martial law in Poland, but does not mention the Caucasus?"[57] The Georgian Tavegeradze also argued for more debate on the issue of autonomy for his homeland, and the congress received telegrams from the Caucasus demanding a resolution calling for an end to the oppressive policies of the central government.[58] Delegate Faibishevich from Vladikavkaz pushed the matter even further: "Why demand autonomy only for Poland, and fail to mention the Caucasus?"[59] But the Russian zemstvoists were intent on discussing only the Polish question, not the nationalities question in general.

It was not just other non-Russians who complained about the preferential treatment received by Poles. Aleksandr Guchkov argued in much the same tenor as he had in September, reiterating his opposition to Polish autonomy. He supported martial law and challenged the statements of Lednicki and others, maintaining that it was introduced for good reason: "[I]n Poland there is an armed uprising."[60] Despite catcalls, Guchkov continued, stating that although the government might be using force, the "violence began from the side of the revolutionaries. If one speaks about protection, then one ought to be protected from both sides."[61] Prince E. Trubetskoi rebuffed these charges, and warned that "martial law...always strengthens the significance of extreme parties. Let us reach out to our Polish comrades, let us give them a helping hand and counsel the government to lift martial law in Poland!"[62]

Representing Kowno, Tadeusz Wróblewski also defended the Polish position; his speech was reported in the press as "the culminating moment in the debate" on Polish autonomy.[63] Closely following Lednicki's line of thought, he argued that the Russian revolution was a struggle for the rights of all peoples, and that "these same people, who are prepared to cut us off from you and from this very liberation movement, stand for martial law in Poland, against its autonomy."[64] Lednicki was one of the last persons to speak that day, reading from telegrams he had just received from the Kingdom that protested tsarist policies.[65]

Two days later Fedor Kokoshkin presented the organizational bureau's resolutions on Poland. He reminded the assembly that in September the zemstvoists had delineated clearly their attitude on this question: the final decision on the exact details of the autonomous system of the Kingdom would have to be left to a national constituent assembly. Repeating the now familiar refrain, the bureau opined that Poles had no desire to separate from Russia, but merely wanted autonomy. Therefore, Kokoshkin added, there was no need for martial law.[66]

Petr Struve, a member of the bureau, spoke out in favor of Polish autonomy. Like many others who addressed the assembly, he pandered to feelings of Slavic unity, explaining that while "martial law is applauded in Berlin, we mourn it. Polish autonomy provokes tears in Berlin, but we, Russia and Poland, we must greet it as a great holiday for Slavic peoples."[67] Petr Dolgorukov also expressed hope that the "great Slavic idea" of a unified Slavdom would become a reality. He testified that he personally "had studied the situation in Poland...read the programs of all parties...and [was] able to attest that Poland does not think at all about separation from Russia."[68] Sergei Kotliarevskii, historian and member of the Kadet Central Committee, went so far as to insist that "Russian patriotism demands" granting Poland autonomy, for it would "give us the possibility to stand more firmly in relation to Germany."[69]

As at the September zemstvo congress, there were plenty of delegates in November who opposed Polish autonomy. Delegate Bodisko, from Petersburg, argued that if Poland got autonomy, then other regions would clamor for similar treatment. He feared that this would lead to the dissolution of the empire.[70] Nikolai Guchkov, brother of Aleksandr, opposed any rash decision. Although he had participated at Lednicki's Russo-Polish conference in November 1904, and was therefore aware of Polish desires, Guchkov now demanded to know why Poles were suddenly seeking autonomy. "At the start of the liberation movement, one year ago," he testified, "when Polish representatives first appeared at our negotiations, they did not speak about autonomy, but only about the equal rights of nationalities. Now, Polish delegates are demanding autonomy."[71]

Lednicki quickly responded to his colleague, denouncing criticism about the vagueness of Polish demands as patently unfair. Besides, he pointed out, Russian oppositionists were probably less united than their Polish counterparts, who universally supported the demand for autonomy. Recalling the November 1904 conference, he insisted that

> at the very start of the liberation movement, when still in the milieu of Russian society a demand for a constitution had not yet crystallized, representatives of Poland (right fraction) came, putting forward a demand for local self-rule with its own sejm. They even were advised not to use the word "sejm," which might appear frightening to many.[72]

Fedor Kokoshkin supported his friend, asserting that it was "better to lose 1,000 votes in the elections, standing on a constitution and autonomy, than to receive one, going together with the Black Hundreds and '*Moskovskiia vedomosti*.'"[73] He added that acceding to Polish desires was really in the best interests of Russia, because

> without autonomy it is possible to hold Poland in submission only with bayonets. But one must not want freedom for oneself, and bayonets for another. A healthy patriotism... must suggest to us that a free Russia must give autonomy to Poland.[74]

On 12 November, Tadeusz Wróblewski stepped up the rhetoric, warning Russians that "there will not be a peaceful world as long as Poland does not receive autonomy: if we will have bayonets, you will have bayonets...."[75] This speech made a huge impression on the audience. In an attempt to calm Russian nerves, Lednicki quickly followed with a more conciliatory speech.[76]

Several delegates expressed the fear that an autonomous Poland would not protect the rights of non-Poles. Nikolai Guchkov raised the matter of Jewish rights, and his brother, Aleksandr, charged that Poles would mistreat minorities living in the Kingdom.[77] The Ukrainian deputy, I. L. Shrag, held that only in Galicia could Ukrainians find free cultural development. Attempting to counter these arguments, Lednicki pointed out that Jews and Lithuanians suppported autonomy for the Kingdom.[78]

Lednicki urged Russians and Poles to quit fighting one another and concentrate their efforts in opposition to the real enemy, the tsarist bureaucracy. He declared that freedom-loving people should never forget that "the Russian system is despotic, not swerving one bit and progressing with ruthless consequence" in its efforts to suppress freedom everywhere.[79] He denounced the Russian nationalism of the tsarist government as a corruption of the nationalism that developed as a result of the French Revolution. This bastardized version was employed by strong nations to oppress weaker ones—the Germans against the Poles, Hungarians against the Slovaks, etc. Autonomy for Poland, Lednicki reassured his audience, was "not a question of the division of Russia, but the liquidation of aggressive nationalism."[80] But in a statement that must have heightened the concerns of men like Guchkov, Lednicki concluded that Polish autonomy would be "only the first step towards the solution of the national question" in Russia.[81]

The Kadets controlled the deliberations, and Miliukov credited them for pushing through a vote confirming the zemstvoists' September decision on Polish autonomy.[82] The three-point resolution called for: 1) an end to martial law in the Kingdom; 2) that the issue of Polish autonomy, on the condition that the integrity of the Russian state remain intact, would be addressed at the first meeting of the national assembly; 3) the free use of Polish, or other local languages, in the Kingdom. The resolution passed 154–14.[83] Rodichev chided those who voted against the resolution, noting that "all opponents of Polish freedom have also been opposed to Russian freedom, beginning with Novosil'tsev and ending with Katkov."[84] And "without autonomy," Rodichev added, "freedom in Poland was a senseless dream."[85] The zemstvoists emphasized, however, that this did not mean the separation of the Kingdom from Russia. Conversely, the November resolution adamantly maintained that it was "vital for the continued preservation of the integrity and power of the empire" that Poles be granted autonomy.[86]

No doubt energized by the success of the Poles, other nationalities began to clamor for autonomy.[87] A national Lithuanian assembly convened in Wilno from 21–22 November, with some 2,000 persons in attendance. Resolutions included demands for autonomy within ethnograpic Lithuania, with a sejm in Wilno chosen on the basis of the four-tail vote.[88] At the All-Estonian Congress in Tartu (27–29 November), more than 800 delegates gathered to discuss the issue of autonomy. The Estonians passed a resolution calling for national and cultural self-determination.[89]

Most important of all, national minorities were coming together to coordinate their actions. From 19–21 November, the First Convention of the Representatives of the Stateless Nationalities (Autonomists-Federalists) convened in St. Petersburg. Jan Baudouin de Courtenay and the Ukrainian zemstvo activist O. O. Rusov organized the gathering, which was attended by 115 deputies—Poles, Ukrainians, Belorussians, Finns, Estonians, Lithuanians, Latvians, Jews, Georgians, Volga Tatars, Azerbaijanis, Armenians, and Kirghiz. Despite the fact that Russians were barred from the proceedings, de Courtenay stressed that "they, all non-Russians, are also for the unity of Russia and are in no way aiming for its disunity."[90] The assembly set up a 20-member central committee, chaired by de Courtenay. In the First Duma, the Union of Autonomists fraction, led by Lednicki, represented the parliamentary wing of this organization.[91]

By the end of 1905, Lednicki's political machinations had born fruit. Beginning with the Russo-Polish Congress in April, Lednicki coordinated an intense propaganda campaign among Russian liberals for the inclusion of Polish demands in their programs. The zemstvo-municipal congresses provided special occasions: after the November congress, for example, Lednicki hosted a meeting between Polish delegates and members of the Moscow Kadet group.[92] Such efforts were not in vain: the zemstvoists had overwhelmingly approved measures in September and November in favor of Polish autonomy, and the new Kadet party he helped found also called for a restoration of the Polish Kingdom's former status. What's more, Lednicki's political colleagues were defending the Polish cause in the provinces. On 15 November, Dmitrii Shakhovskoi defended the November resolution on Polish autonomy at a provincial zemstvo meeting in Iaroslavl', arguing that "'autonomy' does not mean 'separation', or 'isolation': it is little more than local self-rule, but even less than federalism."[93]

Lednicki's own propaganda efforts mirrored those of his friend. At a presentation in the auditorium of the Historical Museum in Moscow on 17 November, he reassured his Russian audience that Poland did not desire separation from Russia, but rather a strengthened relationship that he believed was possible only through the granting of autonomy.[94] The November zemstvo congress was clearly a major victory for Lednicki,[95] and with the coming year he had great hopes that the forthcoming elections to the First Duma would vault him and his fellow *osvobozhdentsy* into a position of power in the Russian parliament. He firmly believed that the Russian liberals would be empowered to resolve the nationalities problem in a just manner.

ENDNOTES

1. Blobaum, *Rewolucja*, 226.
2. Ibid., 228. In response to widespread unrest and large anti-government demonstrations, martial law had been imposed in Lodz on 11 June and in Warsaw on 10 August.
3. Ibid., 215.
4. Ibid., 215–16.
5. Ibid., 270. Additional troops were sent to the Kingdom to keep the peace; by the end of the year, some 250,000 Russian soldiers were on guard in Poland. See Janus, "Polish Koło," 52.
6. Ibid., 275–77.
7. Micewski, *Roman Dmowski*, 116–19; Janus, "Polish Koło," 52–53; and Blobaum, *Rewolucja*, 227–28.
8. Janus, "Polish Koło," 53.
9. Miliukov, "Aleksander Lednicki jako rzecznik," 32.
10. Ibid., 33.
11. Ibid., 34.

12. A. Lednicki, *Mowy polityczne*, 59.

13. Ibid.

14. Ibid.

15. Ibid., 60–61.

16. Ibid., 61. Once again, Lednicki demonstrated his emphasis on the right to develop one's national culture. Political self-determination was not enough, in his mind, to ensure the survival of a nation, whose soul was embodied in its language and traditions. While Lednicki praised the Social Democrats in 1905 for their views on national self-determination, he later came to despise the Bolshevik regime for its destruction of Polish culture in the *Kresy*. See A. Lednicki, *Nasza polityka*, 43.

17. A. Lednicki, *Mowy polityczne*, 61.

18. Ibid.

19. Ibid., 61–62.

20. Ibid., 64–65.

21. Ibid., 65–66.

22. Ibid., 66.

23. Ibid, 67.

24. Ibid., 67–68.

25. Ibid., 68.

26. Ibid., 71.

27. Ibid., 72–73.

28. Ibid., 73. Lednicki also feared a true social revolution. He hoped that a democratic regime would redress social ills through reform.

29. Ibid., 74.

30. Ibid.

31. Ibid.

32. "Zaiavlenie polskoi advokatury," *Pravo* 45–6 (20 November 1905): 3732–34.

33. *Kraj* 43–45 (1905): 28; A. Lednicki, *Mowy polityczne*, 76. In the Union of Liberation, Annenskii had led the radical wing of Petersburg intellectuals.

34. *Nasha zhizn'*, 9/22 November 1905. Also see Wojciech Bułat, "Sprawa polska w walce rosyjskikh obozów politycznych jesienia 1905 r.," in *Polska-ZSRR: Internacjonalistyczna współpraca—historia i współczesność* (Warsaw: Książka i Wiedza, 1977), 1: 241.

35. A. Lednicki, *Mowy polityczne*, 77. For accounts of this speech, see Miliukov, "Aleksander Lednicki," 35; and *Kraj* 43–5 (1905): 28.

36. A. Lednicki, *Mowy polityczne*, 77.

37. Ibid.

38. Ibid., 78–80.

39. Ibid., 80.

40. Ibid., 81.

41. Ibid., 81–82.

42. Ibid., 82.

43. Ibid., 83.

44. *Nasha zhizn'*, 9/22 November 1905.

45. Zbigniew Baranski, *Literatura polska w rosji na przełomie XIX i XX wieku* (Wrocław: Zakład Narodowy im. Ossolińskich—Wydawnictwo, 1962), 8. See also W. Lednicki, *'Entente cordiale'*, 83.

46. *Nasha zhizn'*, 9/22 November 1905. Also see Bułat, "Sprawa polska," 241–42.

47. Ibid.

48. "S"ezd zemskikh i gorodskikh deiatelei," *Pravo* 44 (13 November 1905): 3601.

49. Twenty-three Polish representatives from the Kingdom and seventeen Poles from the *Kresy* attended. In addition to Lednicki, the most vocal deputies were his fellow Kresy native Tadeusz Wróblewski, the Conciliationist Adolf Suligowski, and the *endek* Franciszek Nowodworski. Also present were the endek Zygmunt Balicki and the Conciliationist Marian Zdziechowski. W. Lednicki, *'Entente cordiale,'* 84–85; also Smolen, "Działalność polityczne," 104.

50. *Pravo* 44 (13 November 1905): 3612.

51. Ibid., 3612–13.

52. A. Lednicki, *Mowy polityczne*, 52–53.

53. Ibid.

54. Ibid., 54.

55. Ibid., 55.

56. Ibid.; also *Pravo* 45–6 (20 November 1905): 3708.

57. *Pravo* 44 (13 November 1905): 3626.

58. Ibid., 3617; 3623.

59. Ibid., 3627.

60. Ibid., 3624.

61. Ibid.

62. Ibid., 3625.

63. *Kurier Polski*, 24 November 1905.

64. *Pravo* 44 (13 November 1905): 3629.

65. *Kurier Polski*, 24 November 1905.

66. *Pravo* 45–6 (20 November 1905): 3705–06.

67. Ibid., 3708.

68. Ibid.

69. Ibid.

70. Ibid., 3711.

71. Ibid.

72. Ibid., 3711–2.

73. Ibid., 3712.

74. Ibid.

75. Ibid., 3716. Maklakov regarded Wróblewski's speech as an "amazing

performance." See Vlast'i obshchestvennost', 45.

76. A. Lednicki, *Mowy polityczne*, 42.

77. *Pravo* 45–6 (20 November 1905): 3711, 3715.

78. A. Lednicki, *Mowy polityczne*, 42.

79. Ibid., 39.

80. Ibid., 43.

81. Ibid., 45.

82. Miliukov, "Aleksander Lednicki jako rzecznik," 34–35.

83. *Pravo* 45–6 (20 November 1905): 3717.

84. Ibid., 3718.

85. Ibid.

86. Miliukov, "Aleksander Lednicki jako rzecznik," 34–35.

87. For example, see "Rezoliutsiia musul'man," *Pravo* 50 (18 December 1905): 4052–53.

88. *Pravo* 51 (24 December 1905): 4134–37.

89. Toivo U. Raun, "1905 As a Turning Point in Estonian History," *East European Quarterly* 14 (1980), no. 3: 328.

90. Miliukov, "Aleksander Lednicki jako rzecznik," 37; and Voskobiynyk, "Nationalities Question in Russia," 215. For a first-hand account of a member of the Union, see Topchibashi, A. M. B., "Soiuz avtonomistov," *Spogadi* 7 (1932): 131–41.

91. Voskobiynyk, "Nationalities Question in Russia," 219–20.

92. *Russkiia vedomosti*, 14 November 1905. Lednicki's actions were widely reported. For example, see *Golos Sibiri*, 4 December 1905.

93. *Severnyi krai*, 20 November 1905.

94. *Russkoe slovo*, 17/30 November 1905. Interestingly, the day before *Russkoe slovo* printed the text of Lednicki's address at the zemstvo congress, because of "outstanding interest" that had been expressed. See *Russkoe slovo* 16/29 November 1905.

95. Lednicki noted the special significance of the November congress in an article he wrote the following spring. See A. R. Lednitskii, "Pol'skii vopros," *Moskovskii ezhenedel'nik* (1906), no. 3: 78.

Chapter Nine

THE CAMPAIGN FOR THE
FIRST DUMA, JANUARY–MAY 1906

At the Second Kadet Congress, held 5–11 January 1906, delegates adopted a resolution on Polish autonomy nearly identical to those approved by zemstvoists at their gatherings in September and November. The party's new program promised that one of the first acts of "an all-Russian democratic assembly" would be "the introduction of an autonomous structure for the Polish Kingdom, with a sejm elected on the same basis as the all-Russian assembly, on the condition that state unity be preserved."[1] Although Lednicki was not at this party congress, the inclusion of a demand for Polish autonomy in the Kadet program represented a great political victory for him, seemingly validating his trust in the Russian *osvobozhdentsy*. Autonomy for the Polish Kingdom was now a main point of a Russian political party's legislative agenda. If debate on this issue was not extensive at the Second Kadet Congress, it was not because the nationalities question was "the most glossed of issues." Debate on this point had been so thorough within the liberal community over the last four months that this measure passed without any opposition.[2]

In general, however, the Kadets assumed a more moderate stance on issues than at their first gathering in October. They retreated from confrontation with the government, no longer demanding a constituent assembly but a "duma with constituent functions." Instead of the old demand for a democratic republic, the delegates added in Article Thirteen that "Russia should be a constitutional and parliamentary monarchy."[3] This rightward swing has been attributed to the horrors of the December Days, during which the threat of a social revolution became all too real.[4] It was during the period between the December uprising and the opening of the First Duma that the so-called "Right Kadets"—led by Struve, Rodichev, Maklakov, Evgenii Trubetskoi, Nikolai L'vov and Sergei Kotliarevskii—were in the ascendancy.[5]

But while these men might have been conservative on the issues of agrarian reform or cooperation with the radical left, they were enthusiastic supporters of Polish autonomy. In an article published in Struve's new journal, *Poliarnaia zvezda* (Polar Star), Kotliarevskii claimed that "of all the features of the [Kadet] program..., perhaps the most original is its section relating to the rights and interests of the various nationalities."[6] He argued that

> only an assembly of popular representatives from the whole Empire based on universal suffrage can decide national-regional questions in a peaceful manner, establishing the autonomy of Poland first of all, and opening a legal road for the formation of other autonomous regions. The Constitutional Democratic Party recognizes just such a path of legal satis-faction of national-regional demands, bowing neither before the cult of deadly unity and centralism, nor before the pres-sure of centrifugal elements. Great political tact is demand-ed in order not to cross the boundary on one side or the other....[7]

The Kadets proved incapable of walking this political tightrope. Rather than pleasing everyone, they pleased noone, and critics from the left and right wasted no time in attacking them on the nationali-ties issue. *Russkaia mysl'* complained that "several points of the [Kadet] program remained open, and others were not clearly expressed," including the exact nature of Polish autonomy.[8] Lednicki's fellow Kadet, Pavel Dolgorukov, later reflected on the Kadet quandary. Writing during the Russian Civil War, Dolgorukov recalled that

> the party of Popular Freedom [Constitutional Democrats] was often accused of the un-nationalism of its politics.

> Short-sighted or biased critics to the right said that we were
> cosmopolitans, that we were not a Russian party on account
> of our professed equality of rights of nationalities. They said
> that we would cause the disintegration of the state through
> our granting of regional autonomy.[9]

In truth, the Kadets were eager to disseminate their message throughout the borderlands. The party leadership was well aware of the importance of the non-Russian vote, especially in areas deemed "progressive." At a Central Committee meeting on 14 November, Tadeusz Wróblewski had pointed out that while there were almost no Russian Kadets in the Western regions, there were many progressive democrats. He urged the Kadets to woo them for the upcoming elections.[10] The party turned to Lednicki for help on this matter, dispatching him to proselytize among *Kresy* Poles. Shortly after the end of the November zemstvo congress, Lednicki travelled to Warsaw. There, on 24 November, he spoke at a ZPD rally, informing his comrades that the Kadet party would support Polish rights in the Duma.[11]

In the winter of 1905–06 the Kadets strove to inform the general public throughout the empire of their nationalities policy. At a meeting of the Kadet Central Committee on 12 January 1906, Leon Petrazicki was assigned the task of supervising the translation of the party program into almost a dozen languages, including German, Yiddish, Armenian, Buriat and Mongol.[12] Ten days later, the Central Committee resolved to publish for free distribution 10,000 copies of Fedor Kokoshkin's plan for autonomy entitled "On the Rights of Nationalities." Members of the Central Committee were dispatched to the provinces for agitation; Leon Petrazicki, for example, went to Minsk, while Maksim Vinaver travelled to Wilno.[13]

These actions conformed to the recommendations of V. M. Gessen, who at the Second Kadet Congress had delivered a report entitled "On the Technical Aspects of the Electoral Struggle." Gessen maintained that the party had two main goals: to attract as many members as possible through agitation, and to disseminate Kadet ideas in the press and at public meetings featuring the best speakers. Even before Gessen urged this action, Vasilii Maklakov had established a course to train young party speakers. After Gessen's report, the Central Committee organized more classes on public speaking: in Moscow, Maklakov took the lead, while Tyrkova-Vil'iams and Lomshakov organized them in Petersburg. Also, agitation courses were set up in Moscow and St. Petersburg. In time, the lecture bureaus sent the best speakers on tours around the country. These appearances were often major events in the election campaigns in the borderlands.[14]

The party developed a questionnaire that was distributed to each member; it asked whether the individual would want to "agitate" for the party and in which areas he or she would feel most competent.[15] Lednicki was pegged as a specialist on the nationalities problem, one who could help spread the Kadet message in the *Kresy*. Indeed, the questionnaire specifically asked whether the party member would be willing to go on missions to the provinces.[16] Lednicki did travel to the western territories,[17] not only proselytizing for the Kadets but also preaching his message of concerted action in the struggle against the tsarist regime. He worked tirelessly for the Kadet cause in the *Kresy*, enabling the party to gain a foothold in the region. In elections to the First Duma, the party was able to win several seats.

While the party as a whole was drifting to the right, Lednicki was becoming more radical, a "Left-Kadet": a non-Russian professional, as distinct from the Russian zemstvoists who led the right faction of the party. Leaders of the left wing included Vladimir Gessen, Maksim Vinaver, and Mikhail Mandel'shtam—all Jews—and Aleksandr Koliubakin. In his report on tactics at the Second Kadet Congress, Vinaver advocated the party continue to ally itself with the left, an idea that Lednicki readily supported.[18]

While Lednicki remained a radical democrat and never embraced fully the beliefs and tactics of the Socialists, he did not refrain from contact with leftist revolutionaries. For him, the most important political criterion in his determination of allies was advocacy of equal rights and self-determination for all peoples. Like many Left Kadets, Lednicki associated with terrorists who were using distasteful methods to overthrow the autocracy. Members of the Union of Liberation had often provided refuge for terrorists, and had lent financial support to SRs as well.[19] Lednicki recounted in his memoirs how he hid a Georgian revolutionary fleeing tsarist authorities during the December

Uprising in Moscow. He frequently gave legal aid to political prisoners, at times working extensively behind the scenes and calling on friends in the government to gain their release.[20]

In October 1905, a radical Pole named Julian Klukowski, with whom Lednicki was on friendly terms, asked him for help in liberating three members of the PPS being held in Butyrka Prison in Moscow. They were on a hunger strike, and Klukowski was concerned for their health. Lednicki did not hesitate. There was no question of ideology here: Poles were in need, and that was all any patriot needed to know.[21] He called on long-time friends in the local government, the procurator A. V. Stepanov and the underprocurator Rudniev. Through their intervention he convinced the Moscow Governor-General to free the prisoners.[22]

At this point negotiations bogged down, for the men insisted that some twenty other Poles held at the Butyrka Prison also be released. Again, Lednicki was able to win their freedom. However, they in turn refused to leave unless their benefactor promised to come back the next day and plea for the liberation of their fellow revolutionaries from the Caucasus: Georgians, Ossetians, Ingushi and Armenians. In all, Ledicki used his clout to free over fifty political prisoners from Butyrka in a matter of days. He also arranged for their care and housing as well as their return home.[23]

Lednicki later explained his aid to revolutionaries by noting that he regarded political differences as less important than solidarity in the battle against the tsarist regime.[24] Yet this does not fully explain his regular—at times intimate—contact with extremists. On the night of 13 January 1906, for example, fifteen SR and SD activists—including the chairman of the Moscow SR committee and members of the party's Battle Organization—were arrested at the Lednicki home on the Arbat. Authorities also seized copies of revolutionary brochures and fake passports.[25]

In fact, Lednicki had earned a reputation as a radical revolutionary. In late 1905 he was informed by a friend with police connections that his home was targeted for attack by Black Hundred thugs. The threat was confirmed when right-wing extremists branded the Lednicki house as the residence of an anti-government activist by painting three crosses on its front door. Lednicki's family was spared any violence, however, when his goodwill to the Caucasian political prisoners was reciprocated: he was reassured by Georgian revolutionaries that his home would be protected.[26] Other leading Kadets were also threatened bodily harm by the Black Hundreds. Ivan Petrunkevich noted in a letter to his son, dated 21 January 1906, that he had "already been sentenced to death several times by various 'patriotic' parties, which interpret patriotism as meaning a return to the old regime."[27]

Lednicki's leftist sympathies soon became well known in the *Kresy*. During the spring 1906 election campaign, several members of the Minsk nominating committee feared Lednicki's "radical" politics, and vehemently opposed his candidacy.[28] By this time the government had grown weary of his clandestine activities, and in February the minister of justice issued a warrant for his arrest. Once again, the Moscow Procurator A. V. Stepanov came to the rescue. He warned Lednicki's wife to inform her husband of the dangerous situation: if he returned to Moscow, he would face imprisonment. She immediately passed on the message, and Lednicki thus spent much of his time in Minsk until after the April elections.[29]

While government officials targeted Lednicki as a "radical" who had long participated in underground activities, their immediate cause for concern was the publication in *Prawda* of a speech he delivered at Zakopane on 22 January 1906. Commemorating the anniversary of the January Uprising, Lednicki called on Poles to listen once again to the "bell of liberation, which summons subjegated peoples to a common struggle for freedom."[30] He now spoke of the Russian revolution as a continuation of the French Revolution, truly a "new stage in the development of mankind."[31] He touted the liberating nature of the revolution, claiming that "liberty, equality of all people and peoples...the defense of minority rights—this is one of the factors of the contemporary revolution."[32] He continued to express Slavophile sympathies, urging Poles to turn to the Russian people for help in gaining freedom. Lednicki once again warned Poles that they should not rely on Western aid as they had for the past century, but rather should beware the "treachery and hypocrisy of the West."[33] Condemning narrow nationalism, Lednicki quoted Mickiewicz in calling for a universal battle against oppression: "He who speaks of the interests of only one nation is an enemy of freedom."[34]

For the publication of this speech, Lednicki was charged with a violation of paragraph 129 of the criminal code, which prohibited the publication of inflammatory remarks. In the end, he was fined 2,000 rubles, the editors of the paper 3,000. Lednicki later bitterly recalled that "it was clear that the whole affair aimed only at my removal from the elections."[35] In fact, Kadet candidates were targeted by the government in order to prevent the election of the most popular—and dangerous—candidates to the Duma. When candidates were apprehended, they were tried under the provisions of "extraordinary" legislation.[36] This was another example of the bureaucratic lawlessness so despised by Lednicki and his fellow *osvobozhdentsy*.

Lednicki had delivered another key political speech at the Slavonic Club in Kraków on 20 January. Together with the Zakopane address, these speeches constituted what one scholar has called "an [electoral] campaign conducted without any personal aim, devoid of egoist interest," aimed at bringing together the democratic elements in the Russian and Polish progressive movements.[37] In his emotional Slavonic Club address entitled "The December Days in Moscow," Lednicki described the events of the bloody uprising in Moscow. He argued that the upheaval in Russia threatened to bring about not only political change but also social transformation. He was convinced that social problems, not just issues of parochial interest, had to be addressed. He warned his audience that "neither the government nor the revolution are a creative force, but contain only ruin and destruction...."[38]

The December Days undoubtedly precipitated Lednicki's pessimism. His fear of the wrath of the masses was not unique, however, for other Kadets had also come to realize the potential dangers of revolution.[39] Lednicki knew that revolution could degenerate into anarchy, which would destroy "not only [material] possessions, but also cultural property...libraries and works of art."[40] Lednicki's fear of the masses and the threat of *buntarstvo* grew over the years. At a social gathering shortly after the February Revolution in 1917, friends and family members related to him how happy they were that the revolution was peaceful and orderly. He replied that while he did not know what had transpired in Moscow, in St. Petersburg—during his tenure in the Provisional Government he had an office in the Winter

Palace—there had been considerable mayhem. He shuddered at the thought of a revolution unleashed: "I know the element of anarchy and destructive spirit of the Russian peasantry!"[41]

Largely because he was unwelcome Moscow, Lednicki sought to represent his native *Kresy* in the First Duma. Still, he remained active in Kadet affairs in Moscow. He was scheduled to deliver an address on the Polish question at a local Kadet meeting on 2 February, but just as he was prepared to talk the local police inspector closed down the meeting.[42] Lednicki successfully delivered this address on 26 February. As usual, he stressed Poles' historic struggle against the oppressive Russian government. Poles, he argued, were fighting with the Russian people for the mutual freedom of both nations.[43] Later, during the week of 20–25 March, Lednicki spoke at election rallies in Moscow.[44] In addition, he was a generous benefactor to the party.[45]

The Kadets were undoubtedly pleased to place such a prominent figure on their list in Minsk. Lednicki later recalled that he "went to Minsk after the first of February for self-orientation in the situation."[46] His main goal was "to convince Poles of the necessity of voting in solidarity with other nationalities," an electoral strategy that made good political sense in a region populated mainly by non-Poles. This was not an easy task, for chauvinistic attitudes were common.[47]

While Lednicki ran as a Kadet candidate in Minsk, he did so with the blessing of the ZPD. That party had boycotted the elections until December 1905, when martial law was briefly lifted. When it was reinstated shortly thereafter, the party decided to continue its half-hearted campaign. Polish progressives tried to please too many people—the Socialists who advocated a total boycott as well as the moderates who sought to participate in the Duma—and paid dearly for their vacillation at the polls.[48] Lednicki would be the only member of the ZPD ever elected to the Russian parliament, and he technically was a Kadet candidate.[49]

Lednicki stood for election in the Minsk urban curia, where he owned property. His liberationist rhetoric appealed to the urban constituency of free professionals, intellectuals, and non-Poles (especially Jews). The landed gentry, however, were most concerned with the issue of land reform. The Kadet policy of forced expropriation—albeit with compensation—did not set well with them, nor did

Lednicki's reputation as a radical activist. In the city, this trait was not a hindrance but an advantage.

Lednicki recalled that the voters in the city of Minsk were "about 1/7 Russian; 2/7 or perhaps fewer, Poles; and the rest Jews."[50] Jews may have dominated the city, but landowners and peasants carried more weight in the electoral system, because the government deemed them to be more sympathetic voters. But neither landowners nor peasants could alone gain a majority in Minsk province, and their conflict of interests prevented any cooperation between the two groups, especially because the Orthodox Belorussian peasants regarded the Catholic Polish landlords as aliens. If the Jews could reach an understanding with either the Polish landowners or Belorussian peasants, they would still manage to gain seats in the Duma. With the peasants hostile to both the Polish gentry and the Jews, the latter groups joined forces in the electoral process.[51] Lednicki was uniquely equipped to forge this alliance, for he had support among progressive Polish landowners and Jews.

In March, Lednicki advised Polish activists in Minsk that cooperation with the Jews was the only way to win the election. A nonpartisan election committee composed of Jews and Poles of all political groups—liberals, conservatives and National Democrats—was established in Minsk. There was some Polish-Jewish conflict, as Jews resented the liberals not addressing their concerns fully. The election committee induced some Jewish leaders to cooperate, however, in "reducing the national antagonism, improving mutual relations, and strengthening the old traditions of the mutual work of Jews through Polish social institutions."[52]

There were three stages to the Minsk city elections. Voters first chose seven electors; then, these electors chose two "standing electors" to represent the city in the general election. Finally, in the general election all electors in the province chose nine delegates to the Duma from among standing electors from all curiae.[53] In the urban curia, Lednicki engineered a compromise: of the seven electors, two would be Polish, four Jewish, and one Russian. Lednicki was guaranteed a position as standing elector, for Jews trusted him and knew of his reputation for defending their rights. The other standing elector was to be a Jew. Lednicki promised to use his influence to get that person elected to the Duma, but he warned that he would make no promises concerning the general election.[54]

Aided by the Polish-Jewish alliance and Kadet propaganda, Lednicki had thus won the support of Minsk urban voters, but he had to work behind the scenes with provincial power brokers to win the general election. In a move to gain the support of other electors, he turned to Edward Woyniłłowicz, the long-time president of the Minsk Agricultural Society. The Society had long been a center of Polish resistance to russification in the *Kresy*; in defiance of a government prohibition, it used the Polish language at its meetings and in its correspondence. Agricultural societies had sprung up after 1863 to fill a void; before 1911 there were no zemstva in the region. Although established as instruments for greater Russian influence in the *Kresy*, the societies were "ninety percent dominated by a Polish element" and served as centers of "Polish culture and Polish spirit."[55] As head of the Minsk Agricultural Society, Woyniłłowicz was perhaps the most influential Pole in the province.

Lednicki was not yet widely known among Poles in Minsk. He did have a reputation, however, as a friend to any Pole in need of moral or material support. Moreover, his "phenomenal legal career, as well as his political activities...were often the subjects of discussion" among *Kresy* Poles.[56] Lednicki first came to Woyniłłowicz's attention through his political work in the spring of 1906, when he impressed audiences with his understanding of the needs of *Kresy* Poles. After personal consultations, Woyniłłowicz asked Lednicki to stand as "his candidate" in the upcoming election.[57] Lednicki regarded the relationship with Woyniłłowicz as a natural one: "[T]his humanist aspired, like me, to peace between nationalities."[58]

Woyniłłowicz presented his candidate to the Minsk Agricultural Society and Lednicki addressed the gathering. One witness later recalled how the audience listened with great interest to Lednicki's speech, which he "delivered with rarely seen erudition."[59] The atmosphere was charged with the anticipation of change: those assembled put great faith in the elections and hoped that the First Duma would grant broad concessions. While most spoke of gaining greater cultural freedom, some were hopeful that they might "even win independence."[60] Lednicki's oratical style served him well in such an environment. One colleague, who heard several of Lednicki's campaign speeches, recalled that

> the political speeches of A. R. [Lednicki], almost always lyrical, very often on a Russo-Polish theme, produced a very strong impression on the listener. The strength of these speeches was not in the logic; his manner and style as an orator lay not in a psychological obsequiousness, but always in a strong and magnificent spirit, the impression from which was especially strong thanks indeed to his splendid voice.[61]

In return for the Society's backing, Lednicki pledged not to push for the compulsory expropriation of land even though that was part of the Kadet program.[62]

Challenges to Lednicki's candidacy took various forms and came from several camps. Some regarded him as a Socialist, while others considered him to be an alien, since he was a member of a Russian party. Adam Lenkiewicz, a former colleague at Moscow University, opposed Lednicki's nomination on the grounds that he represented urban interests and had no understanding of the plight of Polish landowners in the *Kresy*. Members of the Union of Russian People charged that Lednicki was ineligible because he was wanted for arrest in Moscow. It was mainly the National Democrats, however, who tried to block Lednicki's nomination. To counter his opponents, Lednicki called on his many friends from his gymnasium and university days, as well as moderate Realists with whom he had relations since the first Russo-Polish conference in November 1904. Above all, it was the crucial support of Woyniłłowicz that enabled Lednicki to overcome the opposition to his candidacy.[63]

His connections with the Church hierarchy also helped. Lednicki believed that the "Catholic Church was the great Polish hotbed, not only religious but also socio-political."[64] He was proven correct, for in the electoral campaign the Church played an integral role. Lednicki wrote in his diary that

> from the pulpits, priests exhorted their people to participate actively in the election [and] explained its significance....

Indeed, the Catholic Church could be proud of the excellence of its chaplains. Words of supreme truth, healing perennial wounds, streamed from the lips of our priests.[65]

The most politically active Catholic clergyman was undoubtedly Lednicki's friend Baron Edward von Ropp, Bishop of Wilno. On 7 February 1906, he founded the Constitutional-Catholic Party in Lithuania and Belorus (Stronnictwa Konstytucyjno-Katolickiego na Litwe i Białorus) in Wilno. The party's program called for a united front made up of all peoples, so that even a huge state such as the Russian empire would have to reckon with the national minorities' demands.[66] Ropp sought a common ground for different nationalities in the *Kresy* to come together in working for reform. The party maintained that the common bond of Catholicism would unite the peoples of the *Kresy* in a joint struggle to topple the tsarist regime. The party's program claimed that "practically all Poles and Lithuanians and a large part of Belorussians living in our country are Catholics. This belief, alongside our joint historical past, is our strongest and most efficacious" weapon in fighting tsarism.[67] The party urged Catholics to consider their commonality when casting ballots in the upcoming elections to the Duma: "Our folk," it pointed out, "will want to choose good Catholics as deputies...."[68]

Bishop Ropp was particularly sensitive to the desires of the local non-Polish population. Elected to the first Duma, he refused to join the *Endecja*-dominated Polish Koło, because "he was apprehensive lest Polish methods repel other nationalities such as the Lithuanians or Byelorussians."[69] Ropp had long been sympathetic to Belorussian cultural aspirations and recognized the needs of other nationalities. Like Lednicki, Ropp sought to mobilize all peoples of the *Kresy*.

Another member of Lednicki's clique from the *Kresy* was Prince Hieronim Drucki-Lubecki. Possessor of vast estates, he became a convert to Christian socialism and in the First Duma pushed for regional control over the redistribution of land.[70] Drucki-Lubecki was a key activist in Kadet politics during the first months of the party's existence and a member of the Moscow chapter's organizational bureau.[71] He also served as envoy for the Kadet Central Committee in the Minsk area. Throughout the spring and summer of 1906, especially during the election campaign, he corresponded frequently with party headquarters. His letters, which were forwarded to Lednicki for his appraisal, repeatedly warned of the danger of the Union of Russian People; that organization had established cells in Minsk and other cities in the *Kresy*.[72] Radical Russian nationalists were a major concern for the party during the first electoral campaign in early 1906, for they threatened to use violence against Kadet candidates in the western borderlands.[73]

It was not only the *Kresy* Poles who rallied around the Kadet banner in the first national elections. The party program, which after the second party congress promised to make Polish autonomy a major issue in the Duma, attracted Poles throughout the empire. Warsaw progressives hailed the party's stand on the decentralization issue, noting approvingly that "the KD vision lies between the absolutist ideal of a federated Slavic state and a socialist utopia."[74] In late February, leaders of the Polish Electoral Committee in St. Petersburg reminded their compatriots that "the long awaited moment draws near," and that Poles should take the elections seriously and cast their votes for the party that would best serve Polish interests in the Duma.[75] The committee—which included the Lednicki allies Aleksander Babianski and Aleksander Więckowski—urged Poles to vote for candidates of the Kadet party, the first party to proclaim "the motto of autonomy."[76]

The St. Petersburg committee promised Poles that they would have a hand in choosing Kadet candidates for the Duma. Poles were urged to forget petty political differences and vote as a bloc for Kadet candidates. The circular argued that "in Petersburg, we have only one goal—the defense of our national rights—a joint goal for all of us."[77]

Thanks in part to support from national minorities throughout the empire, the Kadets won a plurality of seats in the First Duma.[78] From 22–25 April 1906, just one week before the Duma convened, the Kadets held their third congress, known as the "Congress of Victors." The electoral victory made many delegates ebullient, and talk was in the air about the real changes that were in store for Russia. Even the generally moderate Rodichev proclaimed that "we go to the Duma conscious of our strength, conscious that behind it stands the might of Russia."[79] Miliukov posed the question on everyone's mind: "Has the revolution in Russia come to an end already, or is it still in progress?"[80]

Believing that the revolution was just beginning, delegates from the provinces pushed for further commitment to a just solution of the nationalities question. While the Kadets debated this and other matters, the government issued the Fundamental Laws, which curtailed the powers of the Duma. This only served to further radicalize the Kadets, tilting the Third Congress to the left. The Kadets took a more aggressive stand, renewing the old demand for a secret, direct, universal and equal vote for all citizens, including women; a radical agricultural reform project; full amnesty for political prisoners; abolition of capital punishment; a parliamentary inquiry into government actions since 17 October; and satisfaction of the demands of national minorities.[81]

Lednicki warned the assembly that the party had to address the nationalities question in order to fulfill promises it had made at the Second Congress in January. He fully expected his fellow Kadets in the Duma to act quickly on the Polish issue. In pursuit of this goal, he called on the party to create a parliamentary commission for the elaboration of a statement on the nationalities question, and in particular the matter of Polish autonomy.[82] Others argued that the nationalities should be better represented on the Central Committee. Prince Shakhovskoi called for a restructuring of that body to include some of the Kadets recently elected to the Duma as well as representatives from the borderlands.[83] As a result, Lednicki—who was both a non-Russian and a member of the party's delegation to the Duma—was coopted into the Central Committee. A founder of the party and a radical democrat, Lednicki symbolized the Kadet party in the heady days before the opening of the First Duma: multinational, radical, and confident of success.[84]

By the spring of 1906 Lednicki had attained a level of political influence he would not reach again until February 1917, when his fellow *osvobozhdentsy* assumed control of the government upon the tsar's abdication. With his great political prestige Lednicki was able to create two more organizations in 1906, one parliamentary fraction consisting of deputies from the nine Western provinces, and a second, the Union of Autonomists, which was open to all deputies interested in the nationalities question. On 26 April, the day before the Duma opened, the Polish deputies held a joint meeting devoted to the creation of a common Polish parliamentary group. Differences among the delegates were too great, however, and the representatives from the *Kresy* resolved to establish a separate "Group of Deputies from the Western Regions." This group, often referred to as the Territorial Circle or Territorialists, was composed of *Kresy* Poles who refused to join the Polish Koło.[85] They argued that, because they were not elected solely by Poles, they could not represent exclusively Polish interests but the concerns of their entire constituency.[86]

Scholars have explained this move by Lednicki and the *Kresy* Poles differently. Zygmunt Lukawski, for example, argued that these Poles feared joining the Koło lest Russian nationalists accuse them of harboring separatist tendencies.[87] Actually, Polish nationalists were the most vocal critics of the *Kresy* Poles: the National Democrats accused deputies from Minsk and Wilno—Lednicki, Ropp, Skirmunt and Massonius—of "extremely pernicious separatism" and secretly plotting to separate from Russia and Poland.[88] Lednicki's role in the creation of the *Kresy* group angered those Polish nationalists who opposed cooperation with non-Poles. They believed that Polish politicians should concentrate on Polish affairs and not bother with the national yearnings of other peoples in the empire—especially those in the *Kresy* who resented Polish cultural and economic domination of the region. Roman Dmowski and other National Democrats singled out Lednicki as the "mastermind of organizational strategy and political philosophy for the Territorialists."[89] Dmowski was correct on this point: Lednicki did formulate the group's tactical program for the new parliamentary fraction. He told his fellow *Kresy* Poles that

> in spite of the fact that it would be easier and more pleasant for us to organize in the name of nationality, nevertheless we must not do this. If we unite in the name of nationality, that will undermine our position in the country; we will become defenders of a minority and lose the confidence of our electors and consequently our mandates. We must unite only territorially and in our parliamentary programs defend the needs of our entire country. Let the people see in us Poles, but only those who are defending the principles of universal freedom—so that we can better defend the national cause.[90]

This manifesto clearly identified the Territorialist Circle as yet another means for Lednicki to attain his fundamental political goal: a democratic, federated Russia composed of autonomous units in which peoples could freely develop their own national cultures and ways of life.

Signed by 18 *Kresy* deputies to the First Duma on 4 May 1906, the program of the Territorialists was the most concise statement of Lednicki's political philosophy. Emphasizing the uniqueness of the *Kresy*, the program noted that

> taking into account the ethnographic, cultural and economic peculiarities of the Western regions, and also the community of spiritual and material interests of the local populations, the popular representatives of the aforesaid regions deem it necessary to unite for solidarity in parliamentary activities.[91]

The ten-point program called for the following reforms:

1) The establishment of a constitutional and parliamentary system on democratic bases.

2) The freedoms of conscience, speech and press; the right of assembly and the right to form unions; and the inviolability of person and home.

3) Full equality of rights for all citizens without distinction of confession, nationality or estate.

4) Constitutional guarantees of the right of national minorities to cultural self-determination.

5) Broad local self-rule, as a transitional step to an autonomous system within limits defined by the local population, on the condition of the sanctity of state unity. A universal, equal, direct, secret and proportional electoral vote.

6) The right to use local languages on an equal footing with the state [language] in administration, courts, schools, public and social institutions.

7)   Universal compulsory free instruction on the basis of equality of all local languages. Fulfilling compulsory military service, as far as possible, in one's home district.

8)   Freedom of internal church administration.

9)   A resolution of the agrarian problem on the bases of... improvement, regulation and expansion of peasant land-ownership, including obligatory alienation (with compensation) if needed.

10) The organization of a conciliatory chamber for the resolution of disputes between employers and workers, both agricultural as well as industrial.[92]

This encapsulated the main tenets of Lednicki's political ideology: democratism and a deep concern for the rights of all national minorities and a social activism that at times wed him to a radical agenda.

Lednicki's cooperation with the radicals is best revealed by his actions during the last days of the Duma. In a demonstration of solidarity with the Left, Lednicki broke ranks with his fellow Kadets on the issue of a proclamation to the people and supported the planned appeal to the nation. Joined by Socialists and *Trudoviki*, he urged the populace to disregard any government action on the issue of agricultural reform. The strongly-worded declaration called on peasants to instead wait for the Duma to resolve the matter.[93] Lednicki's support of the declaration even merited the approval of V. I. Lenin:

[T]he 'Left' trend...was in favor of explaining to the people that they cannot 'wait peacefully and passively,' and was therefore in favor of a revolutionary and not a 'pacifying' appeal. The views of this last trend were most vividly expressed by the Trudovik Zhilkin, the Polish deputy Lednitsky and the Social-Democrat Ramishvili.[94]

The Bolshevik leader applauded "the correct ideas expressed by Ramishvili, Zhilkin and Lednitsky."[95]

Lednicki's actions in the First Duma may have gained the ephemeral approval of the Left, but it angered the conservative Polish gentry in the *Kresy* who had lent him crucial support in the general election. In the end, his attempt to bring together various special interest groups into a united political movement would prove futile.

ENDNOTES

1. Raymond Pearson, ed. and intro., *Vtoroi Vserossiiskii S"ezd Konstitutsionno-Demokraticheskoi Partii 5–11 Ianvaria 1906 g.* (White Plains, New York: Kraus International Publications, 1986), 25.

2. In his introduction to a recent reprint of the resolutions of the second congress, Pearson gives the Kadets little credit on this point. In addition, he incorrectly asserts that there was "no Polish delegate at the Congress," even though the record clearly shows the eminent legal scholar Leon Petrażicki represented St. Petersburg. Also, de Courtenay reported to the congress on the proceedings of the first congress of autonomists. See *Vtoroi Vserossiiskii S"ezd*, xxxiv.

3. Emmons, *Formation of Political Parties*, 55; also see Abraham Ascher, *Revolution of 1905*, vol. 2, *Authority Restored* (Stanford: Stanford University Press, 1992), 36–37.

4. Emmons, *Formation of Political Parties*, 55–58.

5. Richard Pipes, *Struve: Liberal on the Right, 1905–1944* (Cambridge, MA and London: Harvard University Press, 1980), 15–18; also Pearson, *Vtoroi Vserossiiskii S"ezd*, xxxviii-xxxix.

6. S. Kotliarevskii, "Natsional'no-oblastnoi vopros v programme konstitutsionno-demokraticheskoi partii," *Poliarnaia zvezda* 1 (14 January 1906): 383. Struve published fourteen issues of the journal between December 1905 and February 1906, before authorities shut it down. See Pipes, *Liberal on the Right*, 18–21.

7. Kotliarevskii, "Natsional'no-oblastnoi vopros," 386–87; translation by Zimmerman, "Between Revolution and Reaction," 167.

8. V. L., "Vnutrennee obozrenie," *Russkaia mysl'* 27 (January 1906): 184.

9. Prince Pavel D. Dolgorukov, "Natsional'naia polityka partii Narodnoi Svobody do bol'shevizm," in *Natsional'naia polityka i partiia Narodnoi Svobody* (Rostov na Donu: Svobodnaia Rech', 1919), 5.

10. *Protokoly tsentral'nogo komiteta*, 41.

11. Brykalska, *Aleksander Świętochowski*, 72. Władysław M. Kozłowski, Alojzy Wierzchlejski, and Stanisław Kempner also spoke on behalf of the Kadet party.

12. *Protokoly tsentral'nogo komiteta*, 48; 485, f.n. 99.

13. Ibid., 49–50. Kokoshkin's brochure was apparently scrutinizeded by the censor. See Ibid., 63.

14. Emmons, *Formation of Political Parties*, 156; see also Zimmerman, "Between Revolution and Reaction," 162.

15. GARF, f. 579, op. 1, d. 806a, l. 9.

16. Ibid.

17. In February, for example, he traveled to Smolensk for "agitation meetings." *Riech'*, 24 February/9 March 1906.

18. Pearson, Vtoroi Vserossiiskii S"ezd, xxxix-xl.

19. Geifman, *Thou Shalt Kill*, 210; also see Joseph L. Sanders, *The Moscow Uprising of December, 1905: A Background Study* (New York; London: Garland Publishing, Inc., 1987), 305–18.

20. A. Lednicki, "Z pamiętnika," 40. In his remembrances of his own role in political trials in 1905, M. L. Mandel'shtam recalls Lednicki as a leading defense attorney. See *1905 god v politicheskikh protsessakh. Zapiski zashchitnika*. (Moscow: Izdatel'stvo Politkatorzhan, 1931): 52–3.

21. Throughout his life in Russia, Lednicki was bombarded by such requests. During his tenure as president of the Liquidation Commission, he was inundated with petitions from Poles. See GARF, f. 1041, op. 1, d. 22.

22. A. Lednicki, "Z pamiętnika," 30–37.

23. Ibid.

24. Ibid., 31.

25. GARF, f. 63, op. 26 (1906), d. 300, ll. 18-19. Reports dated 14 January and 14 March. Among the radical propaganda seized were copies of "the revolutionary poem, the 'Marsel'ez'," and the SR brochure, "Bankrotstvo burzhuaznykh idealov" (The Bankruptcy of Bourgeois Ideals).

26. A. Lednicki, "Z pamiętnika," 39–40. Lednicki's reputation as a friend to Georgians led the Georgian National Assembly in Tiflis to grant him the mandate to represent their interests in the First Duma, until elections in that region could be completed. See PIASA, Aleksander Lednicki Collection (006), folder 3. Letters dated 29 April, 4 May, and 8 May 1906.

27. S. Galai, "A Liberal's Vision of Russia's Future, 1905–1914: The Case of Ivan Petrunkevich," in *Russian and East European History: Selected Papers from the Second World Congress for Soviet and East European Studies*, ed. R. C. Elwood. (Berkeley: Berkeley Slavic Specialties, 1984), 105–06.

28. W. Lednicki, *Pamiętniki*, 2 (A. L. *Memoirs*): 533.

29. Ibid., 529–30.

30. A. Lednicki, *Mowy polityczne*, 99.

31. Ibid. Lednicki even referred to the Butyrka Prison in Moscow—from which he had liberated political prisoners—as the "Muscovite Bastille."

32. Ibid., 100.

33. Ibid., 101.

34. Ibid., 100.

35. W. Lednicki, *Pamiętniki*, 2 (A. L. *Memoirs*): 535–36.

36. Emmons, *Formation of Political Parties*, 191–93.

37. Smolen, "Działalność polityczne," 110.

38. A. Lednicki, Mowy polityczne, 95.

39. See Galai, "The Case of Ivan Petrunkevich," 105–06. Galai shows that Petrunkevich was conscious of the "dual polarization" of Russian society; that is, the liberals were isolated from both the government and the masses. In letters to his son, Petrunkevich repeatedly expressed his fear of the *buntarstvo* of the lower classes. Galai drew extensively on Leopold H. Haimson's landmark article, "Dual Polarization in Urban Russia, 1905–1917," *Slavic Review* 23 (1964): 619–42; 24 (1965): 1–22. These articles have been reprinted in *The Russian Revolution and Bolshevik Victory*, ed. Ronald Suny and Arthur Adams (Lexington, MA: D. C. Heath and Company, 1990), 26–49.

40. A. Lednicki, *Mowy polityczne*, 73.

41. W. Lednicki, *Pamiętniki*, 1: 459–60. Late in life, Lednicki still harbored a mistrust for the judgement of the masses. Writing about Polish-German relations in 1931, he noted that "in order to avoid catastrophe and come to an understanding, it is useless to appeal to the reasoning of the 'man in the street,' as he is likely to approach burning political problems only emotionally. The method of logic is not available here..." "Poland and the Corridor." *New York Herald Tribune*, 8 November 1931.

42. *Viestnik Partii Narodnoi Svobody* 1 (26 February 1906): 43.

43. Ibid., 2 (5 March 1906): 111.

44. Ibid., 6 (11 April 1906): 375.

45. Ibid., 3 (12 March 1906): 150. On this occasion, Lednicki donated 100 rubles to the party.

46. W. Lednicki, *Pamiętniki*, 2 (A. L. *Memoirs*): 532.

47. Ibid. Stegner points out that since the PPS was boycotting the elections, a political alliance with Jewish voters presented a logical alternative in Warsaw, too. See *Liberałowie Królestwa Polskiego*, 154–55.

48. Trenam, "Without a Free Poland," 191–92.

49. It is unfair to say, however, that the ZPD "never managed to elect a single candidate." See Blobaum, *Rewolucja*, 216. Since Lednicki was a founder, and Vice-President, of the ZPD, he did represent the party's interests in the Duma.

50. W. Lednicki, *Pamiętniki*, 2 (A. L. *Memoirs*): 530–31.

51. Ibid.

52. Ibid., 533. Also see Sidney Harcave, "The Jews and the First Russian National Election," *Slavic Review* 9 (1949): 33–41.

53. Trenam, "Without a Free Poland," 212–23.

54. W. Lednicki, *Pamiętniki*, 2 (A. L. *Memoirs*): 534. Riech' kept readers abreast of Lednicki's progress in forging a multi-national alliance in Minsk, and he was credited with bringing together Poles, Jews, and Russians. See *Riech'*, 18/31 March; 28 March/10 April; and 1/14 April 1905. Additional reports on

these events were reported in *Viestnik Partii Narodnoi Svobody* 6 (11 April 1906): 401–3.

55. Marian Jodko-Narkiewicz, "Wspomnienia o s.p. Aleksandrze Lednickim," PIASA, Aleksander Lednicki Collection (006), folder 71, p. 2. This handwritten testimony is dated 1959.

56. Ibid.

57. Edward Woyniłłowicz, *Wspomnienia: 1847–1928*, ed. Janusz Iwaszkiewicz (Wilno: Skład Główny w Księgarni Józefa Zawadzkiego, 1931), 1: 113.

58. W. Lednicki, *Pamiętniki*, 2 (A. L. *Memoirs*): 542.

59. Jodko-Narkiewicz, "Wspomnienia," PIASA, Aleksander Lednicki Collection (006), folder 71, p. 1.

60. Ibid., 1–2.

61. N. Tsirikov, "Aleksandr Robertovich Lednits[k]ii: listki vospominanii," PIASA, Aleksander Lednicki Collection (006), folder 71, p. 3. Lednicki believed that lawyers and artists had a lot in common, and conceded that there was a certain "artistic element" in his speeches. See A. Lednicki, *Pamiętniki*, 158. Lednicki was active in the Moscow Literary-Artistic Circle, as evidenced by a photo of him with F. I. Shaliapin, I. E. Repin and other leading lights of the Moscow cultural scene. See F. I. Shaliapin, *Maska i dusha: Moi sorok let na teatrakh* (Paris: Izdatel'stvo "Sovremennyia Zapiski," 1932), 146–47.

62. Woyniłłowicz, *Wspomnienia*, 113–14.

63. W. Lednicki, *Pamiętniki*, 2 (A. L. *Memoirs*): 537–38. The Minsk assembly of electors consisted of 74 landowners, 41 peasants, 20 urban delegates, and 2 workers. There were three distinct groups: the predominantly Jewish urban group; 52 Polish landowners, joined by a few other Polish Catholic electors from other curiae, bringing the Polish total to 57; and the peasants and other Orthodox electors, totalling 63. Since neither rural group had a majority, the matter would boil down to whom the Jews chose as an ally. Lednicki's negotiations had settled the problem, and an agreement was reached between Poles and Jews: seven of the deputies to the Duma would be Poles, and the other would be Jewish. The Jew chosen was S. Ia. Rozenbaum. Four Polish Kadets were elected: Lednicki; V. O. Janczewski, a Minsk lawyer; and the wealthy landowners Prince Hieronim Drucki-Lubecki and E. I. Ljubanski. Other Poles—National Democrats or independents—were R. A. Skirmunt, P. P. Massonius, and J. J. Wisniewski. Emmons, *Formation of Political Parties*, 336–37.

64. W. Lednicki, *Pamiętniki*, 1: 528; also cited in Zaprudnik, "Political Struggle for Byelorussia," 54

65. W. Lednicki, *Pamiętniki*, 2 (A. L. *Memoirs*): 537, cited in Zaprudnik, "The Political Struggle for Byelorussia," 53–54. The Church had recently been empowered to act in such a manner. On 26 December 1905, the Russian government conceded more rights to the Catholics of the *Kresy*. They now could hold public religious processions, funerals and pilgrimages, if local police were notified ahead of time. This concession also resulted in many conversions to

Catholicism among the Byelorussian peasantry. See Zaprudnik, 51.

66. GARF, f. 579, op. 1, d. 688, l. 15. For a complete description of the party, see Roman Jurkowski, "Stronnictwo Konstytucyjno-Katolickie na Litwie i Białorusi w 1906 r. (Szkic do dziejów)," *Acta Baltico-Slavica* 18 (1987): 93–118.

67. GARF, f. 579, op. 1, d. 688, l. 4.

68. Ibid.

69. Zaprudnik, "Political Struggle for Byelorussia," 81, citing an article in *Okrainy Rossii* 24 (13 August 1906): 412. This article was a reprint of a report published earlier in the Kiev Polish-language daily, *Dziennik Kijowski*. Zaprudnik concludes that the author, cited as a "Mr. D.," was Roman Dmowski. His contention is supported by the tone of the report, which attacks Lednicki and others who did not join the Polish Koło.

70. Ibid., 83.

71. *Nasha zhizn'*, 18 September/1 October 1905, citing a meeting on 16 September attended by Drucki-Lubecki, both Dolgorukov twins, and Prince Shakhovskoi.

72. GARF, f. 523, op. 1, d. 243.

73. W. Lednicki, *Pamiętniki*, 2 (A. L. *Memoirs*): 537.

74. GARF, f. 523, op. 1, d. 174, l. 6.

75. GARF, f. 579, op. 1, d. 687, l. 2.

76. Ibid. Together, these two men and Lednicki would later be know as "the three Aleksanders." For a critical commentary on their actions in 1917, see Zygmunt Wasilewski's article, "System Aleksandryjski," in his *Na wschodnim posterunku: Księga pielgrzymstwa, 1915–1918* (Warsaw: E. Wende i Spolka, 1924), 313–20.

77. GARF, f. 579, op. 1, d. 687, l. 2.

78. The Kadets won 182 out of 448, or forty percent, of all seats in the First Duma. See *Emmons, Formation of Political Parties*, 355.

79. Pipes, *Liberal on the Right*, 35.

80. Ibid.

81. Ibid., 35–36. In a development foreshadowing Kadet actions in the First Duma, agricultural reform—not the nationalities question—was the most-discussed issue at the Third Congress. See A. Kaminka, "III s"ezd partii Narodnoi Svobody," *Svoboda i kul'tura* 1 (1906), no. 5: 340–49.

82. "III-i s"ezd delegatov partii narodnoi svobody," *Pravo* 18 (6 May 1906): 1677.

83. Ibid., 1684–85. Ten new members were added to the Central Committee at this time.

84. Lednicki fits the profile of a Central Committee member as described by Iu. D. Margolis, who ascribes eight general characteristics to these persons: 1) noble status, either by birth or service; 2) university education; 3) membership in a 'free profession'; 4) familiarity with Western Europe; 5) financial security; 6) experience in liberal organizations, including illegal ones; 7) a tendency to be a

member of a non-Orthodox faith (fifteen out of fifty-four members in 1906–7 were not Orthodox); and 8) politicization began in underground activities during university years. See "Shtrikhi k portrety elity rossiiskikh liberalov nachal XX v.," in *Rossiiskaia intelligentsi4ia na istoricheskom perelome: Pervaia tret' XX veka. Tezisy dokladov i soobshchenii nauchnoi konferentsii Sankt-Peterburg 19–20 marta 1996 g.*, ed. M. Iudovich (St. Petersburg: Izdatel'stvo Sankt-Peterburgskogo Universiteta, 1996), 36.

85. The Polish Koło was dominated by the National Democrats, who won all seats from the Kingdom. The Koło had about 30 members in the First Duma.

86. Zaprudnik, "Political Struggle for Byelorussia," 95–96.

87. Zygmunt Łukawski, *Koło Polskie w Rosyjskiej Dumie Panstwowej w latach 1906–1909* (Wrocław: Zakład Narodowy imienia Ossolińskich, 1967), 37.

88. Zaprudnik, "Political Struggle for Byelorussia," 96–97; citing *Okrainy Rossii* 24 (13 August 1906): 412. "Mr. D." pointed out that Skirmunt "first of all does not consider himself to be a Pole. In conversation with me he stated that he is a Byelorussian who only acquired Polish culture, that...he has absolutely no need to number himself among those of Polish nationality to whom he is bound only by culture. Mr. Skirmunt, therefore, favored establishment of a local Territorial Circle which would open wide its doors to Poles as well as Byelo- and Little-Russians, Lithuanians, Jews, and Russians." Ibid., 80.

89. Ibid.

90. W. Lednicki, *Pamiętniki*, 2: 568; also cited by Zaprudnik, "Political Struggle for Byelorussia," 97. Aleksander Lednicki delivered this programmatic speech at the first meeting of the Territorialists. Among those Poles in attendance were Bishop Ropp, Prince Drucki-Lubecki, R. Skirmunt, M. Massonius, Count W. Grocholski, Count Tyszkiewicz, and Count Józef Potocki.

91. PIASA, Aleksander Lednicki Collection (006), folder 22.

92. Ibid.

93. Bernard Pares, *Russia and Reform* (London: Archibald Constable & Co., Ltd., 1907), 558.

94. V. I. Lenin, *Polnoe Sobranie sochinenii.* 5th. ed. (Moscow: Gosudarstvennoe izdatel'stvo politicheskoi literatury, 1960), 13: 102. Emphasis in original.

95. Ibid., 103.

ALEKSANDER LEDNICKI AND THE FAILURE OF POLISH LIBERALISM: THE FIRST DUMA TO THE SECOND REPUBLIC

Lednicki's election to the First Duma seemingly heralded a victory for his progressive politics. Veteran of the Russian liberation movement, founder of the Kadet party and member of its Central Committee, Lednicki was one of the most influential Kadets in the First Duma. The Kadets had a plurality of seats; Lednicki was a leading member of the party delegation and was elected to its parliamentary committee. Assigned to the organizational section, which maintained relations with other parliamentary fractions, he was personally responsible for monitoring the activities of the Polish Koło and other minority groups. Through his close relationships with other Duma leaders, he was in a position to demand immediate debate on Polish autonomy.[1] At the precise moment that Lednicki reached the peak of his political power, however, his hopes for a resolution on the Polish question were dashed. Essentially, the Kadets were loathe to promote the volatile issue of Polish autonomy in the First Duma.[2]

Throughout 1905, Lednicki had preached the doctrine of cooperation with Russian liberals to the Poles. Once his fellow *osvobozhdentsy* gained control of a national parliament, he promised, they would vigorously push for Polish autonomy. Although he had always been primarily concerned with Poland, Lednicki consistently sought a just resolution of the nationalities question within the context of all-Russian reforms. Uniquely qualified to bring this about, only he was both a recognized political leader in Poland and a Russian *osvobozh-denets*. This distinguished him from other Polish leaders such as Roman Dmowski, who never warmed up to the notion of cooperation with the Russian opposition movement.

Unwilling to divorce his search for a solution to the nationalities question from its Russian context, Lednicki simultaneously represented no fewer than five constituencies: the Kadet party; the Polish *Związek Postępowej-Demokratyczne* (ZPD); the "Parliamentary Group of the Western Territories"; the Union of Autonomists' parliamentary fraction; and the people of Georgia, who had asked him to represent their interests until elections in their homeland could be completed in July. But Lednicki proved unable to meld together the all-Russian movement he so desired. In the First Duma, his bases of support were undermined by class conflict and national chauvinism.

At first buoyed by the apparent liberal victory in Russia, the ebullient Lednicki acted quickly to mobilize support for his progressive line of thinking. Above all a humanist and democrat devoted to the concept of universal freedom, Lednicki insisted that the struggle for Polish autonomy was only part of a larger war between the reactionary tsarist government and progressive forces throughout the empire. Central to his philosophy was a sincere belief that Polish freedom was meaningless if the other "captive nations" in the empire remained unfree to govern themselves, teach their children in their native languages and nurture their cultures.

Lednicki faced huge obstacles in his search for a united front. Within the *Kresy* group of parliamentarians, he was confronted by the stubborn resistance of Polish landowners, whose parochial interests precluded cooperation with the Kadets, whose devotion to the Polish cause they doubted. Only Lednicki and his fellow Pole and Kadet Central Committee member Leon Petrazycki defended the party's position on Polish autonomy, believing that their Russian comrades would fulfill the promises made during the previous year.[3]

Kresy deputies to the First Duma and the State Council also were opposed to Kadet plans for agricultural reform, which included expropriation of private estates. They argued that the Kadets had moved too far to the left, embracing socialist ideals. These men simply did not favor the enactment of the far-reaching social reforms envisioned by Lednicki and the Kadets. Consequently, Lednicki's search for allies among *Kresy* Poles proved fruitless. Of the sixteen representatives who signed the charter of the "Parliamentary Group of the Western Territories," only six fully agreed with Lednicki's progressive social program.[4]

Clearly, Lednicki's philosophy did not appeal to conservative Polish landowners in the *Kresy*, whose national and class interests had no place on his liberal agenda. In addition to opposing land reform, *Kresy* Poles were reluctant to embrace universal suffrage, a fundamental tenet of Kadet and ZPD liberalism. Many feared a majoritarian regime would jeopardize Polish cultural dominance in the region. As a minority in the *Kresy*, ethnic Poles felt threatened by the prospects of ceding political power to non-Poles.[5] Lednicki's liberal cosmopolitanism, which made him popular among his Russian friends in Moscow, repulsed Polish nationalists. His failure to rally support around his liberal program among the *Kresy* Poles, who were generally more sensitive to the plight of other nationalities than Poles from the Kingdom, foreshadowed his political demise years later in the Second Republic.

While "Kadetism" had some support in cities where there were sizable Russian communities, such as Kiev, the party generally failed to gain support in the western borderlands. Despite its overtures to Poles and other national minorities, and the presence of several prominent non-Russians in its central committee, the Kadet party was largely a Russian phenomenon. The fate of progressive liberalism was particularly gloomy in the Polish Kingdom, where the Kadets only managed to establish five party cells with 162 members.[6] Even indigineous liberal parties fared poorly in the Kingdom: Lednicki was the only ZPD candidate ever elected to the Russian parliament.

Lednicki manifestly had no sizable constituency in the Polish lands, and that largely explains his failure to parlay his political successes in Russia into a new career later in independent Poland. His political doctrine was centered around the notion of Russo-Polish amity and international harmony: mediation and compromise were his mottoes. These tactics served him well in the months prior to the elections to the First Duma, when the leaders of the liberation movement struggled to prevent its splintering into antagonistic political parties. He was a favorite among Russians who sincerely wanted to rectify the wrongs inflicted on the Polish nation. Though an ardent patriot, Lednicki could never place national ambitions above the greater cause—the liberation of all peoples in the empire chafing under the tsarist yoke of oppression and arbitrary rule. In 1905, the Russian *osvobozhdentsy* praised Lednicki for his "moderation" and ability to compromise.

But in the climate of extreme nationalism that prevailed in the Second Polish Republic, Lednicki's cosmopolitanism and universalism branded him an alien, unworthy of citizenship in the new Poland. His emphasis on compromise and peaceful coexistence of peoples reinforced Lednicki's image as a Russian stooge. While other Polish emigres in Russia hailed Lednicki for being "in the first rank of parliamentarians" in the First Duma and praised him for speaking on behalf of all peoples in the Empire, Polish nationalists questioned the loyalty of this Pole who aligned himself with the program of the Russian Kadets.[7]

In the First Duma, Lednicki's passion for the cause of universal liberty induced him to create the Union of Autonomists' parliamentary fraction. In an attempt to quiet those who denied support for national aspirations among "less developed" nations, Lednicki tried to convince the Poles that their

> truest allies will be deputies from countries likewise oppressed or even from those Russian lands that also desire decentralization, wider self-rule, and in the future—autonomy. I long to unite these autonomist groups into a single entity and to create a parliamentary fraction of autonomists. Who will oppose us? Monarchists and Octobrists....[8]

At the fraction's first meeting on 11 May 1906, Lednicki was chosen President; the Ukrainian I. L. Shrag and the Azeri A. M. B. Topchibashii were elected Vice Presidents. The Autonomists issued a six-point program that called for the restructuring of the state on a democratic basis, with full decentralization of state authority. In an overture to sympathetic Russians, the Union made clear that it supported "the indivisiblity of the Russian state as a unified whole."[9]

The Autonomists' exact number has been the focus of some dispute, but it is clear that at least 63 deputies out of 448 belonged to the fraction in the early days of the First Duma.[10] This group embodied the realization of Lednicki's dream of a truly all-Russian political movement devoted to the liberation of all peoples in the empire. The Autonomists, however, proved ineffectual in promoting their agenda. A loosely-knit organization that allowed its members simultaneously to belong to other parliamentary fractions, the Union of Autonomists failed to rally support for a resolution of the nationalities problem and disintegrated over the course of the First Duma.[11]

Agitating for the freedom of all the empire's peoples, Lednicki was one of the leading orators in the Duma, widely hailed as having "all that a speaker needs: voice, gestures, temperament, and enthusiasm."[12] He reminded his fellow *osvobozhdentsy* that representatives of all nationalities had fought alongside Russians in the liberation movement for a better future: "Without exception, the nationalities are fighting for one common ideal, for democratic principles, for one common freedom."[13] While he welcomed debate on the worker and peasant questions, he argued that the Duma must seek "not only the emancipation of all classes, but also the emancipation of all nations."[14]

An indefatigable advocate of Polish autonomy, Lednicki pled his case with his usual force and eloquence, reminding the Duma that Poles were "choking in an atmosphere of gunpowder and smoke, in an atmosphere of arbitrariness and violence."[15] In the parliament's first sessions, he called on the Kadets to fulfill their campaign promises. Ever since the First Russo-Polish Congress in April 1905, Russian liberals had pledged to Lednicki and his fellow Poles that they would address the Polish issue immediately after the convocation of a Russian parliament. Lednicki now expected his Russian colleagues to keep their word. He had risked his political integrity and reputation among Poles by cooperating so closely with a Russian party, and now the Kadets' failure to address the Polish issue in the First Duma—and in the following years—was to thwart his efforts to forge a lasting Russo-Polish understanding. Moreover, he opened himself up to the damaging charges later levelled by Dmowski and other Polish nationalists that he had always served Russian interests.

Contrary to the accusations, Lednicki acted forcefully to promote Polish interests in the First Duma. In its opening days he demanded that the nationalities question be part of the Duma's response to the address from the throne.[16] The response was to be prepared in part by the Kadets Miliukov, Kokoshkin and Vinaver.[17] Despite the apparently auspicious circumstances, the Kadet-inspired response to the Tsar failed to mention Polish demands for autonomy. The Kadet leadership feared antagonizing the government on an issue it regarded as less important than land reform.

Lednicki could not conceal his disappointment. In an open letter to Miliukov he demanded an explanation of his party's indifference to Poland's plight.[18] In his reply, Miliukov argued that, while the Kadets and the Duma still considered the Polish question an important one, it was not appropriate to force the issue of autonomy at the outset. Miliukov insisted that other issues, notably the agrarian question, affected the nation as a whole and had to be addressed immediately. Although Lednicki regarded the agrarian question as more complicated than the nationalities problem, in the end he acquiesced.[19] He noted later that

> As a Pole, I greatly desired that the Polish demands be mentioned and dreaded the inevitable unsatisfactory results of this neglect, but I had to retreat before another danger—the untimely discussion of the Polish question....[20]

In what Vladimir Nabokov described as a "brilliant speech,"[21] Lednicki could only admonish the Duma that it had been elected "to fulfill a solemn bidding, to fight without distinction of nationality for one general ideal, for democratic principles, for one general freedom."[22]

While Lednicki remained faithful to his Russian allies and bided his time, the Polish Koło pushed for immediate Duma debate on Polish autonomy. The pleas went unheeded. Lednicki later recalled that, "when the declaration of the Polish Koło was read, I lost faith in our victory, so utterly cold was the presentation by the Polish delegates received."[23]

Lednicki applauded the Koło for its intentions but criticized its timing. He continued to work for cooperation among Poles and

Russians as Kadet liaison with the Koło, and in talks on Polish autonomy delivered at local Kadet meetings.[24] He had faith that the Kadets would soon place the Polish issue before the Duma, "for if I did not believe that, I would have left them [the Kadets] long ago."[25] Whether or not Miliukov and the Kadets ever intended to discuss the delicate Polish issue in the Duma soon became a moot point. Seventy-two days after he had ceremoniously declared the opening of the First Duma, Tsar Nicholas II dismissed the body for contemplating a direct appeal to the people to ignore any government pronouncements and await Duma action on the land question.

Lednicki's prowess as tactician was sorely tested in the First Duma, where he tried to juggle the interests of his different bases of support: Russian liberals, Polish landowners in the *Kresy*, and Poles in the Kingdom. He was unable to perform this trick and in the end alienated many of his allies. Even fellow Kadets criticized his outspoken behavior in the Duma. But Lednicki would long remain a key figure in the party.

More damaging to Lednicki's long-term political career was the reaction of *Kresy* Poles to his "radicalism" on social issues. Lednicki's actions in the First Duma, and his signing of the Vyborg Manifesto, alienated many *Kresy* Poles who had supported his candidacy to the Duma in 1906.[26] He received a severe upbraiding at a meeting of Minsk landowners on 30–31 July 1906, convened by his former benefactor Woyniłłowicz and the National Democrat Kazimierz Pawlikowski. The landowners rejected Lednicki's progressive social program, especially regarding the volatile issue of land reform. In an ominous note foreshadowing Lednicki's later fate in interwar Poland, the conference voiced its doubts about his devotion to the Polish cause. It opposed his support of the national movements of other peoples, fearing that Belorussian nationalism would incite peasants to overthrow the traditional political, social and cultural hegemony of the landed Polish minority in the *Kresy*. Lednicki's critics concluded that he had not served Polish interests in the Duma. *Kresy* landowners would no longer support his politics.[27]

Nor had Lednicki gained friends among the National Democrats, who dominated the political scene in the Kingdom. He had steadfastly refused to join the Koło, citing his election to the Duma as representative for all people in Minsk as precluding his membership in an exclusively Polish parliamentary fraction. Lednicki consisently refused to place the issue of Polish autonomy above the interests of other peoples in his constituency, the Belorussians, Russians, Lithuanians and Jews. Throughout 1905 he had promoted the motto of "For your freedom and ours": he never wavered in the Duma from his defense of universal freedom and equality of rights for all peoples of the empire.

While Lednicki's devotion to the ideals of the revolution were admirable, he unwittingly lost credibility among Polish nationalists who came to regard the "Russian" Kadet as a traitor to the Polish cause. Lednicki's signing of the Vyborg Manifesto, which the Kolo boycotted on the grounds that it was a purely Russian matter, reinforced Lednicki's repuation as a cosmopolitan Russian liberal to whom the fate of the Kingdom was secondary. While Lednicki's stature among Russians and his reputation as a true *osvobozhdenets* was enhanced by his performances in the First Duma, he was greatly diminished in the eyes of Poles whose sole concern was the fate of Poland. Long before his controversial role in the events surrounding the emergence of the reborn Polish state in 1918, Lednicki had antagonized Polish nationalists.

Indeed, many of their charges ring true. Lednicki had toed the Kadet party line on the Polish question, even if he had complained publicly about the party's seeming indifference. His loyalty to his Russian comrades had been tested, but he emerged from the Duma a staunch defender of the Kadet position. After that body's dissolution he continued to act in solidarity with his fellow liberals.[28] He even travelled to Vyborg, where a majority of Duma deputies had retreated to convene a rump parliament. As Miliukov later recalled, "Lednicki's daring nature and his views...did not allow him to act otherwise."[29]

Unlike the members of the Polish Koło, National Democrats who were solely interested in the Polish question, Lednicki mourned the fate of the Russian Duma as a setback for freedom throughout the empire. For any true osvobozhdenets, protesting the arbitrary closing of the Duma was a knee-jerk reaction. Lednicki did not ponder the consequences: it was his duty to join his Russian brethren in a show of unity. The Kadets would forever remember the *Endecja*'s failure to support the Vyborg Manifesto and shied from cooperation with the Koło in future Dumas. Kadet leader Miliukov concluded that the Koło's reluctance to support the Vyborg Manifesto "decisively separated the Polish question from the general Russian struggle for freedom...."[30]

Lednicki's hasty action doomed him to the political wilderness for the next decade, for he and his collaborators in Vyborg were later stripped of their political rights. All who signed the manifesto were tried in 1907, and Lednicki and others were sentenced to prison for three months. From mid-May to mid-August 1908 he whiled away the time in a Moscow prison with other prominent Duma leaders. In the Butyrka Prison, Lednicki resided in cell 80, which measured seven feet by fourteen feet. President of the First Duma Sergei Muromtsev lived nearby in cell 83, Fedor Kokoshkin was confined to cell 81, and Pavel Dolgorukov served his time in cell 75.[31] Upon his release, Lednicki returned to active party work as a member of the Kadet Central Committee, but he would never again hold an elected office in Russia.

Until the outbreak of World War I, Lednicki would remain "aloof from all political activities," devoting his time to his legal work.[32] During the war, he renewed his call for his Russian colleagues to support Polish claims for autonomy. Now was the time, he urged, for Slavic brethren to join together as equals to repel the German hordes. As early as October 1914 he launched a series of discussions between Russian liberals and Polish leaders. In the final months of 1914 several meetings took place in Petrograd, Moscow, Kiev and Warsaw. Leading Kadets, including his old friends Miliukov, Struve, Pavel Dolgorukov, Nabokov and Rodichev, participated in the discussions, but no headway was made on the matter of Polish autonomy. Once again, the Kadets rejected the "bad timing" of Polish demands.[33]

The wartime catastrophes that befell the Russian army altered the nature of the Polish question. German and Austrian forces occupied the Kingdom, effectively depriving Russia of any right to regard the Polish question as an internal affair. In November 1916 a frustrated Lednicki "unfurled the banner of independence"[34] in reaction to the creation of a rump Polish state by the Central Powers. One last time he urged his fellow Kadets to join him in recognizing the new situation created by this development. He had long argued that the Polish question was an international one, dating back to the Treaty of Vienna in 1815 and the creation of the Polish Kingdom as an autonomous entity under Russian control. He now asked his comrades on the Kadet Central Committee to join him in embracing Polish independence. They balked, and Lednicki quit the party.[35]

He turned to the left, seeking support for the Polish cause among the Petrograd Socialists with whom his fellow Pole and former colleague in the ZPD, Aleksander Więckowski, worked closely. At this time Lednicki also drew closer to the socialist Aleksander Kerenskii, paving the way for Lednicki's participation in the Provisional Government.

The collapse of the tsarist regime in February 1917 suddenly thrust many of Lednicki's former colleagues into power. Prompted by a manifesto issued by the Petrograd Soviet, the Provisional Government was induced to consent to the separation of Poland from Russia. A member of both bodies, Kerenskii was instrumental in convincing them to act on the Polish question. At Kerenskii's urging, the new foreign minister, Miliukov, summoned Lednicki to Petrograd to help draft the Provisional Government's declaration of Polish independence. Lednicki hailed the manifesto as a "glorious testament to the ideals of universal freedom, brotherhood and equality, for which the Polish nation had always shed its blood."[36] On 28 March, Lednicki was nominated to the post of President of the Liquidation Commission, the branch of the Provisional Government entrusted with coordinating the delicate task of unraveling the many administrative ties between Russia and Poland.

Lednicki served in this post for the duration of the Provisional Government. He was nominated to the position of minister but refused the title, recognizing the dangers of being labelled a Russian minister of Polish affairs.[37] Now that Poland would regain its independence, he desperately wanted to play a role in the new state. He did not want to be regarded as a Russian toady. At the same time, he used his position in the Provisional Government to consolidate his power base within the Polish community in Russia. He openly fought the National Democrats, refusing to follow the lead of the Dmowski-led Polish National Committee in Paris. *Endecja* members on the Liquidation Commission resigned in protest, and during the summer of 1917 Dmowski and the National Democrats battled Lednicki's growing influence in Russia. But leaders in the Provisional Government, those same men with whom Lednicki had coordinated the Russian liberation movement in 1905, staunchly supported their old colleague.

Ironically, it was Lednicki's unflagging loyalty to his Russian comrades that crippled his bid to become a major political figure in the new Polish state. The Provisional Government opposed the Polish National Committee's plan to create an independent Polish army in Russia. Eager to buttress the war effort on the eastern front, the Western Allies supported this scheme. But the Provisional Government feared that if the Poles separated from the general Russian army, then other nationalities would follow suit. The Russians believed that such a development would leave the army in shambles.

Lednicki supported this line of thinking, thereby alienating Western policy makers who placed a premium on a two-front war. Despite their personal distrust of Dmowski, he became their Polish "man." Dmowski's support of Western initiatives in the summer of 1917 induced the Allies to recognize the Polish National Committee as the "legitimate" government of the future Polish state. Lednicki would find no backers in the West.

When the Provisional Government was overthrown in October 1917 and his liberal friends fell from power, Lednicki found himself without the support of any foreign government. For a brief time he served as emissary in Russia for the Regency Council, the governing body of the Polish state created by the Central Powers. His "collaboration" with the Germans further antagonized the Polish National Committee and distressed western governments. Finally expelled by the Bolsheviks in early 1918, Lednicki would be greeted rudely upon his return to Poland.[38]

Lednicki simply was not, his many enemies argued, a Pole: he lived his whole life in Moscow, belonged to a Russian political party and served as a sort of Russian minister of Polish affairs. Worse yet, he was accused of trying to bargain away Polish lands to the Germans in return for political patronage. He neither dressed nor spoke like a Pole. In a place and time that did not prize it, Lednicki's cosmopolitanism—a trait which had served him so well in his efforts to forge an all-Russian liberation movement in Moscow—sealed his fate as one of the first casualties of the harsh political climate of the Second Republic.

Lednicki struggled to stay active in his new life in Poland, but he would never hold an elected office.[39] He sought to remedy the damage wrought by the venomous attacks by *Endecja* hacks who so savagely ridiculed his "foreignness" and questioned his integrity. He sued Zygmunt Wasilewski for slander in 1924; he lost the trial but was vindicated on appeal.[40]

As Lednicki strove to keep abreast of political developments, his home in Warsaw became a sort of salon where people from various parties gathered to discuss the issues of the day. The old mediator never gave up hope that he could somehow foster understanding among the splintered Polish parties. In 1927 he rejected the post of President of Wilno as a "provincial" post beneath his dignity.

Lednicki would never get an opportunity to take part in the political life in the new Polish state. Removed from his familiar milieu in Moscow and St. Petersburg, Lednicki was out of his element in Poland. Lednicki had devoted his early life to the Polish cause as an unofficial Polish ambassador in Russia, living as a Pole among Russians. In a brutal twist of fate, he would die an outsider in his beloved Poland, living his final years as a "Russian" among Poles.

ENDNOTES

1. Zimmerman, "Between Revolution and Reaction," 193–99. Lednicki was friendly with the most influential men in the Duma: Sergei Muromtsev, chosen presiding officer; Prince Petr Dolgorukov and N. A. Gredeskul', the two vice-presidents; and Prince D. I. Shakhovskoi, the secretary. All had long been associated with Lednicki in his attempts to bring about a Russo-Polish understanding on the Polish question. Rodichev, Kokoshkin and Nabokov—men who also worked closely with Lednicki on this issue—were also among the Duma leadership.

2. V. Obninskii, "Pervaia shagi russkago avtonomizma," *Ukrainskaia zhizn'* 2 (1913), no. 4: 15–16. For an overview of the Polish question in the Russian parliament, see Edward Chmielewski, *The Polish Question in the Russian State Duma* (Knoxville: The University of Tennessee Press, 1970).

3. PIASA, Aleksander Lednicki Collection (006), folder 24.

4. Ibid.

5. *Kraj* 4 (1906): 14–15.

6. V. V. Shelokhaev, *Kadety—glavnaia partiia liberal'noi burzhuazii v bor'be s revoliutsiei 1905–1907 gg.* (Moscow: Izdatel'stvo "Nauka," 1983), 62–63. In Wilno, only 100 men belonged to the local Kadet organization. By contrast, in Kiev the party had 1,400 members. It had more than 12,000 members in Moscow and 7,500 in St. Petersburg at the peak of its popularity in early 1907.

7. *Kraj* 18 (1906): 4. Roman Dmowski despised the Kadets, who he believed were "financially dependent...[on] Jews. This dependence they did not even try to conceal,...and Jews to a signficant degree dictated its [the Kadet party's] line of progress." "Jews," he added, "have everwhere been very evil politicians." See Roman Dmowski, *Polityka polska i odbudowanie państwa*, Introduction and Commentary by Tomasz Wituch, 2d ed. (Warsaw: Instytut Wydawniczy Pax, 1989), 1: 109.

8. A. Lednicki, "Polacy w Dumie," *Prawda* 21 (1906): 254.

9. PIASA, Aleksander Lednicki Collection (006), folder 24.

10. Emmons, *Formation of Political Parties*, 355. Voskobiynyk has argued that the Autonomists numbered around 125 or more. See "The Nationalities Question in Russia," 243.

11. F. Dan cited a decline in the number of Autonomists from 104 at the outset of the First Duma in early May, to twelve at the time of its dissolution at the end of July. His figures indicate that Autonomists accounted for 24% of Duma membership in May, but only 2.5% in July. See "Obshchaia politika pravitel'stva i izmeneniia v gosudarstvennoi organizatsii v period 1905–1907 gg.," in *Obshchestvennoe dvizhenie v Rossii v nachale XX–go veka*, ed. L. Martov, P. Maslov, and A. Potresov (St. Petersburg: "Obshchestvennaia Pol'za," 1911), vol. 4, part 2: 3.

12. *Kraj* 18 (1906): 4.

13. Gosudarstvennaia Duma. Stenograficheskie otchety. Sessiia 1, zasedanie 4 (3 May 1906): 102.

14. Ibid., 103.

15. Ibid., 102.

16. N. Gredeskul', "Natsional'nyi vopros v pervoi dume," in *K desiatiletii pervoi Gosudarstvennoi Dumoi: 27 aprylia 1906 r.—27 aprylia 1916 r. Sbornik statei pervodumtsev*, ed. N. A. Borodin, et al. (Petrograd: Ogni, 1916), 76–88.

17. Zimmerman, "Between Revolution and Reaction," 223.

18. *Riech'*, 6/19 May 1906; *Prawda* 21 (1906): 253–55; and *Kraj* 20 (1906): 11.

19. See PIASA, Aleksander Lednicki Collection (006), folder 24. Lednicki made these remarks in debate on 14 May at the third meeting of the Group of Deputies from the Western Territories.

20. Milukow, "Aleksander Lednicki jako rzecznik," 40.

21. *Viestnik Partii Narodnoi Svobody* 10 (11 May 1906): 649.

22. Gosudarstvennaia Duma. Stenograficheskie otchety. Sessiia 1, zasedania 4 (3 May 1906): 103.

23. Trenam, "Without a Free Poland," 270–71.

24. On Lednicki's role as liaison, see *Viestnik Partii Narodnoi Svobody* 11 (18 May 1906): 734–35 and 13 (1 June 1906): 849. For a discussion of his address on Polish autonomy delivered at a local St. Petersburg party meeting on June 14, see 16 (24 June 1906): 1057.

25. Trenam, "Without a Free Poland," 271.

26. The Vyborg Manifesto was issued by many of the Kadets and leftist members of the First Duma after the tsar dissolved that body. They urged people to refuse to obey the government because it had illegally dismissed the parliament. The appeal went unheeded.

27. *Kraj* 32 (1906): 14–15; Riech' 17/30 August 1906; Smolen, "Działalność polityczna," 142. One Russian critic questioned the depth of support for Polish liberalism, noting that while the RussianKadet party had its roots in the zemstvo-liberal movement, "the Polish 'progressive-democrats'...arose at the end of 1904, as they say, out of nothing." See L. Vasilevskii, "Russkaia Pol'sha nakanun novykh vyborov." *Russkoe Bogatsvo* 12 (December) 1906: 78. For the time being anyway, Polish liberals recognized Lednicki's service to the Polish nation. A telegram to Lednicki from the Central Committee of the Polish Constitutional Democratic Party of Ukraine, Wolynia and Podolia expressed thanks to this "Polish Patriot" for his activities in the Duma. See PIASA, Aleksander Lednicki Collection (006), folder 2.

28. W. Lednicki, *Pamiętniki*, 2: 574.

29. Milukow, "Aleksander Lednicki jako rzecznik," 40.

30. Ibid.

31. Aleksandr Lednitskii, "S. A. Muromtsev v tiurme," in *Sergei Andreevich Muromtsev: Sbornik statei*, ed. D. I. Shakhovskoi (Moscow, 1911), 351–53.

32. Milukow, "Aleksander Lednicki jako rzecznik," 41.

33. Wieslawa Toporowicz, *Sprawa Polska w polityce rosyjskiej 1914–1917*. (Warsaw: Państwowe Wydawnictwo Naukowe, 1973), 150–51.

34. Milyukov, "Alexander Lednicki," 678.

35. V. V. Shelokhaev, *Liberal'naia model' pereustroistva Rossii*. Moscow: Rosspen, 1996, 106.

36. *Viestnik Vremennago Pravitel'stva*, 18/31 March 1917.

37. Wieslawa Toporowicz, "Komisja Likwidacyjna do spraw b. Królestwa Polskiego w 1917 r.," *Z dziejów stosunków polsko-radzieckich. Studia i materiały* 9 (1972): 11–12. Other studies of Lednicki's activities during this time include Mieczysław Smolen, "Stanowisko Aleksandra Lednickiego w kwestii polskiej w latach 1914–1917," *Zeszyty naukowe Uniwersytetu Jagiellonskiego. Prace historyczne* 66 (1980): 35–59 and Władysław Bułhak, "Aleksander Lednicki i jego koncepcje rozstrzygniecia kwestii polskiej marzec-grudzien 1917 r.," *Kwartalnik historyczny* 99 (1992), no. 2: 51–70.

38. For information on Lednicki's activities at this time, see Mieczysław Smolen, "Przedstawicielstwo Rady Regencyjnej w Moskwie," *Studia historyczne*

32 (1989), no. 2: 239–54 and Władysław Bułhak, "Aleksander Lednicki i Przedstawicielstwo Rady Regencyjnej Krolestwa Polskiego w Rosji Radzieckiej," *Przegląd historyczny* 81 (1990), nos. 2–3: 537–58.

39.   Lednicki founded the Pan-European Union in Poland, and headed the Polish delegation to the first congress in 1925. On these activities, see Jan Tombinski, "Początki ruchu Paneuropejskiego w Polsce," *Zeszyty naukowe Uniwersytetu Jagiellonskiego. Prace historyczne* 118 (1995): 83–93.

40.   For a full discussion of this case, see Zenowiusz Ponarski, "Spór o koncepcje polityczne z okresu I wojny światowej: Studium o procesie Z. Wasilewskiego o znieslawienie A. Lednickiego" (Ph.D. diss, University im. Adama Mickiewicza, 1980).

BIBLIOGRAPHY

ARCHIVAL MATERIALS

Gosudarstvennyi Arkhiv Rossiiskoi Federatsii (GARF). (Moscow)
  Fond 63. Moskovskoe Okhronnoe Otdelenie.
  Fond 102. Departament Politsii Ministerstva Vnutrennykh Del.
  Fond 518. Soiuz Soiuzov.
  Fond 523. Konstitutsionno-demokraticheskaia Partiia.
  Fond 579. P. N. Miliukov.
  Fond 1041. Likvidatsionnaia Komissiia po Delam b. Tsarstva
    Pol'skogo.
  Fond 5086. (Prazhskii arkhiv.) Petr Dolgorukov.

Pilsudski Institute. (New York)
  Archiwum Władysława Studnickiego.
  Komitet Narodowy w Paryż.

Polish Institute of the Arts and Sciences in America (PIASA). (New
    York)
  Aleksander Lednicki Collection (006).
  Wacław Lednicki Collection (007).

Rukopisnyi Otdel Gosudarstvennoi Biblioteki SSR im. V. I. Lenina
    (RO GBL). (Moscow)
  Fond 77. V. A. Gol'tsev.
  Fond 386. Valerii Iakovlevich Briusov.

WORKS BY ALEKSANDER LEDNICKI

Lednitskii, Aleksandr [Aleksander Lednicki]. "Avtobiografiia." In *Russkaia vedomosti*: 1863–1913. Sbornik statei, 102–03. Moscow: Tipografiia "Russkikh Vedomostei," 1913.

————. "L'homme de la rue en Pologne et l'organisation de la Paix." *Revue Mondiale* (15 January 1932): 132–46.

————. *L'idee nationale et son evolution. A l'occasion du XXVIeme Congres International de la Paix reuni a Varsovie le 25 juin 1928.* Warsaw: Messager Polonais, 1928.

————. *Iz proshlago*. Moscow: V. I. Voronov, 1917.

————. "Mariia Konopnitskaia." *Russkaia mysl'* 24 (April 1903): 1–14.

————. *Mowy polityczne*. Przed zwołaniem dumy. Kraków: Świat Słowianski, 1906.

————. *Nasza polityka wschodnia*. Warsaw: Polskie Towarzystwo Wydawnicze "Zjednoczenie," 1922.

————. "Natsional'nyi vopros v gosudarstvennoi dume." In *Pervaia Gosudarstvennaia Duma*. Vol. 1, *Politicheskoe znachenie Pervoi Dumy*, 154–67. St. Petersburg, 1907.

————. *Pamiętnik. 1914–1918*. Edited by Zbigniew Kozinski. Kraków: Nakładem Biblioteki Jagiellonskiej, 1994.

————. "Pamiętniki." Edited by Zbigniew Kozinski. *Biuletyn Biblioteki Jagiellonskiej* 41 (1991): 147–89.

————. "P. N. Miliukov i pol'skii vopros." In *P. N. Miliukov: Sbornik materialov po chestvovaniiu ego semidesiatiletiia, 1859–1929*, 212–17. Paris, 1929.

_______."Pokazaniia A. R. Lednitskogo, 27 sentiabria 1917." In *Padenie tsarskogo rezhima. Stenograficheskie otchety doprosov i pokazanii, dannykh v 1917 v Chrezvychainoi Sledstvennoi Komissii Vremennogo Pravitel'stva*. Edited by P. E. Shchegolev. Vol. 7, 234–55. Moscow and Leningrad: Gosudarstvennoe Izdatel'stvo, 1927.

_______. "Pol'skii vopros." *Russkaia mysl'* 26 (July 1905): 128–36.

_______. "Pol'skii vopros." *Moskovskii ezhenedel'nik* (1906), no. 2: 44–47; no. 3: 76–80.

_______. "Predislovie." In *Istoriia utopii*, by A. Sventokhovskii. Translated by E. Zagorskii. Moscow: V. M. Sablin, 1910.

_______. "S. A. Muromtsev v tiurme." In *Sergei Andreevich Muromtsev: Sbornik statei*, ed. D. I. Shakhovskoi, 350–72. Moscow, 1911.

_______. "V. O. Kliuchevskii kak istorik slavianin." *Izvestiia slavianskoi kultury* (1911): 1–8.

_______. *Zadania chwili*. Warsaw: Polskie Towarzystwo Wydawnicze "Zjednoczenie," 1922.

_______. *Z lat wojny. Artykuły, listy, przemówienia*. Warsaw: Nakładem Księgarni F. Hoesicka, 1921.

_______. "Z pamiętnika." *Niepodległość* 7 (1933): 29–41.

UNPUBLISHED DISSERTATIONS

Antkiewicz, Henry John. "Leon Wasilewski: Polish Patriot and Socialist." Ph.D. diss., The Ohio State University, 1976.

Bensman, Stephen Jeremy. "The Constitutional Ideas of the Russian Liberation Movement: The Struggle for Human Rights

During the Revolution of 1905." Ph.D. diss., University of Wisconsin-Madison, 1977.

Burch, Robert Jean. "Social Unrest in Imperial Russia: The Student Movement at Moscow University, 1887–1905." Ph.D. diss., University of Washington, 1972.

Janus, Glenn Alfred. "The Polish Kolo, the Russian Duma, and the Question of Polish Autonomy." Ph.D. diss., The Ohio State University, 1971.

Ponarski, Zenowiusz. "Spór o koncepcje polityczne z okresu I wojny światowej. Studium o procesie Z. Wasilewskiego o zniesławienie A. Lednickiego." Ph.D. diss., Uniwersytet im. Adama Mickiewicza, 1980.

Sanders, Jonathan E. "The Union of Unions: Political, Economic, Civil, and Human Rights Organizations in the 1905 Russian Revolution." Ph.D. diss., Columbia University, 1985.

Smolen, Mieczysław. "Działalność polityczna Aleksandra Lednickiego w Rosji: 1905–1918." Ph.D. diss., Jagiellonski Uniwersytet, 1979.

Trenam, Tracey. "Without a Free Poland, a Free Russia Cannot Be! Polish Liberals in the Russian Empire, 1904–1907." Ph.D. diss., Columbia University, 1994.

Urbaniak, George. "White Eagle, White Knight: The Polish-Lithuanian Dispute, 1918–1920." Ph.D. diss., University of Toronto, 1985.

Voskobiynyk, Michael Hryhory. "The Nationalities Question in Russia in 1905–1907: A Study in the Origin of Nationalism, with Special Reference to the Ukrainians." Ph.D. diss., University of Pennsylvania, 1972.

Weeks, Theodore R. "The National World of Imperial Russia: Policy in the Kingdom of Poland and Western Provinces, 1894–1914." Ph.D. diss., University of California, Berkeley, 1992.

Witkowski, Peter A. "Roman Dmowski and the Thirteenth Point." Ph.D. diss., Indiana University, 1981.

Zaprudnik, Jan. "Political Struggle for Byelorussia in the Tsarist State Dumas, 1906–1917." Ph.D. diss., New York University, 1969.

Zimmerman, Judith. "Between Revolution and Reaction: The Russian Constitutional Democratic Party: October, 1905 to June, 1907." Ph.D. diss., Columbia University, 1967.

PUBLISHED DOCUMENTS, MEMOIRS AND CONTEMPORARY ACCOUNTS

Ashukin, N., ed. *Valerii Briusov v avtobiograficheskikh zapisiakh, pis'makh, vospominaniiakh sovremennikov i otzyvakh kritiki.* Moscow: Federatsiia, 1929.

Astrov, N. I. *Vospominaniia.* Paris, 1940.

Boduen-de-Kurtene, Prof. I. "Pol'skii vopros v sviazi s drugimi okrainnymi i inorodcheskimi voprosami." *Pravo* 32 (14 August 1905): 2560–70.

Briusov, V. Ia. *Sochineniia.* 2 vols. Moscow: Khudozhestvennaia literatura, 1987.

Delo o Vyborgskom vozzvanii. Stenograficheskii otchet o zasedaniiakh osobago prisutstviia S.-Peterburgskoi sudebnoi palaty 12–18 dekabria 1907 g. St. Petersburg: Obshchestvennaia Pol'za, 1908.

Dmowski, Roman. "A Modern Pole." In *The Meaning and Uses of Polish History*, edited by Adam Bromke, 127–32. Boulder: East European Monographs, 1987.

Dmowski, Roman. *Polityka polska i odbudowanie państwa*. With an
    introduction and commentary by Tomasz Wituch. 2 vols. 2nd
    ed. Warsaw: Instytut Wydawniczny Pax, 1989.

"Doklad organizatsionnago biuro s"ezdy zemskikh i gorodskikh deiatelei
    po voprosy o pravakh natsional'nostei i o detsentralizatsii
    upravleniia i zakonodatel'stva." *Pravo* 40 (9 October 1905):
    3321–42.

Dolgorukov, Prince Pavel D. "Natsional'naia polityka partii Narodnoi
    Svobody do bol'shevizm." Chap. in *Natsional'naia polityka
    i partiia Narodnoi Svobody*. Rostov na Donu: Svobodnaia
    Rech', 1919.

————. *Velikaia razrukha*. Madrid: Imp. Rafael Taravilla Paul, 1964.

Gessen, I. V. "V dukh vekakh. Zhiznennyi otchet." *Arkhiv russkoi
    revoliutsii* 22 (1937).

Gol'tsev, V. "Natsional'nyi vopros v xix veke. (Iz politicheskago nas-
    ledstva proshlago stoletiia." *Russkaia mysl'* 22 (March
    1901): 142–53.

Gosudarstvennaia Duma pervago prizyva. *Portrety, kratkiia biografii i
    kharakteristiki deputatov*. Moscow: Knigoizdatel'stvo
    "Vozrozhdenie," 1906.

Gosudarstvennaia Duma. Stenograficheskie otchety. Sosyv I. St. Peters-
    burg, 1906.

Grabski, Stanisław. *Pamiętniki*. 2 vols. Edited by Witold Stankiewicz.
    Warsaw: Czytelnik, 1989.

Gredeskul', N. A. "Natsional'nyi vopros v pervoi Dume." In K 10–
    letiiu 1-oi Gosudarstvennoi Dumy: Sbornik statei pervo-
    dumtsev, 76–88. Petrograd: Izdatel'stvo Ogni, 1916.

________."Prof. N. A. Gredeskul' ob otnoshenii russkago obshchestva k natsional'nomy voprosy." *Ukrainskaia zhizn'* 5 (1916), no. 4-5: 114–17.

Gross, Feliks. Interview by author, 21 October 1993, New York City.

Kareev, Nikolai. "Novaia pol'skaia partiia." *Pravo* 15 (15 April 1905): 1175–81.

________. "Pol'skaia natsional'nost' v russkoi gosudarstvennosti." *Pravo* 14 (10 April 1905): 1071–72.

Kerensky, Alexander. *Russia and History's Turning Point.* New York: Duell, Sloan and Pearce, 1965.

Kizevetter, A. A. *Na rubezhe dvukh stoletii. Vospominaniia 1881–1914.* Prague: Orbis, 1929.

________. "Pervyia zhertvy. Fedor Fedorovich Kokoshkin." In *Pamiati pogibshikh*, ed. N. I. Astrov, V. F. Zeeler, et. al., 9–25. Paris: Knizhnoe Delo "Rodnik," 1929.

Kokoshkin, Vladimir Fedorovich. "F. F. Kokoshkin." Edited by V. F. Kokoshkin and I. Iu. Guadanin. *Novyi zhurnal* 74 (1963): 207–26.

Kotliarevskii, S. "Natsional'no-oblastnoi vopros v programme konstitutsionno-demokraticheskoi partii." *Poliarnaia zvezda* 1 (1906), no. 6: 383–87.

Kozłowski, Leon. *Rewolucja rosyjska i niepodległość polski: Geneza aktu 30 marca.* Warsaw: Zjednoczenie, 1922.

Lednicki, Wacław [V. Lednitskii]. *Pamiętniki.* 2 vols. London: B. Świderski, 1963–67.

________. "Vokrug V. A. Maklakova. (Lichnye vospominaniia)." *Novyi zhurnal* 56 (1959): 225–28.

Lenin, V. I. *Polnoe Sobranie sochinenii*. 57 vols. Moscow: Gosudarstvennoe izdatel'stvo politicheskoi literatury, 1958–66.

Maklakov, V. A. [W. A. Maklakow] "F. I. Rodichev i A. R. Lednitskii."
Novyi zhurnal 16 (1947): 240–51.

————. *Iz vospominanii*. New York: Izdatel'stvo imeni Chekhova,
1954.

————. "Lednicki, Rodiczew i sprawa polska." *Wiadomości literackie*
15 (1938), no. 17: 14–15.

————. *Vlast' i obshchestvennost' na zakate staroi Rossii. (Vospominaniia sovremennika)*. Paris, 1928.

Mandel'shtam, M. L. *1905 god v politicheskikh protsessakh. Zapiski
zashchitnika*. Moscow: Izdatel'stvo Politkatorzhan, 1931.

Milyukov, Paul. [Pavel Miliukov, Pawel Milukow] "Alexander Lednicki."
Slavonic and East European Review 13 (1934/35): 677–80.

————. "Aleksander Lednicki jako rzecznik polsko-rosyjskiego
porozumienia." *Przegląd współczesny* 18 (1939): 25–71.

————. *Political Memoirs: 1905–1917*. Edited by Arthur P. Mendel.
Translated by Carl Goldberg. Ann Arbor: The University of
Michigan Press, 1967.

————. *Russia and Its Crisis*. With a new forward by Donald W.
Treadgold. New York: Collier Books, 1962.

Nagórski, Zygmunt. "Aleksander Lednicki (1866–1934)." *Zeszyty
histryczny* 1 (1962): 27–66.

————. *Ludzie mego czasu*. Sylwetki. Paris: Księgarnia Polska w
Paryżu, 1964.

Obninskii, V. "Pervaia shagi russkogo avtonomizma." *Ukrainskaia zhizn'* 2 (1913), no. 4: 14–22.

Obolenskii, V. A. *Moia zhizn'. Moi sovremenniki.* Paris: YMCA-Press, 1988.

Olszer, Krystyna M., ed. *For Your Freedom and Ours: Polish Progressive Spirit from the 14th Century to the Present.* 2nd ed. New York: Frederick Ungar Publishing Co., 1981.

O pravakh natsional'nostei i o detsentralizatsii. Doklad biuro s"ezdy zemskikh i gorodskikh deiatelei. 12–15 sent. 1905 goda i postanovleniia s"ezda. Moscow: O. L. Somovoi, 1905.

Orzeszkowa, Eliża. *Listy zebrane.* Vol. 9. Edited by Edmund Jankowski. Warsaw: Wydawnictwo PAN, 1981.

Petrunkevich, I. I. "Iz zapisok obshchestvennago deiatelia. Vospominaniia." Edited by A. A. Kizevetter. *Arkhiv russkoi revoliutsii* 21 (1934).

Polsko-rosyjski zjazd w Moskwie. Kraków: Przedświt, 1905.

Protokoly tsentral'nogo komiteta i zagranichnykh grupp konstitutsionno-demokraticheskoi partii. Edited by Shmuel Galai, et al. Vol. 1, *Protokoly tsentral'nogo komiteta konstitutsionno-demok-raticheskoi partii: 1905–1911.* Moscow: Progress-akademiia, 1994.

Rappaport, Herman, ed. *Narastanie rewolucji w Królestwie Polskim w latach 1900–1904.* Warsaw: Państwowe Wydawnictwo Naukowe, 1960.

Rodichev, Fedor. "K pol'skomu voprosu." *Pravo* 11 (20 March 1905): 794–98.

__________. *Vospominaniia i ocherki o russkom liberalizme.* Edited, annotated and with an introduction by Kermit E. McKenzie. Newtonville, MA: Oriental Research Partners, 1983.

Rostovtsev, G. "Studencheskie volneniia v Moskovskom universitete v 1887 r." In *Moskovskii universitet v vospominaniiakh sovremennikov*, 326–35. Moscow: Izdatel'stvo Moskovskogo Universiteta, 1956.

Shakhovskoi, Dmitri. "Soiuz osvobozhdeniia." *Zarnitsy: Literaturno-politicheskii sbornik* (1909), no. 2, part 2: 81–171.

Shipov, D. I. *Vospominaniia i dumy o perezhitom*. Moscow: Izdatel'stvo M. i S. Sabashnikovykh, 1918.

Śmiarowski, Eugeniusz. *Mowy obroncze (1920–1925)*. Warsaw: M. Borkowski-Marzałkowski, 1926.

Sprawa polska w dzienniku "Rus"/ Pol'skii vopros v gazete "Rus". Vol. 1: 28 marta 1904 g.–18 fevralia 1905 g. St. Petersburg: Rus, 1905.

Startsev, V. I., S. Liandres, and A. V. Smolin, eds. *Aleksandr Ivanovich Guchkov rasskazyvaet...Vospominaniia predsedateliia Gosudarstvennoi Dumy i voennogo ministra Vremennogo Pravitel'stva*. Moscow: TOO Redaktsiia zhurnala "Voprosy istorii," 1993.

Topchibashi, A. M. B. "Soiuz avtonomistov." *Spogadi* 7 (1932): 131–41.

Tyrkova-Williams, A. [Tyrkova-Vil'iams, Ariadna] "The Cadet Party." *Russian Review* 12 (1953), no. 3: 173–85.

________. "F. I. Rodichev (1854-1933)." *Novyi zhurnal* 38 (1954): 207–23.

________. *Na putiakh k svobode*. New York: Chekhov, 1952.

Vinaver, M. M. *Istoriia Vyborgskgo Vozzvaniia (Vospominaniia)*. Petrograd, 1917.

Vinaver, R. G. "Vozhdi kadetskoi partii (Iz vospominanii.)" *Novyi zhurnal* 10 (1945): 250–62.

Vtoroi Vserossiiskii S"ezd Konstitutsionno-Demokraticheskoi Partii 5–11 Ianvaria 1906 g. Edited and introduced by Raymond Pearson. White Plains, NY: Kraus International Publications, 1986.

Wasilewski, Zygmunt. *Na wschodnim posterunku: księga pielgrzymstwa, 1915–1918*. Warsaw: E. Wende i Spółka, 1924.

————. *Proces Lednickiego. Fragment z dziejów odbudowy Polski 1915–1924*. Warsaw: Skład glowny w Księgarni Perzynski, Niklewicz i Sp., 1924.

Wędziagolski, Karol. *Boris Savinkov: Portrait of a Terrorist*. Edited by Tadeusz Świętochowski. Translated by Margaret Patoski. Clifton, NJ: The Kingston Press, 1988.

Woyniłłowicz, Edward. *Wspomnienia: 1847–1928*. Edited by Jariusz Iwaszkiewicz. 2 vols. Wilno: Skład Główny w Księgarni Jozefa Zawadzkiego, 1931.

Żbyszewski, Wacław Antoni. "Dwaj Ledniccy." *Kultura* 22 (1968), no. 8/9: 153–61.

SECONDARY SOURCES

Ascher, Abraham. *The Revolution of 1905. Vol. 1, Russia in Disarray*. Stanford: Stanford University Press, 1988.

————. *The Revolution of 1905. Vol. 2, Authority Restored*. Stanford: Stanford University Press, 1992.

Baranski, Zbigniew. *Literatura polska w rosji na przełomie XIX i XX wieku*. Wrocław: Prace Wrocławskiego Towarzystwa Naukowego, 1962.

———. "Z dziejów polsko-rosyjskikh związków kulturalnykh u progu XX wieku (Leon Kozłowski)." *Acta Universitatis Wratislaviensis* 170. *Slavica Wratislaviensia* 3: 5–13.

Bardach, Juliusz. "O świadomości narodowej Polaków na Litwie i Białorusi w XIX–XX w." In *Polska myśl polityczna XIX i XX wieku*, ed. Wojciech Wrzesinski. Vol. 6, *Mędzy Polska etniczna a historyczna, 225–72*. Wrocław: Zakład Narodowy imienia Ossolińskich Wydawnictwo Polskiej Akademii Nauk, 1988.

———. "Problematyka Polska liberalnej historiografii rosyjskiej schyłku XIX–początku XX wieku: N. I. Kariejew." In *Polsko-Rosyjskie związki społeczno-kulturalne na przełomie XIX i XX wieku*, ed. Marian Leczyk, 104–54. Warsaw: Książka i Wiedza, 1980.

Bashmakov, A. A., ed. *Spravochnaia kniga izbiratelia v Gosudarstvennuiu Dumu*. St. Petersburg: Slovo, 1906.

Biskupski, M. B. "The Poles, the Root Mission, and the Russian Provisional Government, 1917." *Slavonic and East European Review* 63 (January 1985): 56–68.

Blejwas, Stanislaus. "The Jews in the Theory and Practice of Polish Positivism." In *Proceedings of the Conference on Poles and Jews: Myth and Reality in the Historical Context*, ed. Harold B. Segal, 111–39. New York: Institute on East Central Europe, Columbia University, 1986.

———. *Realism in Polish Politics: Warsaw Positivism and National Survival in Nineteenth Century Poland*. New Haven: Yale Concilium on International and Area Studies, 1984.

Blobaum, Robert E. *Rewolucja: Russian Poland, 1904–1907*. Ithaca and London: Cornell University Press, 1995.

Brianchaninov, A. N. *Rospusk Gosudarstvennoi Dumy*. Pskov: Tipografiia gubernskaia zemstva, 1906.

Bromage, Bernard. *Man of Terror: Dzherzhynski*. London: Peter Owen Limited, 1956.

Brykalska, Maria. *Aleksander Świętochowski: Biografia*. 2 vols. Warsaw: Państwowy Instytut Wydawniczy, 1987.

Bułat, Wojciech. "Konferencja partii opozycyjnych i rewolucyjnych Rosji w Paryżu w 1904 r.—kilka uściśleń." *Z pola walki* 18 (1975), no. 1: 167–70.

————. "Korespondencje Leona Wasilewskiego na lamach 'Oswobozhdenija'." *Z pola walki* 19 (1976), no. 1: 167–70.

————. "Sprawa polska w walce rosyjskich obozów politycznych jesienia 1905 r." In *Polska-ZSRR: Internacjonalistyczna współpraca—historia i współczesność*. Vol. 1: 228–56. Warsaw: Książka i Wiedza, 1977.

————. "Zjazd polsko-rosyjski w Moskwie 21–22 kwietnia 1905 r." *Studia z najnowszych dziejów powszechnych* 2 (1962): 187–208.

Bułhak, Władysław. "Kluczowe problemy polityki polskiej w Rosji (marzec-listopad 1917 r.) w działalności Aleksandra Lednickiego." *Przegląd wschodni* 2 (1992/3): 71–95.

Chermenskii, E. D. *Burzhuaziia i tsarizm v pervoi russkoi revoliutsii*. 2d ed. Moscow: Izdatel'stvo 'Mysl'," 1970.

Chmielewski, Edward. *The Polish Question in the Russian State Duma*. Knoxville: The University of Tennessee Press, 1970.

Copeland, William R. *The Uneasy Alliance: Collaboration between the Finnish Opposition and the Russian Underground.* Helsinki: Suomalainen Tiedeakatemia, 1973.

Davies, David A. "V. A. Maklakov and the Westernizer Tradition in Russia." In *Essays on Russian Liberalism*, ed. Charles E. Timberlake, 78–89. Columbia: University of Missouri Press, 1972.

Davies, Norman. *God's Playground: A History of Poland.* 2 vols. New York: Columbia University Press, 1982.

Dumova, N. G., and V. V. Shelokhaev. "Oppozitsiia Ego Velichestva: Kadety." In *Istoriia politicheskikh partii Rossii*, ed. A. I. Zevelev, 114–43. Moscow: Vysshaia shkola, 1994.

Emmons, Terence. *The Formation of Political Parties and the First National Elections in Russia.* Cambridge, MA, and London: Harvard University Press, 1983.

________. "Russia's Banquet Campaign." *California Slavic Studies* 10 (1977): 45–86.

Fischer, George. *Russian Liberalism: From Gentry to Intelligentsia.* Cambridge: Harvard University Press, 1958.

Fountain, Alvin Marcus II. *Roman Dmowski: Party, Tactics, Ideology 1895–1907.* Boulder: East European Monographs, 1980.

Frolich, Klaus. *The Emergence of Russian Constitutionalism 1900–1904.* The Hague: Martinus Nijhoff Publishers, 1981.

Galai, Shmuel. "The Impact of War on the Russian Liberals in 1904–5." *Government and Opposition* 1 (1965): 85–109.

________. "A Liberal's Vision of Russia's Future, 1905–1914: The Case of Ivan Petrunkevich." In *Russian and East European*

History: Selected Papers from the Second World Congress for Soviet and East European Studies, edited by R. C. Elwood, 96–120. Berkeley: Berkeley Slavic Specialties, 1984.

————. *The Liberation Movement in Russia 1900–1905*. Cambridge: Cambridge University Press, 1973.

Geifman, Anna. *Thou Shalt Kill: Revolutionary Terrorism in Russia, 1894–1917*. Princeton: Princeton University Press, 1993.

Gessen, I. V. *Istoriia russkoi advokatury*. Vol. 1, *Advokatura, obshch estvo i gosudarstvo 1864 20/xi 1914*. Moscow: Izdanie sovetov prisiazhnykh poverennykh, 1914.

Giza, Antoni. *Neosławizm i Polacy 1906–1910*. Szczecin: Wydawnictwa Naukowe Wyzszej Szkoly Pedagogicznej, 1984.

Gleason, William. *Alexander Guchkov and the End of the Russian Empire*. Philadelphia: The American Philosophical Society, 1983.

Godlewski, Grzegorz. "Polska myśl kulturalna na progu niepodległości Żeromski, Zdziechowski, Znaniecki." In *Historia i kultura: Studia z dziejów polskiej myśli kulturalnej*, ed. Andrzej Mencwel, 175–208. Warsaw: Wydawnictwo Uniwersytetu Warszawskego, 1987.

Grabski, Andrzej Feliks. "Warszawscy entuzjasci H. T. Buckle'a. Z dziejów warszawskiego pozytywizmu." *Kwartalnik histo-ryczny* 76 (1969): 853–64.

Gross, Feliks. "Kresy: The Frontier of Eastern Europe." *Polish Review* 23 (1978), no. 2: 3–16.

Grossman, Jean Delaney. "Autumn 1914: A Russian Poet in Poland." In *Language, Literature, Linguistics: In Honor of Francis Whitfield on his Seventieth Birthday, March 25 1986*, ed. Michael S.

Flier and Simon Karlinsky, 72–88. Berkeley, CA: Berkeley Slavic Specialties, 1987.

Grynberg, Henryk. "The Jewish Theme in Polish Positivism." *Polish Review* 25 (1980), no. 3/4: 49–57.

Jankowski, Maciej. *Polska myśl liberalna do 1918 roku.* Kraków: Spółeczny Instytut Wydawniczy Znak; Warsaw: Fundacja im. Stefana Batorego, 1998

Jedlicki, Jerzy. "Holy Ideals and Prosaic Life, or the Devil's Alternatives." In *Polish Paradoxes*, ed. Stanislaw Gomulka and Antony Polonsky, 40–62. London and New York: Routledge, 1990.

Jurkowski, Roman. "Stronnictwo Konstytucyjno-Katolickie na Litwie i Białorusi w 1906 r. (Szkic do dziejów)." *Acta Baltico-Slavica* 18 (1987): 93–118.

Kaminka, A. "III s"ezd partii Narodnoi Svobody." *Svoboda i kul'tura* 1 (1906), no. 5: 340–49.

Kassow, Samuel D. *Students, Professors, and the State in Tsarist Russia.* Berkeley: University of California Press, 1989.

Kiepurska, Halina. *Warszawa w rewolucji 1905–1907.* Warsaw: Wiedza Powszechna, 1974.

Kmiecik, Zenon. *"Kraj" za czasów redaktorstwa Erazma Piltza.* Warsaw: Państwowe Wydawnictwo Naukowe, 1969.

__________. *Prasa polska w rewolucji 1905–1907.* Warsaw: Państwowe Wydawnictwo Naukowe, 1980.

Koroleva, N. G. *Zemstvo na perelome (1905–1907 gg.).* Moscow: Institut Rossiiskoi Istorii, 1995.

Koshevoi, V. "Mechte pol'skikh natsionalistov i deistvitel'nost'." *Ukrainskaia zhizn'* 2 (1913), no. 11: 13–23; no. 12: 30–49.

Krzemiński, Zdzisław, ed. *Zarys historii adwokatury polskiej.* Warsaw: Państwowe Wydawnictwo Naukowe,1978.

Kulczyck-Saloni, Janina. *Włodzimierz Spasowicz. Zarys monograficzny.* Wrocław: Ossolineum, 1975.

Lednicki, Wacław, ed. *Adam Mickiewicz in World Literature.* Berkeley and Los Angeles: University of California Press, 1956.

————. "Aleksander Lednicki (oszczerstwa i prawda)." *Zeszyty historyczny* 1 (1962): 67–93.

————. "Cracow Celebration—A Retrospective Presentation of Aleksander Lednicki's Report." *Polish Review* 9 (1964), no. 2: 5–18.

————. "Panslavism." Chap. in *European Ideologies: A Survey of 20th Century Political Ideas.* Edited by Feliks Gross, with an introduction by Robert M. MacIver. New York: Philosophical Library, 1948.

————. *Rosyjsko-polska 'entente cordiale,' jej początki i fundamenty 1903–1905.* Paris: Instytut Literacki, 1966.

Łukawski, Zygmunt. *Koło Polskie w Rosyjskie Dumie Państwowej w latach 1906–1909.* Wrocław: Zakład Narodowy imienia Ossolińskich, 1967.

————. * Łudność polska w Rosji 1863–1914.* Wrocław: Wydawnictwo Polskiej Akademii Nauk, 1978.

————. "Rosyjskie ugrupowania polityczne wobec sprawy autonomii Królestwa Polskiego w okresie 1905–1917. (W świetle archiwalnych materiałów rosyjskich)." *Zeszyty Naukowe*

Uniwersytetu Jagiellonksiego. Prace historyczne 9 (1962): 145–70.

Margolis, Iu. D. "Shtrikhi k portrety elity rossiiskikh liberalov nachal XX v." In *Rossiiskaia intelligentsiia na istoricheskom perelome: Pervaia tret' XX veka. Tezisy dokladov i soobshchenii nauchnoi konferentsii Sankt-Peterburg 19–20 marta 1996 g.*, ed. M. Iudovich, 35–38. St. Petersburg: Izdatel'stvo Sankt-Peterburgskogo Universiteta, 1996.

Martiukhova, M. A. *Na perelome revoliutsii: Obshchestvenno-politicheskoe dvizhenie v Belorussii v sviazi s uchrezhdeniem gosudarstvennoi dumy v Rossii (avgust 1905-iiul' 1906 g.).* Minsk: Nauka i Tekhnika, 1986.

McKenzie, Kermit. "The Political Faith of Fedor Rodichev." In *Essays on Russian Liberalism*, ed. Charles E. Timberlake, 42–61. Columbia: University of Missouri Press, 1972.

Medushevskii, A. N. "F. F. Kokoshkin i teoriia pravovogo gosudarstva v Rossii." *Mir Rossii* (1997), no. 3: 115–54.

Micewski, Andrzej. *Roman Dmowski*. Warsaw: Verum, 1971.

Miłosz, Czesław. *The History of Polish Literature*. 2d ed. Berkeley, Los Angeles, London: University of California Press, 1983.

Naimark, Norman. "Warsaw Positivism and the Origins of Polish Marxism." *Candadian-American Slavic Studies* 10 (1976), no. 3: 328–50.

Najdus, Walentyna. *Polacy w rewolucji 1917 roku*. Warsaw: PWN, 1967.

Namyslowska, M., ed. "Historia stypendium im. Adam Mickiewicza przy uniwersytecie moskiewskim." In *Puszkin: 1837–1937*. Vol. 2, edited by A. Bruckner, et al, 73–82. Krakow:

Nakladem Polskiego Towarzystwo dla Badan Europy Wschodniej i Bliskiego Wschodu Sklad Glowny, 1939.

Opalski, Magdalena. "The Concept of Jewish Assimilation in Polish Literature of the Positivist Period." *Polish Review* 32 (1987), no. 4: 371–83.

Pares, Bernard. *Russia and Reform*. London: Archibald Constable & Co., Ltd., 1907.

Petrozolin-Skowrońska, Barbara. "Problem genezy 'Zarania' (w świetle listu Aleksandra Świętochowskiego do Aleksandra Lednickiego z 11 listopada 1907 roku)." *Roczniki dziejów ruchu ludowej* 10 (1968): 516–21.

————. "Z dziejów liberalizmu polskiego. Partie liberalno-demokratyczne inteligencji w Królestwie Polskim, 1905–1907." Dzieje najnowsze 3 (1971), no. 3: 3–38.

Piotrovskaia, A. G. *Tvorcheskii put' Marii Konopnitskoi*. Moscow: Izdatel'stvo akademii nauk SSSR, 1962.

Piszczkowski, Tadeusz. *Odbudowanie Polski, 1914–1921. Historia i polityka*. London: Orbis, 1969.

Pól, Krzysztof. "Aleksander Lednicki (1866–1934)." *Zeszyty historyczne* 129 (1999): 3–43.

Ponarski, Zenowiusz. "Aleksander Lednicki (1866–1934)." In *Biblioteka palestry. Szkice z dziejów adwokatury polskiej*. 2d series. Edited by Roman Lyczywka, 60–88. Warsaw: Wydawnictwo Prawnicze, 1978.

Pulaski, Michal. "Z historii projektow stanow zjednoczonych Europy w latach 1923–1932." *Zeszyty naukowe Uniwersytetu Jagiellonskiego. Prace historyczne* 80 (1985): 94–113.

Raun, Toivo U. "1905 As a Turning Point in Estonian History." *East European Quarterly* 14 (1980), no. 3: 327–33.

Riha, Thomas. *A Russian European: Paul Miliukov in Russian Politics.* Notre Dame: University of Notre Dame Press, 1969.

Rothstein, Robert A. "The Linguist as Dissenter: Jan Baudouin de Courtenay." In *For Wiktor Weintraub: Essays in Polish Literature, Language, and History presented on the occasion of his 65th Birthday*, ed. Victor Erlich, et al, 390–405. The Hague; Paris: Mouton, 1975.

Sadowski, Lesław. *Polska inteligencja prowincjonalna i jej ideowe dylematy na przełomie XIX i XX wieku.* Warsaw: Państwowe Wydawnictwo Naukowe, 1988.

Sanders, Joseph L. *The Moscow Uprising of December, 1905: A Background Study.* New York & London: Garland Publishing, Inc., 1987.

Shanin, Teodor. *The Roots of Otherness: Russia's Turn of Century.* 2 vols. New Haven, London: Yale University Press, 1986.

Shatsillo, K. F. "Iz istorii osvoboditel'nogo dvizheniia v Rossii v nachale XX veka (O konferentsii liberal'nykh i revoliutsionnykh partii v Parizhe v sentiabre-oktiabre 1904 goda." *Istoriia SSSR* (1982), no. 4: 51–70.

________. "Novoe o 'Soiuze Osvobozhdenie.'" *Istoriia SSSR* (1975), no. 4: 132–45.

Shelokhaev, V. V. *Kadety—glavnaia partiia liberal'noi burzhuazii v borb'e s revoliutsiei 1905–1907 gg.* Moscow: Nauka, 1983.

________. *Liberal'naia model' pereustroistva Rossii.* Moscow: Rosspen, 1996.

Sinel, Allen. *The Classroom and the Chancellery: State Educational Reform in Russia under Count Dmitry Tolstoi*. Cambridge: Harvard University Press, 1973.

Slavinskii, M. A. "Russkaia intelligentsiia i natsional'nyi vopros." In *Intelligentsiia v Rossii. Sbornik statei*, ed. K. K. Arsen'ev, 220–34. St. Petersburg: Knigoizdatel'stvo "Zemlia", 1910.

Slisz, Andrzej. *Prasa polska w Rosji w dobie wojny i rewolucji (1915–1919)*. Warsaw: Książka i Wiedza, 1968.

Smith, Jr., C. Jay. "Miljukov and the Russian National Question." *Harvard Slavic Studies* 4 (1957): 395–420.

Smolen, Mieczysław. "Aleksander Lednicki (1866–1934). Pierwsze kroki na niwie spolecznej i politycznej." *Prace historyczne* 92 (1990): 55–70.

————. "Działalność Aleksandra Lednickiego w I Dumie Państwowej." *Studia historyczne* 34 (1991): 415–28.

Solak, Zbigniew. "Marian Zdziechowski i Klub Słowianski." *Studia historyczne* 30 (1987), no. 2: 219–39.

Spustek, Irena. "Jan Boudouin de Courtenay a carska cenzura." *Przegląd historyczny* 52 (1961): 112–26.

————. *Polacy w Piotrogrodzie 1914–1917*. Warsaw: 1966.

Startskova, E. V. "*Russkaia mysl'*." In *Literaturnyi protsess i russkaia zhurnalistika kontsa xix—nachala xx veka. 1890–1904: Burzhuazno-liberal'nye i modernistskie izdaniia*, 44–90. Moscow: Nauka, 1982.

Stegner, Tadeusz. *Liberałowie Królestwa Polskiego 1904–1915*. Gdańsk: Studencka Spółdzielnia Pracy "Techno-Service," 1990.

________. "Liberałowie Królestwa Polskiego wobec kwestii żydowskiej na początku XX wieku." *Przegląd historyczny* 80 (1989): 67–88.

________. "Postępowa demokracja a inteligencja." In *Inteligencja Polska XIX i XX wieku*, ed. Ryszard Czepulis-Rastenis, 278–92. Warsaw: Państwowe Wydawnictwo Naukowe, 1985.

Sukiennicki, Wiktor. *East Central Europe During World War I: From Foreign Domination to National Independence.* 2 vols. Edited by Maciej Siekierski, with a preface by Czeslaw Milosz. Boulder: East European Monographs, 1984.

Tombinski, Jan. "Początki ruchu Paneuropejskiego w Polsce." In *Zeszyty naukowe Uniwersytetu Jagiellonskiego. Prace historyczne* 118 (1995): 83–93.

Tsitron, Aleksandr. *72 dnia pervago russkago parlamenta.* St. Petersburg: Knigoizdatel'stvo Baum, 1906.

Uzhakov, S. N. "Polityka." *Russkoe bogatstvo* (March 1905), no. 3: 138–63.

Vasilevskii, L. "Russkaia Pol'sha nakanun novykh vyborov." *Russkoe bogatsvo* (1906), no. 12: 64–92.

Vetrinskii, Ch. "Viktor Aleksandrovich Gol'tsev. Biograficheskii ocherk." In *Pamiati Viktora Aleksandrovicha Gol'tseva. Stat'i, vospominaniia, pis'ma*, ed. A. A. Kizevetter, 1–92. Moscow: N. N. Klochkova, 1910.

Vinaver, M. M. *Konflikty v pervoi dume.* St. Petersburg: Tsentral'naia Tipolitografiia M. Ia. Minkova, 1907.

Walicki, Andrzej. "The Conceptions of Nation in the Polish Romantic Messianism." *Dialectics and Humanism: The Polish Philosophical Quarterly* 2 (1975), no. 1: 103–19.

Wapiński, Roman. *Narodowa demokracja 1893–1939. Ze studiów nad dziejami myśli nacjonalistycznej.* Wrocław: Zakład Narodowy imienia Ossolińskich Wydawnictwo, 1980.

Weber, Max. *The Russian Revolution.* Translated and edited by Gordon C. Wells and Peter Baeh. Ithaca: Cornell University Press, 1985.

Weeks, Theodore R. "Defining Us and Them: Poles and Russians in the 'Western Provinces,' 1863–1914." *Slavic Review* 53 (1994): 26–40.

Whyte, Frederic. *The Life of W. T. Stead.* 2 vols. London: J. Cape, Limited; New York & Boston: Houghton Mifflin Company, 1925.

Wieczorkiewicz, Pawel Piotr. "Udzial Polaków w ruchu neosławianskim a stosunki polityczne polsko-rosyjskie (1908–1910)." *Pamiętnik słowianski* 28 (1978): 133–68.

Wierzchowski, Mirosław. "Problematyka polska w rosyjskiej prasie liberalnej w latach 1907–1912." *Studia z dziejów ZSRR i Europy Środkowej* 1 (1965): 164-95.

Wladyka, Wiesław. *Działalność polityczna polskich stronnictw konserwatywnych w latach 1926–1935.* Wrocław: Zakład Narodowy imienia Ossolińskich Wydawnictwo Polskiej Akademii Nauk, 1977.

Zimmerman, Judith E. "Russian Liberal Theory, 1900–1917." *Canadian-American Slavic Studies* 14 (Spring 1980): 1–20.

CONTEMPORARY NEWSPAPERS AND JOURNALS

Kraj
Kurier polski
Listok "Osvobozhdenie"

Nasha zhizn'
New York Herald Tribune
New York Times
Osvobozhdenie
Pan-Europa
Poliarnaia zvezda
Pravo
Prawda
Riech'
Rus'
Russkaia mysl'
Russkii vestnik
Russkiia vedomosti
Russkoe bogatstvo
Russkoe slovo
Segodniia
Severnyi krai
Svoboda i kul'tura
Ukrainskaia zhizn'
Viestnik Partii Narodnoi Svobody
Viestnik Vremennago Pravitel'stva